Learning Resource Centre

Park Road, Uxbridge, Middlesex UB8 1NQ

UXBRIDGE COLLEGE

£25·99

Renewals: 01895 853344

Please return this item to the LRC on or before the last Date stamped below:

1 1 APR 2016

0 5 MAY 2016

Working with

Young People

362.7

This Reader forms part of the Open University module *Working with Young People, an introduction* (E108). This is a 60-credit module and is part of the BA (Hons) in Youth Work. Details of this and other Open University modules can be obtained from the Student Registration and Enquiry Service, The Open University, PO Box 197, Milton Keynes MK7 6BJ, United Kingdom (tel. +44(0)845 300 60 90, email general-enquiries@open.ac.uk).

www.open.ac.uk

Working with
Young People
Second Edition

edited by Sheila Curran, Roger Harrison
and Donald Mackinnon

Los Angeles | London | New Delhi
Singapore | Washington DC

Los Angeles | London | New Delhi
Singapore | Washington DC

SAGE Publications Ltd
1 Oliver's Yard
55 City Road
London EC1Y 1SP

SAGE Publications Inc.
2455 Teller Road
Thousand Oaks, California 91320

SAGE Publications India Pvt Ltd
B 1/I 1 Mohan Cooperative Industrial Area
Mathura Road
New Delhi 110 044

SAGE Publications Asia-Pacific Pte Ltd
3 Church Street
#10-04 Samsung Hub
Singapore 049483

Editor: Alison Poyner
Assistant editor: Emma Milman
Production editor: Katie Forsythe
Copyeditor: Rosemary Campbell
Proofreader: Sharon Cawood
Indexer: Elske Janssen
Marketing manager: Tamara Navaratnam
Cover design: Lisa Harper
Typeset by: C&M Digitals (P) Ltd, Chennai, India
Printed and bound by CPI Group (UK) Ltd,
Croydon, CR0 4YY

MIX
Paper from
responsible sources
FSC
www.fsc.org   FSC® C013604

First edition published 2005. Reprinted in 2006,
2007, 2008 (twice), 2009, 2010 (twice) and 2011

This edition first published 2013

The Open University
Walton Hall
Milton Keynes
MK7 6AA
United Kingdom
www.open.ac.uk

Library of Congress Control Number: 2013933872

British Library Cataloguing in Publication data

A catalogue record for this book is available from
the British Library

ISBN 978-1-4462-7327-2
ISBN 978-1-4462-7328-9 (pbk)

Contents

Notes on the Contributors

Janet Batsleer, Manchester Metropolitan University.
Dave Beck, University of Glasgow.
Jeremy Brent, formerly of Southmead Youth Centre in Bristol.
Liesl Conradie, University of Bedfordshire and The Open University.
Sheila Curran, The Open University.
Carol Devanney, Youth Worker.
Alison J. Fielding, Canterbury Christ Church University.
Tyrrell Golding, The Open University.
Jean Harris, Sheffield Hallam University.
Roger Harrison, The Open University.
Jean Hine, De Montfort University.
Gina Ingram, Youth Worker.
Mary Jane Kehily, The Open University.
Donald Mackinnon, The Open University.
Jane Melvin, University of Brighton.
Tomas Paus, University of Toronto.
Rod Purcell, University of Glasgow.
Hazel L. Reid, Canterbury Christ Church University.
Kate Sapin, University of Manchester.
Howard Sercombe, University of Strathclyde.
Jean Spence is a member of the Youth and Policy editorial group.
Naomi Stanton, YMCA George Williams College.
Etienne Wenger, independent consultant.
Aniela Wenham, University of York.
Jane Westergaard, Canterbury Christ Church University.
Jason Wood, Nottingham Trent University.
Tom Wylie was chief executive of the National Youth Agency from 1996 to 2007.

Publisher's Acknowledgements

Chapter 1 is the author's revision of Wood, Jason and Hine, Jean (2009) 'Introduction: The changing context of work with young people', Chapter 1 in Wood, Jason and Hine, Jean (eds) *Work with Young People*, SAGE.

Chapter 2 is the author's revision of Kehily, Mary Jane (2007) 'A Cultural Perspective', Chapter 1 in Kehily, Mary Jane (ed.) *Understanding Youth*, SAGE.

Chapter 3 is a revision of Brent, Jeremy (2005) 'Trouble and Tribes: Young people and community', Chapter 13 in Harrison, Roger and Wise, Christine (eds) *Working with Young People*, SAGE, which was a revised version of the original text that appeared in *Youth and Policy*, the journal of critical analysis edited by Ruth Gilchrist, Tony Jeffs and Jean Spence, published by The National Youth Agency. Republished with kind permission of *Youth and Policy* journal, www.youthandpolicy.org.

Chapter 4 is a newly commissioned chapter by Aniela Wenham.

Chapter 5 is the author's revision of Sercombe, Howard and Paus, Tomas (2009) 'The Teen Brain Research: Implications for practitioners', *Youth and Policy* No. 103, pp. 25–38, and Sercombe, Howard (2010) 'The Teen Brain Research: Critical perspectives', *Youth and Policy* No. 105, pp. 71–80. Republished with kind permission of *Youth and Policy* journal, www.youthandpolicy.org.

Chapter 6 is the author's revision of Wylie, Tom (2010) 'Youth Work in a Cold Climate', *Youth and Policy* No. 105, pp. 8–10. Republished with kind permission of *Youth and Policy* journal, www.youthandpolicy.org.

Chapter 7 is a revision of Ingram, Gina and Harris, Jean (2005) 'Defining Good Youth Work', Chapter 1 in Harrison, Roger and Wise, Christine (eds) *Working with Young People*, SAGE, which was a revised version of the original text that appeared as Chapter 4 in Ingram, Gina and Harris, Jean (2001) *Delivering Good Youth Work*, Russell House Publishing. Republished by kind permission of Russell House Publishing, www.russellhouse.co.uk.

Chapter 8 is edited from Spence, Jean and Devanney, Carol (2006) 'Every Day is Different', Chapter 3 in *Youth Work: Voices of Practice – A Research Report* by Durham University and Weston Spirit, Leicester: National Youth Agency. Republished by kind permission of Jean Spence and Carol Devanney.

Chapter 9 is edited from Reid, Hazel and Fielding, Alison (2007) 'Helping: Definitions and Purpose', Chapter 2, *Providing Support to Young People*, Routledge. Copyright 2007 Routledge. Reproduced by permission of Taylor & Francis Books UK.

Chapter 10 is the author's revision of Batsleer, Janet (2008) 'Informal Learning and Informal Education', Chapter 2, *Informal Learning in Youth Work*, SAGE.

Chapter 11 is edited from Sercombe, Howard (2010) 'Thinking Ethically', Chapter 7, *Youth Work Ethics*, SAGE.

Chapter 12 is a revision of Wenger, Etienne (2005) 'A Social Theory of Learning', which appeared in Harrison, Roger and Wise, Christine (eds) *Working with Young People*, SAGE, which was a revised version of the original text that appeared as pp. 3–17 in *Communities of Practice* by Etienne Wenger. First published in 1998 © Cambridge University Press, reproduced with permission.

Chapter 13 is a newly commissioned chapter by Sheila Curran and Tyrrell Golding.

Chapter 14 is edited from Sapin, Kate (2013) 'Enhancing Young People's Participation', Chapter 9, *Essential Skills for Youth Work Practice*, 2nd edn, SAGE.

Chapter 15 is edited from Beck, Dave and Purcell, Rod (2010) 'Developing Generative Themes for Community Action', *Popular Education Practice for Youth and Community Development Work*, Learning Matters.

Chapter 16 is edited from Westergaard, Jane (2009) 'The Role of Youth Support Workers with Groups of Young People', Chapter 1, *Effective Group Work with Young People*, Open University Press. Reproduced with the kind permission of Open University Press. All rights reserved.

Chapter 17 is a newly commissioned chapter by Jane Melvin.

Chapter 18 is a newly commissioned chapter by Naomi Stanton.

Chapter 19 is a newly commissioned chapter by Liesl Conradie.

Figures republished from third-party sources are credited in the relevant captions.

Introduction

Sheila Curran, Roger Harrison and Donald Mackinnon

The aim of this second edition of *Working with Young People* is the same as the first: to bring together a collection of writing about the theory and practice of working with young people which reflects, and is a product of, the changing times in which we live and work. It is also designed to support students studying for the Open University's professional qualification in Youth Work, particularly in the first two years of their study. We were gratified to see the extent to which the first edition was adopted as recommended reading for a range of other courses in the field of working with young people, and hope that this new edition achieves a similar level of acceptance.

In introducing the first edition in 2005, we noted the diversity of this field of practice and also the speed with which it was realigning itself with changes in the political and social landscape. Since then changes to the landscape show no signs of slowing down, as publicly funded services adjust to times of austerity and new forms of work with young people emerge. Our intended audience also remains the same as in 2005: practitioners working with young people in a variety of contexts and roles. As a reader of this volume you might be, for example, a youth worker, a learning mentor, a Scout/Guides leader, a sports or after school club leader, or a specialist young people's worker in a training or housing organisation. You might be working with a young men's group in Belfast, with young black women in Leicester, or with young people who are leaving care in London. You might be working in a youth centre or as a detached worker, with young people in school or with those who have been excluded from school. Taken together these practices form a complex pattern of provision which has been recognised by successive governments as a highly significant force in the lives of young people (DfES, 2001; DfE, 2011).

Since 2005 there have been significant changes in the social, economic and political contexts in which work with young people takes place. Political change has arrived with a new UK government in 2010, but we have also seen a significant devolution of powers to governments in Scotland and Wales and a consequent divergence of policies, priorities and practices across the different parts of the UK. Reductions in public funding have led to significant cuts in youth services and even the complete disappearance of some youth services, particularly in England. Connexions services, which were in the early stages of development in England in 2005, have largely disappeared as a result of changes in policy and funding. Organisations such as the Children's Workforce Development Council (CWDC) no longer exist. At the same time, we can observe new practices emerging, growing out of new contexts and settings, including in churches, temples and mosques, in hospitals, schools and housing organisations. There has been an increasing emphasis on partnership work, with practitioners from across a range of professional backgrounds working together to support young people's learning and development. There is a growing recognition of the role that youth work can play in supporting young people's learning and achievement in schools and colleges, and in helping to prevent school exclusion and underachievement, particularly in the Celtic nations.

As public provision for young people has contracted, voluntary and community organisations, including faith-based organisations, are playing an increasingly significant role in the provision of youth services. Private sector organisations are also taking a larger role, and it looks as though this will grow further. There have also been significant changes in the professional education and training of those working with young people. For example, youth work is now a graduate profession in each of the different nations of the UK.

We are also writing in what are challenging times for many young people. The youth unemployment rate is currently around 20 per cent, compared with 12 per cent in 2005, when our first edition was published (Evans, 2013). Changes in welfare look likely to result in benefit cuts which may have a particularly adverse impact on the most vulnerable young people, including young parents, young people with disabilities and young people living in parts of the country with high-cost housing. This environment brings new challenges for those working with young people, but also indicates the continuing need for young people to have access to knowledgeable, skilled and committed practitioners who can provide them with support and encouragement, especially at those times when life is difficult.

No single volume can claim to be representative of all the issues and viewpoints which are available in this diverse and dynamic field. The selection we have made here is a mixture of edited versions of texts which have already been published, together with chapters specially commissioned for this book. They span over a decade of researching, writing, debating and developing the ideas and the practices which constitute this field. Some are included because they offer a timely reminder of the values and purposes which remain fundamental to working with young people; others because they present new insights into the world of young people and the possibilities for working with them. The last decade has seen a considerable expansion of the literature from and about this field, reflecting changing social and economic conditions, new priorities and new voices. We have tried to represent at least some of these changes and some of these new voices, whilst also recognising the continuity of ideas and approaches which have always underpinned this work.

The book is divided into three overlapping parts.

Part 1 looks at how young people are characterised and defined, both through government policy initiatives and through academic research, for example in sociology, psychology and neuroscience. These understandings are important since they powerfully influence debates about what is practical and desirable in working with young people. Jason Wood and Jean Hine introduce this idea that young people's place in society is constituted through a complex interaction between public attitudes, government policies and academic knowledge. Mary Jane Kehily develops this further, focusing on the role of knowledge, popular culture and the market as factors shaping the identities of young people. Her analysis shows how young people are not simply the victims of these larger social forces, but also active agents in shaping their own identities. Jeremy Brent and Aniela Wenham both draw on their research into particular groups of young people to illustrate how our ideas about, and responses to, these groups are constructed in policies which view them first and foremost as problems. Both chapters present powerful arguments for why it matters for those who work with young people to take a critical stance towards assumptions and prejudices that often lie behind such policies, and the practices they produce. These chapters also illustrate how knowledge about young people is powerful in shaping our understandings and interpretations of their actions. Howard Sercombe and Tomas Paus introduce us to a relatively new branch of knowledge – neuroscience – which is beginning to provide insights into how the brain works, and in doing so change the way we think about young people and their behaviour. Their chapter provides a lucid and balanced description of a complex field of research, and touches on some of the implications for those working with young people. Finally in this section, Tom Wylie assesses the implications of the current rather austere context for work with young people, and the challenges it presents for young people and for those working with them.

Part 2 investigates the nature of this field of practice: what are its defining features; what are the ideas about ethics, about learning, about helping, which underpin the practice; how are these ideas mobilised in practice settings? Gina Ingram and Jean Harris give us a succinct characterisation of youth work, covering the diversity of the practices used, the subtlety of the skill set required, and the quality of the relationship between the practitioner and the young person which lies at the heart of this work. Jean Spence and Carol Devanney take us from the general to the particular with their illuminating account of the realities of day-to-day youth work practice, and the challenges faced by practitioners as they seek to be responsive to young people whilst at the same time responding to externally determined agendas and organisational priorities. The chapters by Hazel Reid and Alison Fielding and Janet Batsleer both examine the theory and practice of different kinds of work with young people: individual advice and guidance on the one hand and informal education on the other. Both of these approaches can provide valuable interventions in the lives of young people but require different skills and techniques if they are to be used successfully. Howard Sercombe discusses the place of ethics in work with young people, looking both at why ethics matter and how ethical decision making plays an integral part in the everyday work of practitioners. Finally in this section, we return to the subject of learning. Etienne Wenger's chapter does not directly address youth work but is nevertheless highly relevant to the kind of informal education described in this volume by Janet Batsleer. Drawing on research into the learning which occurs in real-life contexts, Wenger suggests that learning should be understood not as a distinct activity which can be organised and regulated, but as a natural result of participation with others in meaningful activity. The role of the practitioner then becomes one of setting up and facilitating situations which are rich in learning opportunities, rather than attempting to achieve pre-arranged learning outcomes.

Part 3 examines a diversity of practices and practical dilemmas which are present in contemporary work with young people. It is here that most of the newly commissioned chapters are to be found as we attempt to keep up to date with an ever- changing field. Sheila Curran and Tyrrell Golding discuss the dilemma for those who work informally with young people of adapting these approaches to more formal settings such as schools and colleges. They are able to draw on their own experiences of practice to provide examples of how these challenges can be met. Meeting the needs of young people and devolving responsibility back to them is often stated as a priority in most forms of youth and community work. Kate Sapin's chapter deals with how to involve young people more directly in decisions which affect their lives, including the design and delivery of services intended to meet their needs. Again, she is able to draw on her own direct experience, as well as that of others, in describing strategies for making young people's participation something more than tokenistic. Dave Beck and Rod Purcell pursue this question of how to engage with young people on a more equal and democratic footing. Their chapter describes both the theory and practice of a community development model for participative approaches in work with young people. Group work is another form of practice which has always been valued for its ability to engage young people in purposeful social interactions. Jane Westergaard considers ways in which practitioners from different professional backgrounds can work with groups of young people to support their learning and personal development. Jane Melvin reviews the growth of digital technologies, drawing on her own research to explore their impact on the way young people communicate and interact with each other, and some of the implications for practitioners, including organisational policies and safeguarding. Faith-based youth work now constitutes a significant proportion of the professional field of work with young people. In her chapter, Naomi Stanton draws on her own research to examine the origins of this work, the nature of young people's involvement and some of the tensions which occur between the aims of youth workers and those of the churches involved. Finally, Liesl Conradie discusses the importance of supervision in supporting and developing capable and reflective practitioners, and examines some of the skills and qualities that practitioners need to develop as they engage in supervision and prepare to become supervisors themselves.

In putting together the contents of this volume, we have tried to cover a number of dimensions in this 'infinitely fluid, flexible and mobile' (Bradford, 2005: 58) field of practice: from the timeless to the contemporary; from individual to group; from formal to informal; from research to practice. The selection we have made cannot claim to be comprehensive or even representative of the richness and diversity of the literature available, but it does cover what we see as some of the key themes currently being discussed in the field.

References

Bradford, S. (2005) 'Modernising youth work: from the universal to the particular and back again', in R. Harrison and C. Wise (eds) *Working with Young People*, London: Sage.

Department for Education and Skills (DfES) (2001) *Transforming Youth Work*, London: The Stationery Office.

Department for Education (DfE) (2011) *Positive for Youth Statement*, www.education.gov.uk/ childrenandyoungpeople/youngpeople/positive%20for%20youth/b00200933/positive-for-youth-the-statement (accessed 18/02/13).

Evans, J. (2013) *Youth Unemployment Statistics*, SN/EP/5871, London: House of Commons Library, www.parliament.uk/briefing-papers/sn05871 (accessed 04/07/13).

Part 1

Young People in Society

1

Policy, Practice and Research in Work with Young People

Jason Wood and Jean Hine

In recent years there have been significant shifts in the landscape of work with young people. These have followed changes in policy, in social and economic conditions and in the knowledge base through which we understand young people. This chapter examines some of these changes, drawing attention to their implications for practice and practitioners. In particular it points up the tendency to view young people as 'at risk', either to themselves or others, as a driver for changes in policy and practice.

Introduction

The past ten years have seen significant expansion and change in work with young people. The field once occupied predominantly by youth services, social work and education now contains a wider network of agencies that seek to intervene in a young person's life. A qualified youth worker today is one who can be called upon to make a contribution to a number of agencies and organisations that, in many cases, did not exist ten years ago. In statutory youth offending partnerships and crime prevention teams, they work to prevent and reduce the reoccurrence of youth crime. In information, advice and guidance services, they undertake work to reduce the number of young people excluded from education, training or employment. Through various health initiatives, they work preventatively in reducing the health risks that young people face. Positive activities and structured programmes of leisure, once the cornerstone of youth work, persist, but in a wide variety of contexts provided by a range of statutory, voluntary and private agencies. This broad range of work with young people frequently takes place in multi-agency contexts, where

---

This chapter is the authors' revision of Wood, Jason and Hine, Jean (2009) 'Introduction: The Changing Context of Work with Young People', Chapter 1 in Wood, Jason and Hine, Jean (eds) *Work with Young People*, London: Sage.

the disciplinary boundaries between professions are increasingly characterised as porous. As a result, the professional identity of a youth, health or social worker is under challenge as partnership working becomes more commonplace.

Many of the policy initiatives that have underpinned these changes have done so on the basis of a desire to improve things for all children and young people. In England, the *Every Child Matters* (ECM) framework offered five laudable outcomes for children and young people: being healthy, staying safe, enjoying and achieving, making a positive contribution and achieving economic well-being (DfES, 2003). Similarly, the ambitions of the overarching *Youth Matters* and *Aiming High for Young People* strategies indicated both a desire to empower young people in the delivery of positive activities and for them to access high quality support in terms of advice and guidance (DfES, 2005; HM Treasury/DCSF, 2007). More recently the coalition government's Positive for Youth policy (https://www.education.gov.uk/publications/eOrderingDownload/DFE-00198-2011.pdf) promotes similar aspirations for young people's development, though its strategy for achieving them is rather different. For example, it proposes:

> a common goal of young people having a strong sense of belonging, and the supportive relationships, strong ambitions, and good opportunities they need to realise their potential.

It specifically supports the value of young people's voices being heard and taken notice of:

> Young people have a right to have their views taken into account in all decisions that affect their lives. We must give them a stronger voice and celebrate their positive contribution and achievements.

And it aims to work through collaboration between government departments, councils, schools, charities and businesses. These positive messages are also evident at a European level where youth policy is governed by a commitment to advocating youth citizenship, promoting better participation and listening to the voice of young people (Williamson, 2009).

However, such developments also invite wide-ranging criticism. The dominant message about young people is one of ambivalence: they are to be protected and improved through increased intervention, but society must be protected from some of them. They are to be active participants in public life, yet are increasingly excluded from public spaces through dispersal and curfew measures. They are held up as responsible for making decisions, yet are often characterised as lacking the necessary skills to exercise this responsibility in an acceptable way. All of which results in young people being labelled in neat, dichotomous ways that do not necessarily reflect the complexity of young people's real lives and circumstances.

At the same time as seeking to expand the range of work with young people, policy has also become more prescriptive, specifying how this work should be done and introducing a wide range of targets to be met by agencies delivering it. Practitioners are increasingly required to demonstrate how their work results in accredited learning outcomes for young people. These targets are underpinned by an espoused commitment to evidence-based practice, though it is sometimes difficult to see the value of the evidence chosen. This is all the more surprising given the extent to which research and wider theory has increased understandings of young people over the past decade. The relationship between this growing body of research, much of it focused on young people, and the definitions and approaches found in policy is clearly not as strong as it could be.

Developments in theory and research

Research studies of youth and work with young people have produced different understandings, not only of young people's lives, but of 'education, family, the media, popular culture, (un)employment transitions, the life course, risks and so on' (Kelly, 2003: 167). Despite this expansion in knowledge about young people, exactly what is meant by 'youth' is still open to question (see Hine, 2009). A central concept in traditional definitions is the notion of it being a stage in life between childhood and adulthood. But more recent sociological perspectives have shown that the period in the life course that is defined as 'youth' is as much a social construction as it is a period of individual change. Mizen defines youth as a 'socially determined category' (Mizen, 2004: 5) and in this respect it is little use to rely solely on individual biological markers as a frame for understanding youth. What this 'social turn' tells us is that the cultural, social and political contexts in which young people grow up will invariably shape definitions of what is childhood, adolescence and adulthood.

Studies of childhood show it as a similarly contested and socially constructed period of the life course (Foley et al., 2001; James and James, 2004). Like youth, childhood 'cannot be regarded as an unproblematic descriptor of the natural biological phase' (James and James, 2004: 13). The experiences of a child growing up in the 1990s compared with that of those today will vary dramatically. Further complexity arises in any cross-cultural comparison of childhood, especially in the values ascribed to certain definitions of childrearing practices as compared to 'Western notions of what all children should aspire to' (Sanders, 2004: 53). Such perspectives open up a challenge to claims of a neutrally defined 'normal' childhood since 'childhood as a social space is structurally determined by a range of social institutions and mechanisms' (James and James, 2004: 213). These institutions and mechanisms reflect the dominant cultural and social adult expectations of childhood, either in response to the individual and collective behaviours of children or in the wide variety of macro determinates that influence the wider structure of society (James and James, 2004).

Adulthood is also subject to social categorisation. What is meant precisely by adulthood is highly contested. Economic indicators would suggest full and continuous participation in the economy and the acquisition of property. Social indicators include the formation of stable family units, characterised by the reproduction and socialisation of the next generation of children. Civil indicators would suggest political and civic participation. All of these claims though can be subject to dispute. For instance, if full economic participation and property acquisition are indicators of responsible adulthood, are we to conclude that those who engage in further and higher education are not behaving as responsible adults?

What we can say with some certainty is that young people in late modern societies are characterised as leading immensely complex and fragmented lives. Their social identities are subjected to far-reaching, diverse and interconnected influences, many of which have not been experienced by previous generations. These new challenges include changing macro forces arising from globalisation and the risk society (which now operate together with longstanding issues of social stratification relating to class, gender, race, disability, sexuality, and so on).

Two strands of recent research are worthy of exploration here since they have direct implications for the significant changes in work with young people over the past ten years. The first examines expanding knowledge about youth transitions in a markedly changing and complex world. The second reviews the interplay of risk and resilience in young people's lives.

Changing, complex and extended transitions

Young people are frequently referred to as being in a state of transition, of moving between the life stages of childhood and adulthood: a stage termed adolescence or 'youth'. Age boundaries are often applied to this stage and are embedded in legislations related to education, voting rights and marriage, but in the modern Western world a range of economic and social indicators of adulthood are primary signifiers of the transition. In the discussion above, the idea that childhood and adulthood are problematic concepts was put forward. In any discussion around transition as a journey, one perhaps must accept some sort of a destination. For Coleman et al., adolescence is 'best understood as a complex transition between the states of childhood dependence and adult independence' (2004: 227). The extensive study of this transition period has provoked much recent empirical and theoretical interest, not least because of the complex changes associated with the risk society. Such research has been useful in considering:

- The interaction between personal capacity, biology and personality ('agency') and the systems and structures that influence young people ('structure').
- The ways in which institutions, social policies and systems intervene within a key stage of the life course.
- The ways in which other problems or situations emerge, particularly at the point of transition from education to employment. This is of particular interest to policy makers, often concerned with the interconnectedness of 'social exclusion'. (Bynner, 2001: 6)

While there has perhaps always been a great deal of confusion over what constitutes arrival at adulthood (Coleman and Warren-Adamson, 1992), transitions that were once understood to be linear are now recognised as fluid, changing and increasingly without a fixed end-point (Dwyer and Wyn, 2001). Consequently, young people growing up in the modern world 'face new risks and opportunities' (Furlong and Cartmel, 2007: 8) perhaps only glimpsed by previous generations. It certainly makes one's own reflections on childhood in many cases redundant.

Regarded as 'an important phase in the life cycle' (Furlong and Cartmel, 2007: 34), the transition from education to employment is one such example. Pathways from post-16 education are now beset by a range of further training opportunities, increased uptake at higher education and new uncertainty in traditional, skilled and unskilled labour (Furlong and Cartmel, 2007). Government recognition that the nature of the labour market has shifted towards a 'knowledge economy' ultimately means that more young people are required to attend further and higher education and training for longer periods. Indeed, at the time of writing, government policy for England and Wales is to raise the statutory school leaving age from 16 to 18 by 2015. One consequence of fragmented employment patterns and extended education is the changing relationship that young people have with their immediate families. In the UK, for instance, extended periods of financial dependency on parents and carers may mean home ownership takes place increasingly later on in the life course.

A key indicator for arrival at 'adulthood' is the shift from dependence on parents and family to independent living, including obtaining employment, forming a relationship and family, and moving into accommodation. Research by Bynner (2005) shows that across Europe there is a trend towards the achievement of the markers of adulthood coming at a later age now than previously, as the transition from childhood to adulthood becomes extended. His research also draws attention to the different experiences of young people in different socio-economic groups: '… over the 24-year period examined, the most dominant feature was growing polarization between the advantaged and the disadvantaged' (Bynner, 2005: 377). Involvement in extended education and training delays the onset of employment for some, but rates of such participation are lower for the more disadvantaged, with higher levels of early parenthood and early entry into work.

The focus on the notion of transition is accompanied by the view that young people are adults in the making, and thus do not have the awareness or competencies of adults. This view is informed by the dominant developmental perspectives of childhood presented by psychologists such as Piaget and Inhelder (1969). Children are seen to develop adult attributes gradually over their early and adolescent years in an additive and linear fashion, with normative age bandings identified as significant for the acquisition of particular competencies. It is argued that recent times have seen significant changes in young people's transitions, because the nature of the world in which they live has changed dramatically (e.g. Bynner, 2005; Spence, 2005). In this new world young people have greater opportunity but less certainty about their futures, requiring them to be more self-aware, flexible and responsive to changing social and economic conditions (Beck, 1992). This instability and fluidity in social and economic conditions has meant that transitions can be more difficult for young people to achieve and that this transitional phase of life is becoming longer and more complex (Valentine, 2003), though, as noted above, these changes have not affected all young people in the same way, with those from disadvantaged backgrounds tending to have different patterns of transition than those from more privileged backgrounds (Bynner, 2005).

Young people, risk and resilience

Nowhere is the tension between the need to prevent risk and the necessity of learning to manage and take calculated risks more apparent than in the process of growing up from childhood to adulthood. (Thom et al., 2007: 1)

Certainly, young people are leading lives of increasing uncertainty and 'heightened risk' (Furlong and Cartmel, 2007: 8), an idea located within the now well rehearsed framework of the 'risk society' (Beck, 1992). Life is literally prone to risks that once did not exist and 'people are seen to both cause risks and be responsible for their minimization' (Lupton, 2006: 12). Whether these risks are the consequence of seemingly uncontrollable forces (such as global warming) or understood within the more localised or personalised experiences of the population (health-related risky behaviours such as smoking, for instance), the overwhelming consequence is an increased feeling of insecurity and a desire for risk prevention and protection (Beck, 1992; Kemshall, 2002; Furlong and Cartmel, 2007). This 'culture of caution' (Thom et al., 2007) leads us ultimately to see risk through a negative lens.

The association of 'youth' with 'risk' is prominent in relation to young people's social activities and debates around youth welfare, criminal justice, employment and sexuality. The expanding knowledge base about young people's personal and social risks is driven by research that gives increasing attention to young people as problems: sexual behaviour (Hoggart, 2007); substance misuse and 'binge' drinking, with grand but contested claims about alcohol misuse (see France, 2007: 137–138); and the links between truancy and long-term social exclusion (Social Exclusion Unit, 1998) are just three examples. This concern with risky behaviour drives a desire to predict it and stop it, using the idea of 'risk factors': literally what key determinants impact upon whether young people will grow up as integrated members of society, or as somehow deviant (Hayes, 2002). This growing body of work seeks to understand 'protective factors' and the idea of 'resilience' to address the question: what capacities do young people 'need' in order to ward off risk? Resilience is not simply located at the level of individual agency but is increasingly seen as a cultural and structural concept. Particular approaches to building resilience through community youth development (Perkins, 2009) and the building of social capital (Boeck, 2009) demonstrate the importance of strategies which acknowledge and work with the social contexts in which young people are growing up, rather than viewing young people only as sites of individual (in)capacity.

Developments in policy

Throughout history, youth policy has responded to different political, public and social imperatives, since 'youth has always been under the microscope and of central concern to adults and the state' (France, 2007: 1). Even in times of economic austerity and the closure of many local authority youth services in England, politicians of all major political parties have expressed concern about the dangers of young people not engaging in education and training, with consequences for their future employment prospects, and their involvement in crime, drug use and teenage pregnancy. The question of how to engage young people as socially and economically productive citizens is beset by a curious mix of anxiety, fear, hope and aspiration. Key themes in policy development over the past ten years include the prominence of risk-based social policy over traditional welfarist models. This includes an increasing emphasis on fostering conditions that promote 'self-reliance' and 'responsibility'. For young people in particular, there has been an increase in strategies designed to ward off social exclusion through the use of early intervention strategies. In some cases, the preoccupation with risk has led to a widening of the criminal justice net (Yates, 2009). Services that were not traditionally classed as within the criminal justice arena find themselves increasingly contributing to outcomes related to the reduction of the risk of offending.

Dealing with young people for what they might become

In any welfare system, resources are prone to economic rationalisation, and targeting offers a politically attractive option for addressing the most pressing social problems (Kemshall, 2002). The argument suggests that the more entrenched a difficulty becomes, the more costly and less effective interventions become. So policy responds by seeking to address early warning signs: the truancy, rather than the long-term exclusion from school; the cigarette smoking rather than the diseases that plague the individual in later life; the healthy eating of children in schools rather than the health consequences of obesity. The approach is often argued as common-sensical: if it is known that someone is more likely to do X, if they are displaying Y, then surely one should intervene? As former Prime Minister Tony Blair observed:

> Where it's clear that children are at risk of being brought up in disadvantaged homes where there are multiple problems, then instead of waiting until the child goes off the rails we should act early enough to prevent that. (Blair, 2006, cited in *The Guardian*)

This emphasis on risk factors and precaution have ultimately led us towards a focus on the potential futures of young people via targeted policy and away from universal, open access welfare that deals with problems in the present (France, 2008). Risk factors serve as 'targets' helping to identify 'populations at risk' (Schoon and Bynner, 2003).

Early intervention is realised through a number of policy measures. All children and young people have access to universal education and health care, with minimum standards in both. But those children and young people who embody certain risk factors face greater levels of state intervention. Families in the most deprived communities in Britain are the targets of specialist, multi-disciplinary Children and Family Centres that seek to address the interconnected problems of health, education, child development and parenting. In criminal justice, the expansion of programmes of structured activity and the development of youth prevention services are targeted at those areas with higher crime rates in the hope that such programmes will divert potential offenders. Similarly, those young people Not in Education, Employment or Training (NEET) may find themselves subject to a raft of initiatives such as alternative curricula and dedicated personal advisers, both on compulsory and voluntary terms. The last ten years have seen a prioritisation of engagement in education, in whatever new forms it takes hold, including most recently through private enterprise seeking to offer alternative qualifications for those children most at risk of exclusion.

From entitlement to conditionality

A key theme in social policy has been the reframing of welfare from one of entitlement to one of conditionality (Dwyer, 2004), putting at the centre the balance between individual rights and obligations. Increasingly, welfare is based on the 'something for something' society (Blair, 1998), where the expected duties of the individual are more clearly prioritised. Welfare reform then is more than an economic imperative: it literally becomes a 'remoralising' exercise, redefined as a system that encourages active participation of its citizens over passively dispensing compensation to those in need (see Kemshall, 2002: 111–112).

The theme of rights and responsibilities is then witnessed through a number of policy initiatives, and when seen in terms of a broader social framework can be applied to almost all aspects of youth policy. Rights in this case are often framed as a right to participate, with the UN Convention on the Rights of the Child often underpinning the rationale for encouraging the 'duty to consult'. Recent youth policy in the United Kingdom has sought to engage young people in the process of formulation, for instance through *Youth Matters* consulting the views of nearly 20,000 young people, and through the commitment in *Positive for Youth* to give a stronger voice to young people.

Social responsibility is a more complex policy development. Obligations on young people are either quite specific (children will not truant, or they/their parents will face financial penalties) or rather more ambiguous (increasing 'respect', for instance). In whatever form they take, the desired moral and social behaviour of young people is increasingly determined by policy and instructed through education and welfare services (Armstrong, 2009).

Implications for practice

The start of this chapter indicated that work with young people in the UK now offers a more diverse employment market driven by new and expanding policy intentions. This market includes housing authorities, the police, youth offending teams, health services, education, and welfare and guidance services. Much of the work is prescriptive and targeted, but creativity and diversity still flourish: practitioners do indeed seek to empower young people and develop meaningful relationships built upon increased trust (Yates, 2009).

The guiding principles of youth work have in recent tradition been bound to those of informal education: an emphasis on voluntary association, starting from where the learner is at and encouraging them to reflect on their own experiences (Jeffs and Smith, 2005) in order to engage in a process of moral philosophy (Young, 2006).

However, these principles are under challenge: how, for instance, to ensure voluntary association in a court-ordered programme for young offenders? Or does a youth worker cease to be a youth worker when joining such a system? What is clear from the changing knowledge and policy landscape is that those with a training in youth work can contribute much to these newer contexts, perhaps offering creativity in working within these new frameworks and changed agendas. They can play a significant role that re-examines the problems that young people present, and attempt to negotiate more holistic problem definitions and solutions. It is therefore important to see the picture as far from gloomy.

Practitioners are increasingly promoting ways of engaging young people in influencing and shaping their social worlds. The increased attention to active citizenship and social capital offers a gateway to an alternative focus on young people as agents who can shape their social contexts with the support of trusted adults. This relies, however, on learning the lessons from research and practice where young people's views actively shape adult understanding of their worlds. It also requires practitioners to re-evaluate and restate their own values and ethical positions so that these can act as lamplights in a complex, challenging and constantly changing set of environments.

References

Armstrong, D. (2009) 'Educating youth: assimilation and the democratic alternative', in J. Wood and J. Hine (eds) *Work with Young People*, London: Sage.

Beck, U. (1992) *Risk Society: Towards a New Modernity*, London: Sage.

Blair, T. (1998) *The Third Way*, London: Fabian Society.

Blair, T. (2006) 'Our nation's future – social exclusion', speech to the Joseph Rowntree Foundation, York, 5 September.

Boeck, T. (2009) 'Social capital and young people', in J. Wood and J. Hine (eds) *Work with Young People*, London: Sage.

Bynner, J. (2001) 'British youth transitions in comparative perspective', *Journal of Youth Studies*, 4(1): 5–23.

Bynner, J. (2005) 'Rethinking the youth phase of the life course: the case for emerging adulthood?', *Journal of Youth Studies*, 8(4): 367–384.

Coleman, J. and Warren-Adamson, C. (eds) (1992) *Youth Policy in the 1990s: The Way Forward*, London: Routledge.

Coleman, J., Catan, L. and Dennison, C. (2004) 'You're the last person I'd talk to', in J. Roche, S. Tucker, R. Thomson and R. Flynn (eds) *Youth in Society*, 2nd edn, London: Sage.

Department for Education and Skills (DfES) (2003) *Every Child Matters*, London: DfES.

Department for Education and Skills (DfES) (2005) *Youth Matters*, London: DfES.

Dwyer, P. (2004) 'Creeping conditionality in the UK: from welfare rights to conditional entitlements?', *Canadian Journal of Sociology*, 29(2): 265–287.

Dwyer, P. and Wyn, J. (2001) *Youth, Education and Risk: Facing the Future*, London: Routledge Falmer.

Foley, P., Roche, J. and Tucker, S. (eds) (2001) *Children in Society: Contemporary Theory, Policy and Practice*, Basingstoke: Palgrave.

France, A. (2007) *Understanding Youth in Late Modernity*, Basingstoke: Open University Press.

France, A. (2008) 'Risk factor analysis and the youth question', *Journal of Youth Studies*, 11 (1): 1–15.

Furlong, A. and Cartmel, F. (2007) *Young People and Social Change*, 2nd edn, *Berkshire*: Open University Press.

Hayes, M. (2002) *Taking Chances: The Lifestyles and Leisure Risk of Young People*, London: Child Accident Prevention Trust.

Hine, J. (2009) 'Young people's lives: taking a different view', in J. Wood and J. Hine (eds) *Work with Young People*, London: Sage.

HM Treasury/Department for Children, Schools and Families (DCSF) (2007) *Aiming High for Young People: A Ten Year Strategy for Positive Activities*, London: HM Treasury.

Hoggart, L. (2007) 'Young women, sexual behaviour and sexual decision making', in B. Thom, R. Sales and J. J. Pearce (eds) *Growing up with Risk*, Bristol: Policy Press.

James, A. and James, A. L. (2004) *Constructing Childhood: Theory, Policy and Social Practice*, Basingstoke: Palgrave.

Jeffs, T. and Smith, M. K. (2005) *Informal Education: Conversation, Democracy and Learning*, 3rd edn, Nottingham: Educational Heretics Press.

Kelly, P. (2003) 'Growing up as risky business? Risks, surveillance and the institutionalised mistrust of youth', *Journal of Youth Studies*, 6(2): 165–180.

Kemshall, H. (2002) *Risk, Social Policy and Welfare*, Buckingham: Open University Press.

Lupton, D. (2006) 'Sociology and risk', in G. Mythen and S. Walklate (eds) *Beyond the Risk Society: Critical Reflections on Risk and Human Security*, Maidenhead: Open University Press.

Mizen, P. (2004) *The Changing State of Youth*, Basingstoke: Palgrave Macmillan.

Perkins, D. (2009) 'Community youth development', in J. Wood and J. Hine (eds) *Work with Young People*, London: Sage.

Piaget, J. and Inhelder, B. (1969) *The Psychology of the Child*, New York: Basic Books.

Sanders, B. (2004) 'Childhood in different cultures', in T. Maynard and N. Thomas (eds) *An Introduction to Early Childhood Studies*, London: Sage.

Schoon, I. and Bynner, J. (2003) 'Risk and resilience in the life course: implications for interventions and social policies', *Journal of Youth Studies*, 6(1): 21–31.

Social Exclusion Unit (1998) *Truancy and Social Exclusion*, London: HMSO.

Spence, J. (2005) 'Concepts of youth', in R. Harrison and C. Wise (eds) *Working with Young People*, London: Sage.

Thom, B., Sales, R. and Pearce, J. J. (2007) 'Introduction', in B. Thom, R. Sales and J. J. Pearce (eds) *Growing up with Risk*, Bristol: Policy Press.

Valentine, G. (2003) 'Boundary crossings: transitions from childhood to adulthood', *Children's Geographies*, 1(1): 37–52.

Williamson, H. (2009) 'European youth policy and the place of the United Kingdom', in J. Wood and J. Hine (eds) *Work with Young People*, London: Sage.

Yates, S. (2009) 'Good practice in guidance: lessons from Connexions', in J. Wood and J. Hine (eds) *Work with Young People*, London: Sage.

Young, K. (2006) *The Art of Youth Work*, 2nd edn, Dorset: Russell House Publishing.

2

Youth as a Social Construction

Mary Jane Kehily

> The idea that youth is a social construction – that it is made and shaped by the society we live in and will therefore change time and place – can have a powerful influence on how we look at young people and interpret their behaviour. This chapter explains what is meant by social construction and explores some of the processes through which our understandings of young people are being shaped.

This chapter will introduce you to the concept of *youth*. Generally referring to an age-bound stage in the life course, the term has particular associations and meanings in Western societies. This chapter will demonstrate how the idea of youth can be understood as a *social construction* that is made and shaped by the society in which we live. To explore the processes involved in the social construction of youth, the chapter will consider the following themes:

- The 'birth' of the adolescent through psychological studies of human development and the emergence of the teenager as a cultural phenomenon;
- The construction of youth through the market, commercial forces and consumer practices;
- Youth as a creation of representational field, the media and popular culture;
- The self-defining practices of young people themselves, through youth cultures and subcultures.

The purpose of this exploration is to reveal how individuals and groups participate in the construction of their social worlds. This approach does not imply that changes taking place in the teenage years are imagined or do not exist, but it does involve recognising that people create their own reality and that reality is multiple and not

This chapter is the author's revision of Kehily, Mary Jane (2007) 'A cultural Perspective' Chapter 1 in Kehily, Mary Jane (ed) *Understanding Youth*. London: Sage.

fixed. The truth, like reality, is a social construct; it can be found but will vary over time and place. The social construction of reality is an ever-changing process dependent on the way people make sense of the world around them. To claim youth as a social construct implies that there are no universals of age or experience. The transition to adulthood will take on different meanings across time and place. As Margaret Mead (1971 [1928]) demonstrated in her study of young women in Western Samoa, the stress associated with Western adolescence is not a feature of all societies. This chapter will consider how *youth* is given meaning through processes that create dominant ways of thinking and speaking about young people and their activities in, for example, leisure spaces and sites of consumption. A central theme of the chapter considers the perspective of young people themselves, providing examples of youth culture and subculture in which young people become active co-constructors, engaged in interpreting their social worlds and defining reality for themselves.

The 'birth' of the adolescent and the emergence of the 'teenager'

Youth as a life phase in Western cultures is commonly seen as socially significant and psychologically complex. But how did it become so? Large-scale socio-economic changes in Europe and North America such as industrialisation, education and legislation regulating child labour created the conditions for children and young people to be separated, to some extent, from the adult world. Schooling, for example, organises children and young people into age-based cohorts, subjects them to similar experiences and, of course, delays the onset of economic activity. Within the changing social context of the late nineteenth century, in which the young spent less time with adults and more time with each other, the emergent discipline of psychology played a part in constructing the concept of *adolescence* rather than youth. American psychologist G. Stanley Hall was influential in charting adolescence as a stage of development within the life course in a two-volume study, *Adolescence: its Psychology, and its Relations to Anthropology, Sex, Crime, Religion and Education*. Hall described adolescence as a transitional period in the journey from childhood to adulthood. He drew upon the notion of *recapitulation* – the idea that individual development mirrors the development of humankind throughout history – from primitive being to civilised adult. Hall's approach assumed that all human development followed the same pattern regardless of time and place. This universal model runs counter to social constructionist perspectives that emphasise the importance of socio-cultural context in shaping development and the meanings that can be ascribed to it. Hall is best known for his characterisation of adolescence as a period of *storm and stress*:

> It is the age of natural inebriation without the need of intoxicants, which made Plato define youth as spiritual drunkenness. It is a natural impulse to experience hot and perfervid psychic states, and it is characterised by emotionalism. We see here the instability and fluctuations now so characteristic. (Hall, 1904, vol. 2, pp. 74–5)

For Hall adolescence is marked by physiological change and bodily development that in popular discourse conjures up an image of the stereotypical teenager, subject to 'raging hormones', mood swings and an inability to communicate with adults. Hall's account of adolescence and the contemporary image of the teenager in popular culture suggest that young people are at the mercy of biological change that they are not entirely in control of. Hall's ideas about young people rest upon biology as a driving force in their lives; young people remain in the grip of hormonal and psychological changes that produce an erratic range of feelings and behaviour. Approaches to understanding youth from a cultural perspective have been critical of research traditions that prioritise the importance of biology. The two contrasting terms adolescence and youth signal some of the differences between the perspectives. Though both terms refer to young people in the same age range, the term adolescence is usually used by researchers concerned, like Hall, with matters of biology, psychology and human development. From this perspective, adolescence is viewed as a developmental stage; the term youth, on the other hand, suggests a more social orientation, a concern with young people as a socially constituted group and an interest in the ways in which young people are positioned and defined within society.

Adolescence as a stage of development

The idea of adolescence as a stage of development has been influential in shaping many psychological and psychotherapeutic studies of young people. A contrasting perspective on psychoanalytic development during adolescence can be found in the work of Erik Erikson (1902–94). Erikson focused upon the concept of identity as it emerged and changed in developmental stages across the life course. He used the term *identity confusion* to describe the conflict of adolescence in which young people appear to be at war with themselves and the society they live in. Erikson's account of the development of identity begins in infancy when the child incorporates or interjects adult images that arise in the trustful parent–child relationship. Later childhood is marked by *identification*; the incorporation of roles and values of others who are most admired. Adolescence places emphasis on *identity formation* in which the individual retains some earlier childhood identification and rejects others in accordance with their developing interests and values. Erikson's account of adolescent development is distinctive in that he considers young people within the context of their society, paying attention to work, prevailing ideologies and cultural milieu:

> As technological advances put more and more time between early school life and the young person's final access to specialised work, the stage of adolescing becomes an even more marked and conscious period and, it has always been in some cultures in some periods, almost a way of life between childhood and adulthood. Thus in the later school years young people, beset with the physiological revolution of their genital maturation and the uncertainty of adult roles ahead, seem much concerned with faddish attempts at establishing an adolescent subculture with what looks like a final rather than a transitory or, in fact, initial identity formation … (Erikson, 1968, p. 128)

Erikson notes the significance of the broader context in which young people experience their teenage years and comments upon some of the interrelationships to be found. A striking feature of Erikson's account is the way in which he views youth subcultures as 'faddish' and disruptive cliques that young people may be in danger of over-identifying with. The account of adolescent development presented by Erikson treats young people as an important group that requires attention. Understanding young people and taking them seriously is regarded as important for parents, other adults and for society as a whole. Erikson places emphasis upon psychological development in adolescence, focusing upon matters of identity formation.

The teenager as a cultural phenomenon

From a cultural perspective, youth is not defined as a biological state. Rather, the idea of young people as a special category is regarded as a product of the way society is organised. The visibility of young people in the West can be seen as a post World War II phenomenon associated with growing affluence and young people's participation in the workplace as economic subjects with the ability to develop particular interests. The 'birth' of the 'teenager' can be understood as a social phenomenon of the post-war years; part of the cultural narrative of modern times. Green (1999) locates the primal scream of the modern teenager as a 1950s event. For the first time, he suggests, young people found themselves in forms of employment that gave them free time and a disposable income. In the past young people moved from school to work and from the family home to the marital home with little time or money for carefree pleasure. But the optimism and relative affluence of the post-war years provided the space for something else to emerge. Increased employment opportunities and greater financial independence provided young people with some of the resources for the pursuit of cultural 'play'. The mass production of everyday items such as food, clothes, music and literature provided further resources for young people to create cultural groups based on a shared style and attitude. The emergence of the teenager in the West defined young people in terms of age and gender. Young women and men were differently marked as gendered subjects, defined in relation to each other in ways that reflected the normative gender relations of the culture.

'Bird on the wire': the construction of femininity through leisure activities

Mary Celeste Kearney's (2005) study of teenage girlhood and telephony illustrates the ways in which the trope of the teenage girl on the phone has been used as a symbol of American girlhood from the 1940s. She suggests that in the immediate post World War II period teenage girls were presented in media culture as resistant to domesticity and the prevailing gender order in ways that posed a threat to traditional Western values at a time when the US was attempting to reconstitute itself through domestic containment strategies. In this context the telephone worked symbolically as a sign of social progress and social disruption, representing, simultaneously, girls' liberation and containment within the domestic sphere. Like young people's use of mobile phones in contemporary times, the ability to communicate can give individuals greater independence while also subjecting them to increased forms of surveillance and control (Henderson et al., 2007). The image of the teenage girl on the phone was used across a range of media throughout the 1940s, 1950s and 1960s to symbolise an expression of emergent new femininities that could be mediated and contained. This period also saw changes in marketing strategies that recognised young women as an emergent consumer market. The Bell Telephone Company, for example, began marketing the 'Princess Line' as a second telephone for the teenage girl in the house, whose long calls and idle chatter could be viewed with a mixture of disdain and amusement. Images from the 1950s and 1960s pursued the idea of girls' sociability through talk that could be ridiculed as idle, vulgar and frivolous, to the point where girls' excessive use of the telephone was represented as a disease – 'telephonitus'. Kearney's study offers an interesting insight into the ways in which femininities are shaped by time and place. Her study demonstrates how youthful femininity has been seen as a vehicle for societal concerns in the US at least since the 1940s and the way concerns can be focused around a technology such as the telephone.

Moral panic: media constructions of young masculinities as 'trouble'

The activities of young people in general became a cause for concern among adults in the post-war years, but it was the activities of working-class young men that raised particular concerns. There are many ways in which youth and the activities of young people have been cast as 'deviant'. Young people's reluctance to conform to societal norms has routinely been seen as a form of deviance incorporating moments of rebellion and/or criminality. The notion of 'moral panics' can be seen as a counter interpretation that attempts to understand young people's activities rather than see them as disruptive and troublesome. The term 'moral panic' describes the reactions to social or cultural phenomena that appear out of proportion to the actual threat posed. The term is drawn from the influential research of Stanley Cohen. Taking a sociological approach, Cohen (1972) focused upon the emergence of two UK-based youth subcultures with contrasting modes of dress and lifestyle. Cohen's study of Mods and Rockers in south-east England illustrated the ways in which media coverage of their activities turned young people into 'folk devils' that in turn generated widespread 'moral panic' about their behaviour:

A crucial dimension for understanding the reaction to deviance both by the public as a whole and by agents of social control, is the nature of the information that is received about the behaviour in question. Each society possesses a set of ideas about what causes deviation – is it due say to sickness or to wilful perversity? – and a set of images of who constitutes the deviant – is he an innocent lad being led astray, or is he a psychopathic thug? – and these conceptions shape what is done about his behaviour. In industrial societies, the body of information from which such ideas are built, is invariably received at second hand. That is, it arrives already processed in the mass media and this means the information has been subject to alternative definitions of what constitutes 'news' and how it should be gathered and presented. The information is further structured by the various commercial and political constraints in which newspapers, radio and television operate. (Cohen, 1972, p. 16)

Cohen turns his attention to the now infamous encounters between Mods and Rockers at south-coast holiday resorts on Bank Holiday weekends in the mid-1960s. He documents the journalistic styles of exaggeration, melodrama and distortion that 'enter into the consciousness and shape societal reaction at later stages' (p. 33). In a detailed analysis of the events and media coverage of the events, Cohen powerfully suggests that the activities of young people only exist as reportable stories of youthful rivalry: 'The Mods and Rockers didn't become news because they were new; they were presented as new to justify their creation as news' (Cohen, 1972, p. 46). Rather, through the act of reporting, Mods and Rockers become associated with 'trouble' that is regarded as symptomatic of imminent social breakdown.

The self-defining practices of young people: youth culture and subculture

Folk Devils and Moral Panics, discussed above, marked the emergence of a new and highly influential approach to youth; using the concept of 'subculture' as an approach to understanding the social lives of young people. In simple terms a subculture can be seen as a group within a group. The social group frequently referred to as 'youth' has thrown up many sub-groups over the years which have come to be regarded as subcultures. Over time these subcultures acquire names and identities such as Teddy-boys, Skinheads, Punks and Goths. There is a rich vein of research that uses the concept of subculture to illustrate the many ways in which young people can be observed and studied. It is through the concept of subculture that the activities of many young people have become visible.

Subcultural groups are commonly marked by distinctive modes of appearance, a particular style, modes of dress and adornment that make the participants look different, sometimes even spectacular and shocking. In the context of subcultural groups, style takes on a particular meaning as 'the means by which cultural identity and social location are negotiated and expressed' (O'Sullivan et al., 1994, p. 305).

It is also worth drawing attention to the emotions and the lived experience of being a member of a subculture. Being a member of a subculture is not about being a victim. Individuals involved in subcultural activity often speak of the highs and lows of life as part of a subculture; the mundane inertia of 'doing nothing' (Corrigan, 1979) contrasted with moments of risk and excitement when *something happens*.

Albert K. Cohen (1955) explored the concept of subculture as a means of better understanding *what people do*. In Cohen's analysis subcultures arise when people with similar problems get together to look for solutions. It is then through interaction with one another that members of a subculture come to share a similar outlook on life and evolve collective solutions to the problems they experience. This process, however, often creates a distance between the subculture and the dominant culture. Indeed, achieving status within a subculture may entail a loss of status in the wider culture. This definition makes it clear the subcultures exist in relation to the society in which they emerge and that their existence may provide an insight into the experiences of young people, especially in the areas of education, work and leisure. Sociologists and those working with young people may be interested to consider why particular subcultures emerge at certain times and remain an enduring feature of the era. The relationship between the anti-war movement and 'hippies', for example, or Punk as an expression of shrinking opportunities for young people suggest productive lines of enquiry for understanding youth subculture. Subsequent studies have challenged the concept of subculture itself. Steve Redhead's (1993) study asserted that subcultures have been replaced by 'clubcultures'. Redhead's analysis signals the impact of globalisation upon youth culture. He defines clubcultures as global and fluid youth formations that are based upon the media and the niche marketing of dance music as a youth-culture-for-all.

Tokyo girls: the globalisation of youth subcultures

Early studies of youth subcultures tended to focus on young men's dominance of public space in which the street functioned as a backdrop to the unfolding of male subcultural activity. Girls and young women were often invisible in these studies and were positioned within the domestic sphere – the home and the bedroom. This was, at least in part, a reflection of gendered social relations in the 1970s which have been challenged and altered through processes of feminist struggle and social change in the intervening decades. Contemporary research into girlhood indicates that there are different ways of being a girl and that femininity is no longer so rigidly defined. This has allowed young women more freedom to shape their own identities and to create interesting new subcultural spaces (as well as participating in established subcultures).

In twenty-first century Japan, youth cultures often revolve around a constantly evolving set of very distinctive 'street fashions'. Yuniya Kawamura (2006) explains that these fashions are not produced or controlled by professional fashion designers, but by teenage girls who rely on their distinctive appearance to produce a subcultural identity. Loli or 'Loli' is a particular subcultural aesthetic, which is often associated with the Harajuku area of Tokyo, where many Lolis gather to socialise and to pose for photographs (Figure 2.1). Although the subculture is not exclusively female, there are far more female Lolis than male.

Figure 2.1   Sweet Lolitas posing for a photograph
Source: Christian Kadluba, available at www.flickr.com/photos/pokpok/3557137042

In the Western world, the term Loli is likely to evoke images of the sexually precocious title character from Vladimir Nabokov's 1955 novel. Yet, while the subculture does reference this character in its name, Loli takes on a completely different meaning in the context of Japanese youth culture. The roots of the Loli subculture can be traced back to the *kawaii* or cute trend in 1970s and 1980s Japan. In the 1980s, band members within the newly emerging visual-*kei* (or visual style) music scene began to wear elaborate costumes and make-up which explored what has become known as the Loli aesthetic. This very distinctive style of dress draws upon and adapts a wide range of influences, including British Victoriana, particularly porcelain dolls and Lewis Carroll's *Alice in Wonderland* books, and Japanese popular cultural forms. In addition to visual-*kei* bands and celebrities, the style is influenced by characters from anime and manga (Japanese animation and comics).

By the beginning of the twenty-first century, the Loli subculture had grown exponentially in popularity both within Japan and internationally. A wide variety of Loli-style clothes and accessories can be bought in specialist boutiques and, increasingly, in mainstream shops. The Loli aesthetic centres around an idealised image of Victorian childhood. Lolis wear clothes designed to de-emphasise the features of an adult female body; they use flattened bodices, high waists and full skirts with voluminous underskirts in order to conceal their bust and hips. They often wear their hair in ringlets with a bonnet, and make use of a range of accessories, including aprons, small bags, stuffed animals or parasols. This style of dress is complemented by striking poses intended to evoke the illusion of a very young girl or of a porcelain doll. When posing for photographs, Lolis often stand with their knees together and toes pointed inwards and their head inclined to one side.

This 'classic' or 'traditional' Loli aesthetic has diversified into a wide range of different subgenres. 'Sweet Lolis' emphasise the *kawaii* (or cute) aspects of the style and incorporate overtly Romantic or Rococo elements, and 'Gothic Lolis' incorporate influences from Victorian mourning dress into the overall aesthetic and make use of a range of cute yet macabre accessories (like coffin-shaped bags or injured teddy bears). Indeed, the Gothic Loli look is so popular that it is often said to have produced its own subgenres, such as Elegant Gothic Loli or Elegant Gothic Aristocrat Loli, who wear longer dresses and use different accessories.

Kawamura (2006) argues that Loli identities are resolutely not political or ideological; Loli is primarily an aesthetic and the subculture is concerned with the production and display of innovative fashion. Despite this claim, she argues that Japanese street fashions are a way for young people to express shifting cultural values in contemporary Japanese society. For Osmud Rahman and colleagues (2011) the Loli subculture in Japan, and in south-east Asia more generally, is as much a way of reacting to societal pressures as it is an expression of their dreams and fantasies. The subculture provides young Lolis with a way to escape from their immediate realities and to express their feelings about their lives and experiences as young women. Far from being resolutely a-political, then, the Loli subculture is intricately interwoven with contemporary Japanese sexual and gender politics.

Theresa Winge (2008) argues that the Loli subculture in Japan is a combination of both distinctive dress and what she calls 'ritualised performance' in particular public spaces. She describes the experience of these performances in terms of the 'carnivalesque' in so far as they allow Lolis some release from the usual norms of Japanese society. By performing as part of this subcultural community, Lolis are able to assert their difference from mainstream society without entirely abandoning the collectivism privileged in Japanese culture. Winge explains that Lolis attempt to prolong childhood through the extensive use of *kawaii* or cuteness. As a result, the Loli subculture may appear to be anti-feminist because it portrays an ideal of feminine passivity by valorising the image of virginal youth. However, Winge argues that the doll-like Loli aesthetic creates a safe space for young women to perform their sexuality.

The Loli subculture has caused controversy both within Japan and internationally. Much of this controversy centres around issues of female sexuality and sexualisation, particularly surrounding *lolicon* (a Japanese portmanteu of 'Loli complex') or sexual attraction to prepubescent girls. Winge argues that the Loli subculture is entirely separate from *lolicon* as a sexual fetish. She explains that although Lolis attempt to prolong childhood through the use of *kawaii*, they are striving to create the appearance of living dolls, rather than young girls. In contrast, Vera Mackie (2009) argues that the Loli aesthetic and *lolicon* are different manifestations of the same anxiety about female sexuality: Lolis are attempting to escape from the pressures within Japanese society by prolonging their girlhood, while adult men choose to focus on the image of young girls which they find less threatening than adult women.

Since its emergence as a subculture some decades ago, the Loli subculture has grown in popularity and influenced popular culture both within Japan and internationally. A range of dedicated fashion labels and accessory boutiques have emerged to supply the subculture, although many Lolis continue to adapt these items or make their own. The subculture has also been commodified for consumption within Japanese popular culture more generally, particularly in manga, anime and video-game franchises. The relationship between subcultures and the commercial world sets in motion a long-standing tension between the DIY spirit of subcultural membership and the encroachment of the market into every aspect of human experience. Postcards of Punks with 'Greetings from London' captions illustrate how the 'alternative' can be incorporated into the mainstream as a unique selling point, promoting tourism by marketing London as an exciting city inhabited by this spectacular urban species.

Conclusion

This chapter has explored the idea of youth as a social construction that varies over time and place. Pointing out the differences embedded in the academic disciplines of psychology and sociology, the early sections of the chapter considered how the terms adolescence and youth signalled different ways of looking at young people and making sense of what they do. The chapter offers an account of the teenager as a feature of a historical moment in Western societies that is marked by economic and social change. The chapter provides contrasting examples of how youth as a social category is shaped by gender as well as age. Young people, however, speak back to ideas that position them. Through subcultural activity, the style and attitude of particular groups cross national boundaries to connect with each other and produce meanings for themselves. Finally, we may want to ask, why does it matter what young people do? Christine Griffin (1993) points to some of the implications when she suggests that, in Western societies, the category 'youth' is 'treated as a key indicator of the state of the nation itself'. The values, behaviour and attitudes of young people can be read as a comment upon the society at present and can also be seen to hold the key to the nation's future. Viewed in these terms, youth as a social category always represent something bigger than themselves.

References

Cohen, A.K. (1955) *Delinquent Boys: the Culture of the Gang*, New York, Free Press.
Cohen, S. (1972) *Folk Devils and Moral Panics*, London, Paladin.
Corrigan, P. (1979) *Schooling the Smash Street Kids*, London, Macmillan.
Erikson, E. (1968) *Identity, Youth and Crisis*, New York, Norton and Co.

Green, J. (1999) *All Dressed Up: the Sixties and the Counterculture*, London, Pimlico.

Griffin, C. (1993) *Representations of Youth*, Cambridge, Polity.

Hall, G.S. (1904) *Adolescence: its Psychology and its Relation to Anthropology, Sociology, Sex, Crime, Religion and Education* (2 vols), New York, Appleton.

Henderson, S., Holland, J., McGrellis, S., Sharpe, S. and Thomson, R. (2007) *Inventing Adulthoods: a Biographical Approach to Youth Transitions*, London, Sage/The Open University.

Kawamura, Y. (2006) 'Japanese teens as producers of street fashion', *Current Sociology*, 54(5), pp. 784–801.

Kearney, M.C. (2005) 'Birds on the wire: troping teenage girlhood through telephony in mid-twentieth-century media culture', *Cultural Studies*, 19(5), pp. 568–601.

Mackie, V. (2009) 'Transnational bricolage: gothic Loli and the political economy of fashion', *Intersections: Gender and Sexuality in Asia and the Pacific*, 20, available at http://intersections.anu.edu.au/issue20/mackie.htm#n47.

Mead, M. (1971 [1928]) *Coming of Age in Samoa: a Study of Adolescence and Sex in Primitive Societies*, London, Pelican.

O'Sullivan, T., Hartley, J., Saunders, D., Montgomery, M. and Fiske, J. (1994) *Key Concepts in Communications and Cultural Studies*, London, Routledge.

Rahman, O., Wing-sun, L., Lam, E. and Mong-tai, C. (2011) '"Loli": imaginative self and elusive consumption', *Fashion Theory*, 15(1), pp. 7–28.

Redhead, S. (ed.) (1993) *Rave Off: Politics and Deviance in Contemporary Youth Culture*, Aldershot, Avebury.

Winge, T. (2008) 'Undressing and dressing Loli: a search for the identity of the Japanese Loli', *Mechademia*, 3, pp. 47–63.

3

Trouble and Tribes: Young People and Community

Jeremy Brent

Young people and adults often have quite different understandings and experiences of 'community'. The chapter describes some of the strategies used by young people on a particular housing estate to establish their own sense of community. Whilst the behaviour of these young people can be read as disruptive and even illegal, the analysis draws out attention to how collective action is being used to build solidarity, enforce boundaries and give young people a sense of belonging, identity and security.

In Southmead, an area in which I have worked and researched over a number of years, young people are persistently seen as a major problem that stands in the way of the formation of community, which itself is seen as an almost magical solution to the ills of the area. It is as if young people are held responsible for holding the area back. However, young people too continually engage in collective activities that bear certain strong resemblances to what is generally labelled 'community', except that their activities are not approved of, and are not given the accolade of having this term applied to them.

For me, this leads to a difficult question: 'What is community, anyway?', which I have explored more fully elsewhere (Brent, 2004). In this chapter, I want to look at young people in relation to ideas of community, including issues of sociality, collectivity, locality and power. I give examples of adult views of young people, followed by accounts of young people's own communal actions, and relate these to theories of community, including that of 'neo-tribes', described as unstable 'effervescent communities' (Maffesoli, 1996: 66) that challenge the nostalgic idea of community as 'warm togetherness' (Bellah, 1997: 388).

This is a revised version of the original text which appeared in *Youth and Policy*, the journal of critical analysis, edited by Ruth Gilchrist, Tony Jeffs and Jean Spence and published by The National Youth Agency.

Southmead itself is a large housing estate on the northern edge of Bristol. No thumbnail sketch can do the area justice ... [but] to show the context of the argument, here are some bare facts and figures.

Southmead has a population of over 10,000. It was primarily developed over a twenty-five year period between 1930 and 1955, with later infill. The housing is low density – the vast majority of it being three-bedroom houses with gardens. Ever since it was built Southmead has had a reputation for trouble and poverty. It was the subject of a major action research study by the Bristol Social Project in the 1950s, and in one of the papers from that project, tellingly entitled *Difficult Housing Estates*, it is described as: 'containing areas of bad reputation which caused the whole neighbourhood to be held in low esteem' (Wilson, 1963: 3). Three decades later a survey stated that:

> Throughout its history, Southmead has received attention in the media as a problem estate where crime, lawlessness and anti-social behaviour are rife. Riots and fire bombings in the early and late 1980s and the problem of joyriding, which recently received national coverage, have all seemed to firmly establish Southmead as 'Bristol's trouble-plagued estate'. (Safe Neighbourhoods Unit, 1991: 7)

In the 1999 *Audit of Crime and Disorder in Bristol*, Southmead was named as a major 'crime hot-spot' in the city, the only area with as many as five entries out of eight police priority categories (Bristol Community Safety Partnership, 1999). The 'problem' tag therefore has a long history – from at least 1952, when the Bristol Social Project research was set up, until at least the end of the 1990s.

Southmead has also always featured as one of the poorest areas in the city in the *Poverty in Bristol* reports that Bristol City Council issue, with the 1996 report stating that the estate falls within the 'highest' fifth of the five indicators used to measure deprivation in Bristol. In 1998 the Southmead ward was scored as having the third worst quality of life out of 34 Bristol wards, and in DETR statistics it figures among the worst 10% of wards in England (Bristol City Council, 1996, 1999; DETR, 1998).

Southmead is not alone as an area with such statistics. There are some 2000 such estates throughout Britain, the main feature of Southmead being its size – four to nine times larger than the '20 of the most difficult' that were surveyed in a Joseph Rowntree Foundation study (Power and Tunstall, 1995). Nor is it alone in being seen as an area where, despite all the figures of poverty, it is young people that are seen as the major social problem.

There is one distinction often made between different young people – the 'good' versus the 'bad', or 'disaffected' – which needs to be treated with care, if not scorn. This distinction is far too neat, bears little close examination, and is even 'wicked' in the way that it is used (Piper and Piper, 1999). Certainly in my experience some young people that are involved in 'bad' activities, are, in other circumstances, categorised as 'good' (as can be seen in my examples later). The argument as to whether young people are *either* bad *or* good is finally a sterile approach to looking at the issues involved in young people living in a 'community', and puts all the onus of good behaviour on to them.

Adult views of young people and community

Like many poor areas, Southmead has been exhaustively researched and surveyed. Without fail, all the various official surveys of Southmead cast young people as a, even *the*, major problem of the area. The very first research into community in the area was set up because of the problem of young people: 'Juvenile delinquency was the initial problem and starting point for the project' (Spencer et al., 1964: 24). Later reports continually reiterate that theme. Out of the blue, with no lead up of argument or evidence, a 1983 report states that: 'youth problems [are] a major factor in Southmead' (Bristol City Council, 1983). A report written in 1991 is full of disparaging references to young people, including the one that states: 'There was almost universal agreement that those largely responsible for crime in Southmead are young people' (Safe Neighbourhoods Unit, 1991: 46). The 1999 *Audit of Crime and Disorder in Bristol* gives as one of the reasons for Southmead being a priority ward for crime and disorder that there are more than 25% young people in the population (Bristol Community Safety Partnership, 1999: 28).

In all the reports young people are seen as a cause of crime, their behaviour a problem. The Crime Audit answers its own question about Southmead: 'Who are the offenders and why are they offending?' thus:

> In keeping with the largest concentrations of young people in the city the area has high levels of truancy and youth unemployment. A minority of young people on the estate experiment with drugs and some have become addicted to hard drugs. Many burglaries and thefts are committed to fund drug habits. There is boredom and a lack of prospects amongst young people leading to crimes such as criminal damage. (Bristol Community Safety Partnership, 1999: 33)

Throughout the reports on Southmead, young people are the *only* group that are identified as criminal, their large concentration seen as a problem. Even in discussion of domestic violence, men are not named as the major responsible group.

In the 1991 survey, there was a separate section in which under-18-year-olds were surveyed. They were asked questions that the adults were not asked. Had they ever played truant? Had they been involved in crime? And 'During the last year have you had an alcoholic drink or taken any drugs?' (Safe Neighbourhoods Unit, 1991). Asking these questions shows clearly how surveys create a perception of young people as a problem and manufacture data that maintain this perception; the questions asked in surveys are not themselves innocent.

That there is a problem with the behaviour of some young people in Southmead cannot be denied. F—, a long-time youth worker with a strong commitment to young people in Southmead, told me:

> Walking around the estate on Saturday I was so ashamed. The kids were being really horrible. I saw them attack X—, and another old woman who used to work in the Post Office. They were throwing bricks at buses, and opening and closing the bus doors. Wherever I went on the estate there were kids behaving badly. They were collecting penny-for-the-guy. When people refused to give them any money, they followed them

into the shops and pestered them. I feel that it is getting so bad that it can't get better. I was gutted and ashamed that I knew these kids. With this old lady they were jostling her in the street, and almost hit her.

Much of the conflict between adults and young people is about behaviour in public space. A noticeable facet of Southmead life is the number of young people using the public space of the streets; in common with many poor areas, young people are a high proportion of the population. Their use of the street is not unusual, as is pointed out in a work on the geographies of youth culture: 'Studies on teenagers suggest that the space of the street is often the only autonomous space that young people are able to carve out for themselves' (Valentine et al., 1998: 7). This attempt at autonomy brings them into conflict with other street users, challenging adult rules of sociality. In Brown's research, in place of a reciprocal sociality between young people and adults, there was a 'perpetual, never ending conflict over space which characterises much of the relationship between the generations in public' (Brown, 1995: 40).

In these descriptions of conflict, young people are always mentioned in the plural. There are always more than one of them. The behaviour is collective. Melucci writes that collective behaviour is 'never a purely irrational phenomenon. It is always to a degree meaningful to its participants ...' (Melucci, 1989: 191). I want to use his insight to examine this behaviour, as collectivity is another important facet of the idea of community. Used with the idea of public space, it is closely linked to another idea often used as an ingredient of community: that of control over locality. In looking at examples of young people's collective actions in Southmead, and their relation to public space and locality, wider issues of community are raised than just that of the behaviour of young people. Youth behaviour may be seen as destructive to community, but nostalgia for past youth is one aspect of community building. People love the shared history of remembering themselves as young. In 1993 there was an exhibition, called '40 Years of Youth Work in Southmead'. This was extremely popular, much more popular in the area than the exhibitions of contemporary work done by young people, and led to more people bringing in their even older photographs, and eventually the compilation of the book *Alive and Kicking!*, full of memories of youth (Truman and Brent, 1995). As Stuart Hall has put it: 'organic community was just always in the childhood you left behind' (Hall, 1991: 46). Shared memories of youth can be an important ingredient of adult community. Now, though, I want to give examples of the communal activities created by young people themselves.

Young people, collective action and neo-tribes

One of the features of the social life of young people in Southmead is the way certain sites – street corners, park areas, shops – by some mysterious way become the place where crowds of young people congregate and socialise. These places become young people's space for a time, with their own shorthand titles, until eventually the police are called, and the crowds dispersed until, a few weeks or months later, a new site emerges as that place to be. One area, 'the Green', was used so often as a gathering place and centre of joyriding and battles with the police, that in 1996 it was built over. 'They've taken *our* green away', I was told by young people at the time. Three months later the crowds met up again at 'the woods', as described below. These gatherings are comparable to the concept of 'neo-tribes'. Neo-tribes have been characterised as 'recently invented communities involving some membership choice', which occur in '"wild zones" ... where aesthetic and other resources are thin on the ground' (Lash and Urry, 1994: 318). They are arguably a modern version of 'community' in a mass society, with young people in Southmead being active and creative inventors of their own such communities.

The sight of large numbers of teenagers meeting together and enjoying themselves should be a cause for celebration for all those interested in their welfare. Especially when the young people feel 'empowered' enough to organise all their own activities – sitting around campfires, cooking food in the open, chatting, laughing, playing games, all with no adult supervision. However the headline in one local newspaper was: '*BIKER GROVE! Beauty spot is ravaged by teen hoodlums*'. The story went on:

> Police and park rangers are joining forces to clamp down on teenage motorcyclists who have turned a woodland beauty spot into an off-road race track.

> The move follows complaints from residents walking their dogs at Badocks Wood, in Southmead, about noise and dangerous driving.

> ... The area has been plagued by gangs of youths in recent months, who meet up on mopeds and use the wooded slopes and paths as an off-road adventure circuit. (*Bristol Observer*, 4 April 1996)

Despite its sensationalism, the newspaper coverage missed the full dramatic importance of the events in Badocks Wood for young people. The newspaper's perspective was that of the outraged adults, and in no way reflected young people's perspective of pleasure as that area was taken over and used for a carnival of collective action and transgression (that this transgression worked was confirmed by the affronted tone of the article).

Going around the area in the day (at night I would have been out of time and out of place; even as a youth worker, I am excluded from young people's communities), I could get a sense of the excitement that the young people must have felt, as well as seeing the destruction caused. It was like a scene after a carnival. I could almost hear the shrieks of delight from the evening before. On a long stretch of grassland one could see the marks of wheels running up and over a dip. The ground in the woods was covered in skid marks from racing around amongst the trees and slopes. There were the remains of bonfires and food wrappers, and burnt out wrecks of cars. Branches had been pulled off trees for firewood. There was the dramatic sight of a burnt out Metro on top of the old burial mound. The fence around the mound and the post with its Ancient Monument information had gone, the wood used for fires.

Entry to the area was through a hole in the fence. The hole was small, so only small cars (hence the Metro) were being used. In the course of one week there were eight wrecks in the area. The motorbikes were taken home at night.

The authorities cleared the area of this activity by a concerted operation; the aftermath of this was extreme anger amongst young people and antagonism towards the police and all other adults. It was a difficult time for staff at the Youth Centre, as angry young people moved there and vented their rage. The community police team felt the antagonism – they had a meeting with me to discuss the events, and struck me as being totally frustrated. They saw the issue as a matter of the law, as shown by this piece they put in the community newspaper:

> Once again, as spring approaches, the problem of off-road motorcyclists has re-surfaced in Badocks Wood … Offences include dangerous riding and riding without due care and attention, for which fines of up to £1,000 can be levied … One youth was arrested recently for theft of a bike. We hope in the coming months to counter this danger to lawful users of the parks. (*Southmead Community News*, May 1996)

All this illicit activity had resulted in a total of one arrest. The events were virtually unpoliceable, with the collective activity of the young people leaving the police powerless until they used semi-military tactics.

At around the same time there was a minor collective event which I witnessed directly. One evening young people started to pull up brick pavers from the courtyard in front of the Youth Centre. Once one was loose, they could all be pulled up. This turned into a tremendous group effort, pulling up the bricks and loading them into trolleys taken from the local shops, wheeling them up to the side of the Youth Centre and building a wall from them – a proper wall, with the headers and stretchers of proper brickwork, if no mortar. I was struck by the immense enjoyment this collective activity brought, the creativity of the wall building, the great effort being put into a 'meaningless' activity – for the wall did virtually nothing, in fact a gap was left at one end for people to walk through. K in particular was working hard and enjoying it – calling for people to help her push the loaded trolley. It did greatly annoy – because of its meaninglessness? – and of course because of its destructiveness of the yard. It frightened old people, who took another way to walk through. It unsettled place, made people unsure whether the path was blocked or not, safe or not.

Both these examples show a challenge to accepted modes of sociality, but also display an alternative, transgressive form of collective social behaviour. These are not orderly forms of community which might offer solutions to problems of neighbourhood crime, but are transgressive – deliberately breaching boundaries, pushing the limits and challenging the law – crucially establishing a different kind of community, one which belongs to these young people. This transgressive impulse leads groups of young people to embrace and celebrate (and even extend) the negative labelling of the area that respectable community activity is working hard to overturn.

Only, of course, for a short time. These were not sustainable communities. Even without police action, their transgressive moment would have passed, even if reappearing in other guises at other times (as has happened since). These short-lived communal gatherings have been described as: 'the efflorescence and effervescence of neo-tribalism … whose sole *raison d'etre* is a preoccupation with the collective present' (Maffesoli, 1996: 75). They are not stable: 'neo-tribalism is characterized by fluidity, by punctuated gathering and scattering', like a ballet, 'the arabesque of sociality' (Maffesoli, 1988: 148). The basis of neo-tribalism (Maffesoli and others who use this term ignore any racial/racist or primitive connotations of the word tribe – they see them as thoroughly modern and universal phenomena) is sensation, touch, performance, not causality or utilitarianism: 'the communal ethic has the simplest of foundations: warmth, companionship – physical contact with one another' (Maffesoli, 1996: 16). This is not a description of community as being necessarily good – in fact, Maffesoli uses the phrase 'group egoism' to describe such groups. He sees neo-tribes as being aesthetically, not ethically or politically, based, though he argues that an ethics may develop from those aesthetics (1991, 1996).

This description by a joy rider from Southmead, being interviewed for *The Place We're In*, a multimedia project at Southmead Youth Centre, has a similar aesthetic quality:

How do you get into a car?

You need a good screw driver ... right ... flat head ... make sure the end bits nice and thin bit ... fit in the door lock ... put in ... put in the door lock ... turn in round whatever open the door ... door open ... climb inside ... put your foot inside the steering wheel, someone else grabs the other end ... turn it round ... snaps – steering wheel snaps ... grab the casing from the back of the steering column ... rip it off ... get the ignition barrel head – file it down, put a screw driver in the back of it, pop the black box off, put something in the black box that'll fit in it – turn it, start it, drive off.

What happens next?

Drive round, drive it round, spin it round, kill it off – burn it out.

So last night, how many people would you say were on the street?

Thirty, twenty, thirty.

Do you get a really big rush when you get it together?

Yeh, sound funny ... watching the cars getting spun round, smoked whatever.

How do you manage to get the tyres to smoke?

Foot down, handbrake up – put your foot down really fast, let the clutch off fast and it smokes on the spot for ages, or some times you put a brick on the accelerator ... leave it on its own ... just goes round ... smokes on its own.

Accounts like these, with their disobedient, errant view of what is 'good', puncture the worthiness of much community rhetoric. These examples of collective behaviour have a romantic edge to them – in witnessing them and describing them there is a sense of the strong desire for shared, communal excitement. Freie writes that we are highly susceptible to what he calls counterfeit community: 'lacking genuine community, yet longing for the meaning and sense of connectedness that it creates – the feeling of community – people become vulnerable to the merest suggestion of community' (Freie, 1998: 2).

The desire for connectedness can also be more vicious than this expansive, if destructive longing. Forms of collective organisation are concerned with inclusion, exclusion and control, as in this episode I witnessed of control in a girl gang:

> E came to club, asked for Y, told her about party. Y said she wasn't going. Later a group of girls came up, all done up, hair especially, carrying cans of lager and cider. E and E (12), L and R (15), J (16). Called Y out. Went around side of building, then J dragging Y by hair to front of building, where all could see – punching her, kicking her, banging her head against railing. I went over, stopped fight. Y kept asking for J to stop. Y went off, cut under left eye. Blokes standing round took no part in it – not even to stop it when it became unfair. Consensus – showing her power – do not leave my group, do what I want you to do – was the message. People predict that Y will toe the line.

My very strong impression was of the establishment of an alternative power structure making sure that no one left the gang, maintaining itself very deliberately in public in the rawest possible way.

By contrast here is an example of forceful public exclusion. One evening the Hs, a family living down the road from the Youth Centre, were driven out by young people. On the evening it happened there was a whole crowd in front of the house, hurling missiles and attacking the police even as they escorted the family away. I was told ferociously by the young people to keep away, that 'This is the way we do things'. There was a strange sense of righteousness about this riot, despite its viciousness. Several were arrested. A few weeks later, in a quieter conversation that took place while young people were creating large paintings for an exhibition (a 'good' communal activity), I discovered what some of the girls involved saw as their reasons for the attack:

> The atmosphere was relaxed, and they started to talk about the Hs. They had a lot of stories to tell – to each other, to O [another girl], and by proxy to me, though they did not seem certain as to what I should know. They were amused at how they had welcomed the Hs, and taken R (girl of their age) under their wing, as she seemed so naive. In the light of what subsequently happened, 'We were the naive ones!'

> They obviously went round to the Hs' house a lot, and were there on the birthday of the father. There was drink, so they knew that they were doing forbidden things that their parents would not allow. The father then invited them to play strip poker, wanted them to sit on his lap, give him a birthday kiss, locked the door and wanted them to stay the night, helped in all of this by his sons. The daughter had gone to bed. The only way they got out was by pretending to be ill. They were laughing about all this as they talked about it, in the way one laughs about something that had been frightening at the time.

Though Maffesoli sees neo-tribes as aesthetic rather than political groupings, they can also be formed to political effect. In the autumn of 1996 there was a campaign against cuts to the Bristol Youth Service. K, whom we last met destroying a pavement to build a useless wall, became a leader of the campaign amongst young people in Southmead.

The young people assembled a mass petition, made up of their hand prints, each signed with a statement as to why they liked the Youth Centre. K met with councillors, and presented this document to Bristol City Council, being the first person under 18 to be allowed to address a full Council meeting, thereby taking part in an approved form of community activity. The collective had been turned to a partially successful political purpose – the cuts in Southmead were less than originally proposed.

Young people and place

A major ingredient in the make-up of these moments of collective activity by young people has been that of place. Southmead itself can feel very bleak, a landscape in which aesthetic resources are sparse. This is felt strongly by young people: 'spaces send messages to young people about how an external world values or fails to value the quality of their lives' (Breitbart, 1998: 308). Young people in Southmead told the youth worker discussing a survey they had done (Kimberlee, 1998) that 'Southmead is a shithole'. Lefebvre argues that it is only by way of revolt that adolescents 'have any prospect of recovering the world of difference – the natural, the sensory/sensual, sexuality and pleasure' (Lefebvre, 1991: 50). In the events around Badocks Wood, this was a suitable space, in terms of size and potential, for such revolt, such a recovery of an aesthetic enjoyment of life.

In some ways, the issue is simple. Place is important for young people who have not the qualifications or other resources to move away. Locality therefore becomes recognised by young people as their 'community of destiny' (Maffesoli, 1996: 125). This relationship is much stronger than that of communities of choice.

Local, known place has its own security. France and Wiles relate the creation of locations of trust – 'small bubbles of security in an insecure world' (France and Wiles, 1998: 68/9) as a reaction to the risks of late modernity. These locations are created by big business in, for example, secure guarded shopping malls that so often exclude young people. As spatiality is controlled against young people, it is no surprise that young people create counter-locations for themselves, their own bubbles where they, if no one else, feel allowed. However, while for some young people this may create a security, for others it creates terror. Thirty per cent of young people surveyed in Southmead in 1998 said that they felt unsafe, and the discussions after the survey highlighted the desire of many young people for safe places to go (Kimberlee, 1998). The rough and transgressive actions of some young people terrify others. The constitutive attachment to place is coupled with acts that are destructive of that very place, an everlasting conundrum: why are young people destroying their own [spaces]? Piven and Cloward, in their work on poor people's movements, point out that people rebel at what is around them as they do not know what the outside forces are that are affecting their lives, nor how to reach them. Without strategic opportunities for defiance, people attack what is around them, act where they are located and with people that they know. The very powerlessness of their situation explains why their defiant behaviour can appear to be so inchoate. They conclude that 'it is difficult to imagine them doing otherwise' (Piven and

Cloward, 1977: 18–22). The combined anger and zest of young people are often not *directed* towards a goal, but are emotions that are *expressed* where they live. Only when there are clear-cut issues, like cuts to the Youth Centre, is anger directed at a political decision affecting their lives.

However, despite actions often being aggressively local (young people in South-mead have their own symbol, the Southmead 'S', and fight against young people from other areas), the cultural symbols of youth are global. The youth culture of Southmead is not a closed culture, similar to the way the youth culture of Yucatec Maya investigated by Massey, where romantic preconception might lead one to expect a local 'authenticity', is also not 'a closed, local culture'. She writes:

> all youth cultures … are hybrid cultures. All of them involve active importation, adoption and adaptation. This challenges the idea that 'local cultures' are under-stood as locally produced systems of social interaction and symbolic meaning. (Massey, 1998: 122/3)

Young people in Southmead probably play the same electronic games she found in Mexico. As the action of young people is about giving a centrality to their own existence, so they will wear the designer clothes of the global market. Campbell observed in the early 1990s: 'All over peripheral estates across Britain teenagers were wearing designer casuals that signified their refusal to be peripheral, to be on the edge of everything' (Campbell, 1993: 271). In a photograph in *The Place We're In* exhibition, the Nike swoosh is highly visible amongst those crowding around a stolen car. The Nike slogan, 'Just Do It' does summon up an impulse of rebellion, even if from the safety of corporate headquarters thousands of miles away. There is a continual interplay between the global and the local elements of youth culture, with both having a major effect. Locality is not an easy autonomy, not separation from the rest of the world, but is still an important stage for collective formations.

Conclusion: young people and questions of community

The various examples I have given of communal activity amongst young people may be disruptive to a peaceful sociality of Southmead, yet contain many of the elements associated with community – solidarity, collective action, boundary enforcement, and control of space – and indicate a central component left out of more utilitarian descriptions of community – a strong aesthetic desire for connec-tion. What they do not do is provide community as a solid and stable entity. The neo-tribes, or micro-groups, formed and re-formed by young people give a speeded up version of the way a range of different ingredients are used, similar to that used in ideas of the construction of communities, though without the approbation that the term provides. As Raymond Williams has famously written, community as a term is one that 'seems never to be used unfavourably'. It is always 'warmly persuasive' (Williams, 1983: 76). To say that what young people are doing when joyriding is building community appears to be a contradiction in terms, but I would argue that this is what they are doing, and also what is being done with even more controversial activities, like heroin use, another collective activity that ties people into a group. Others too have questioned whether strong community does lead to lower crime rates, as criminal activity can be part of an oppositional collective culture (Warner and Rountree, 1997). This means that community is not, of itself, an *answer* to these activities, though thinking about the needs and desires expressed through them might provide fruitful material for forming less destructive forms of collectivities (to use a less loaded term than community). These would have to take into account the issues of identity, activity, aesthetics, control and place that these collectivities raise:

- *Identity.* The formation of young people's collectivities is connected to the formation of their identity as young people, as opposed to being children or adults. The joy rider who gave such an open interview said that in five years' time he would not be doing the same kind of stuff; he would be 'Probably working an' shit'. It is the uncertainty of the identity 'youth' that leads young people to form such dramatic tribal groupings. The lack of solidity in their lives leads to a search for it. This solidity is also what drug addiction promises, when choice is surrendered to an external force. Identity is craved for when it is least stable.
- *Activity.* This identity is achieved by activity and involvement, working together to be part of something, not being left on the sidelines as a mere spectator. All the examples given are active, even involving hard work, and in the case of joyriding, a range of different skills. Neo-tribes flourish in areas without resources: the reasons for collective activities being mostly illicit may not only be about the joys of transgression, but reflect the paucity of licit skilled activity for young people to be involved with.
- *Aesthetics.* A major spur to these activities was to gain pleasure from otherwise barren physical and social landscapes. The activities were not utilitarian, are even a shock to a narrow idea of what is useful; there is often a popular horror that cars are not stolen to sell for cash, but for the pleasure of driving and destroying them. Theatricality and performance are major factors in these activities, with the spectacle being the substance, a performance of community with strong similarities to adult community rituals.
- *Control.* Control can, of course, also be a pleasure, and all these activities involved some form of control, taking power over place and people. These forms of control can be violent, the forms used by rebellious groups countering the ways that they feel controlled. Control both by and against these groups can be raw, but that itself is part of the pleasure, part of the aesthetics.
- *Place.* The connection of community to place in these activities is both clear and obscure. There are strong reasons for emphasising the importance of place, both social and geographical, in all the events described. They always happen in place, each activity is very localised, and could not be otherwise. However, they are not unique to specific places – such activities are replicated over Britain, and further afield. Specific locality does not create these activities, but it is the milieu in which they are created, and a milieu that they create. The activities themselves are used to create the meaning of localities, using any cultural and physical means available.

How does this leave us with an idea of community? While I have identified these ingredients in young people's collective action, they are also used in adult community action (Brent, 2004). There are several things that these actions are not: not necessarily utilitarian; not conformist; not lacking conflict; not permanent; and finally, not necessarily 'good', in the way that many modern communitarian arguments are about its necessity as a social good (e.g. Atkinson, 1994; Bellah, 1997; Etzioni, 1995).

Community, or lack of it, is not the only factor involved in young people's behaviour. There are issues of power involved, issues that communitarians too often ignore (Frazer and Lacey, 1993). All the activities described are gendered, even if they challenge traditional ideas of gendered behaviour. The behaviour is related to Southmead being a place of class and poverty. It involves the power position of young people, in terms of their rights, in terms of the resources available to them, and in terms of the way power is exercised upon them. The punitiveness of many adults would like to achieve, in Foucault's words, 'docility and utility' (Foucault, 1977: 218). However, it is this very negative use of power that strengthens transgressive resistance. The most successful adult initiatives with young people in the area have been based on tolerance and reciprocity, and have generated their own excitement and feelings of connectedness (Greenhalgh, 1999; Kimberlee, 2000). The proponents of discipline as the major tool to be used with young people have not understood the dictum that 'If power were never anything but repressive, if it never did anything but to say no, do you really think anyone could be brought to obey it?' (Foucault, 1980: 119). Any community building that wants to include young people needs to be creative and exciting, not disciplinary and forbidding, and has to recognise those strong aesthetic desires for excitement and connectedness amongst young people as well as amongst adults.

References

Bellah, R. N. (1997) 'The Necessity of Opportunity and Community in a Good Society'. In *International Sociology* 12(4): 387–393.

Breitbart, M. M. (1998) '"Dana's Mystical Tunnel": Young People's Designs for Survival and Change in the City'. In T. Skelton and G. Valentine, *Cool Places: Geographies of Youth Culture*. London, Routledge.

Brent, J. (2004) 'The Desire for Community: Illusion, Confusion and Paradox'. In *Community Development Journal* 39(3): 213–223.

Bristol City Council (1983) *Southmead Report – Report of Southmead Working Group.*

Bristol City Council (1996) *Poverty in Bristol 1996 – An Update.*

Bristol City Council (1999) *Indicators of Quality of Life. Sustainability Update 1998/1999.*

Bristol Community Safety Partnership (1999) *Audit of Crime and Disorder in Bristol.*

Brown, S. (1995) 'Crime and Safety in Whose "Community"? Age, Everyday Life, and Problems for Youth Policy'. In *Youth & Policy* 48: 27–48.

Campbell, B. (1993) *Goliath: Britain's Dangerous Places*. London, Methuen.

Department of Environment, Transport and the Regions (1998) *Index of Local Deprivation.*

France, A. and Wiles, P. (1998) 'Dangerous Futures: Social Exclusion and Youth Work in Late Modernity'. In C. J. Finer and M. Nellis (eds), *Crime & Social Exclusion*. Oxford, Blackwell.

Freie, Ú. P. (1998) *Counterfeit Community: The Exploitation of Our Longing for Connectedness.* Lanham, Rowman & Littlefield Publishers Inc.

Hall, S. (1991) 'The Local and the Global: Globalization and Ethnicity' and 'Old and New Identities, Old and New Ethnicities'. In A. D. King (ed.), *Culture, Globalization and the World System: Contemporary Conditions for the Representation of Identity.* Basingstoke, Macmillan.

Kimberlee, R. H. (1998) *Young People's Survey of Southmead 1998.* Bristol, Southmead Youth Centre.

Lash, S. and Urry, J. (1994) *Economies of Signs and Space.* London, Sage.

Lefebvre, H. (1991) *The Production of Space.* Oxford, Blackwell.

Maffesoli, M. (1988) 'Jeux De Masques: Postmodern Tribalism'. In *Design Issues* IV (1/2): 141–52.

Maffesoli, M. (1991) 'The Ethics of Aesthetics'. In *Theory, Culture & Society* 8: 7–20.

Maffesoli, M. (1996) *The Time of the Tribes: The Decline of Individualism in Mass Society.* London, Sage.

Massey, D. (1998) 'The Spatial Construction of Youth Culture'. In T. Skelton and G. Valentine *Cool Places: Geographies of Youth Culture.* London, Routledge.

Melucci, A. (1989) *Nomads of the Present: Social Movements and Individual Needs in Contemporary Society.* London, Hutchinson Radius.

Piper, H. and Piper, J. (1999) '"Disaffected Youth". A wicked issue: a worse label'. In *Youth & Policy* 62: 32–43.

Piven, F. F. and Cloward, R. A. (1977) *Poor People's Movements: Why They Succeed, How They Fail.* New York, Pantheon Books.

Power, A. and Tunstall, R. (1995) *Swimming against the Tide. Polarisation or Progress on 20 Unpopular Council Estates, 1980–95.* York, Joseph Rowntree Foundation.

Safe Neighbourhoods Unit (1991) *The Southmead Survey 1991.* Prepared for Bristol City Council and Bristol Safer Cities Project.

Spencer, J., Tuxford, J. and Dennis, N. (1964) *Stress and Release in an Urban Estate.* London, Tavistock.

Truman, J. and Brent, J. (1995) *Alive & Kicking! The Life and Times of Southmead Youth Centre.* Bristol, Redcliffe Press.

Valentine, G., Skelton, T. and Chambers, D. (1998) 'Cool Places: an Introduction to Youth and Youth Cultures'. In T. Skelton and G. Valentine *Cool Places: Geographies of Youth Culture.* London, Routledge.

Warner, B. D. and Rountree, P. W. (1997) 'Local Social Ties in a Community and Crime Model: Questioning the Systemic Nature of Informal Social Control'. *Social Problems* 44(4): 520–36.

Williams, R. (1983) (Revised edition) *Keywords: A Vocabulary of Culture and Society.* London, Fontana.

Wilson, R. (1963) *Difficult Housing Estates.* London, Tavistock.

4

Teenage Pregnancy and Parenthood: Implications for Policy and Practice

Aniela Wenham

Teenage pregnancy and parenthood are usually presented as problems for society, as well as for the individuals concerned. Much of the research that has looked at teenage pregnancy has focused on the negative impact it has on young women, and the poor outcomes experienced by their children. This chapter encourages us to examine the negative stereotypes that are often held of young parents and to consider a different account of their experiences, one that is informed by what teenage parents themselves have to say.

Contemporary understandings of teenage pregnancy and motherhood: a cause for concern?

The dominant view of teenage pregnancy and parenthood is of something that is a problem. This viewpoint is part of a much broader perspective that sees teenage pregnancy and parenthood as a threat to the well-being of society, encapsulating practices and behaviour that directly oppose society's conventional norms that surround parenting. It is argued that the result of such behaviour is a wide range of 'poor' outcomes, with society as a whole ultimately having to bear the costs (SEU, 1999; UNICEF, 2001). Within this dominant discourse, or set of ideas, teenage pregnancy tends to be represented as a calamity for all concerned. These sorts of ideas are reflected in comments made by policy makers and in the statements that accompany policy pronouncements:

Too many teenage mothers – and fathers – simply fail to understand the price they, their children and society, will pay … Our failure to tackle this problem has cost the teenagers, their children and the country dear … the consequences of doing this can be seen all around us in shattered lives and blighted futures. (Blair in SEU, 1999: 4)

Teenage parenthood is bad for parents and children. Becoming a parent too early involves a greater risk of being poor, unemployed and isolated. The children of teenage parents grow up with the odds stacked against them. (SEU, 1999: 90)

The claim that teenage pregnancy is problematic often involves emotive and sensationalist language. Arai argues that teenage parents stand out when compared to other stigmatised groups: 'the language used and imagery evoked are such as to suggest that there are few population subgroups who appear to embody so many social and moral "evils"' (Arai, 2009: 48). Similarly, Alexander et al. draw our attention to the pervasiveness of this discourse: 'teenage mothers are seen as emblematic of an "underclass" which is outside of mainstream British society, and which is defined through pathologised moral and cultural values, "lifestyles and behaviour", seemingly transmitted across generations' (Alexander et al., 2010: 136). Duncan argues that these discourses are powerful signifiers of divisions based around social class. He states that 'the fear of teenage pregnancy is bound up in stereotypes of working-class young women whose out-of-control sexuality has historically concerned the ruling classes as having a dangerous potential for social and moral disorder' (Duncan et al., 2010: 311).

The view of teenage pregnancy and motherhood as something that is problematic also lies at the heart of much mainstream social policy research. These studies often rely on statistical evidence to highlight the link between teenage pregnancy and the consequent poor outcomes for both mother and child. For instance, it has been found that teenage parents are more likely not to finish their education, and more likely to bring up their children alone in poverty (Dennison, 2004; Hobcraft and Kiernan, 2001). Teenage mothers and their children are also believed to be at an increased risk of poor health outcomes, including a 60 per cent higher rate of infant mortality; a 25 per cent increased risk of low-birthweight babies; and three times the rate of postnatal depression (SEU, 1999). There is also evidence that the daughters of teenage mothers have a higher chance of becoming teenage mothers themselves (Ermisch and Pevalin, 2003; Hobcraft and Kiernan, 2001), leading, it is argued, to a 'cycle of disadvantage' where social exclusion is passed down from one generation to another. Overall this research data has been used to support the argument that teenage pregnancy not only requires policy intervention, but preventative measures to stop it occurring in the first place (DfES, 2006; SEU, 1999).

However, whilst policy tends to focus on the problems associated with teenage pregnancy, it has yet to determine whether these are caused by long-standing structural determinants or the passing on of cultural expectations and behaviour from generation to generation (Arai, 2003; Hawkes, 2010). For instance, to what extent are the poor outcomes often associated with teenage pregnancy caused by pre-pregnancy social disadvantage rather than teenage childbearing in itself?

The policy landscape – The National Teenage Pregnancy Strategy (TPS)

Under New Labour (1997–2010), a distinct policy agenda emerged putting teenage pregnancy and parenthood high on the policy agenda for central and local government. New Labour developed a 10-year co-ordinated 'National Teenage Pregnancy Strategy' (TPS), the main impetus behind this being the contention that early childbearing was both a cause and consequence of social exclusion (SEU, 1999). This emerging policy framework was distinctly different to that used by previous governments. The notion of social exclusion was a key concept for New Labour and one that shaped and informed social policy over their time in office.

According to the 1999 Social Exclusion Unit report, the three main causes of teenage pregnancy are: *low expectations* (of education or the labour market); *ignorance* (about contraception); and *mixed messages* (confusion about sex) (SEU, 1999). The SEU Report has been highly influential in policy developments directed at teenage pregnancy and parenthood and has set the framework for UK government policy since its publication. The overall ethos of this policy discourse saw young women's attitudes (namely young women within deprived communities), their beliefs and behaviour, as key risk factors. The focus of intervention was on 'tackling' the problem of teenage pregnancy and parenthood (SEU, 1999).

There were also three main policy strands to address 'the problem of teenage pregnancy': a national campaign involving all sections of the community in order to change attitudes to teenage sex and parenthood; prevention through better education about sex and relationships and clearer messages about contraception, with a specific focus on 'at risk' groups; and finally better support for pregnant teenagers and parents to finish their education and learn parenting skills, alongside changes to housing rules so young parents were not housed in independent tenancies (SEU, 1999: 90–91).

New Labour's 'Teenage Pregnancy Strategy' (TPS) was described as highly ambitious (Arai, 2003). The TPS encompassed a range of targets and indicators that evaluated how well the government was doing in tackling the issue. The establishment of the Teenage Pregnancy Unit (TPU) also played a vital role in overseeing the TPS. This involved setting up a network of local teenage pregnancy co-ordinators whose role was to implement the strategy in every local or health authority area in England. Its overall aim was that of preventing teenage pregnancy (wherever possible) and supporting teenage parents (where teenage births had proved unpreventable) (DfES, 2007; SEU, 1999).

The end of the 'National Teenage Pregnancy Strategy'

The year 2010 marked the end of the TPS, and whilst a reduction of 18.1 per cent had been achieved, this was far from the initial 50 per cent first envisaged (DfE, 2011). The Teenage Pregnancy Independent Advisory Group (TPIAG), who monitored the strategy over 10 years, produced a final evaluation of the strategy. The TPIAG outlined what they believed to be the successes, missed opportunities and disappointments over the course of the 10 years:

> England's under-18 pregnancy rate is currently at its lowest level for over 20 years, but it is still unacceptably high. In 2000 we welcomed the launch of the Teenage Pregnancy Strategy but felt the timescale for halving under-18 conceptions by 2010 was too short. Teenage pregnancy is closely interlinked with poverty which is a major issue to tackle in just one decade … despite our reservations many local areas around England used the Teenage Pregnancy Strategy to achieve great success … Some areas managed to reduce their under-18 conception rates by up to 45 per cent from the 1998 base line which proved the strategy worked when it was applied properly. But some local areas failed to implement the strategy effectively and as a consequence their teenage pregnancy rate stayed high – or in some cases increased. (TPIAG, 2010)

Since the development of the TPS there has been a huge amount of interest in exploring the experience of teenage pregnancy and motherhood. This accumulation of research evidence identifies some of the limitations of the TPS, as well as the factors that may have led to the strategy failing to meet its targets. The key messages from this research are outlined below.

What we have learnt

One of the main criticisms of the TPS has been that the policy approach it adopted was based on assumptions, particularly about teenage sexual and reproductive behaviour, that were not backed up by research evidence. For instance, despite weak evidence that sex education programmes are actually successful in changing behaviour (Arai, 2009: 99), the technical/educational approach to the strategy still took centre stage.

A further crucial omission is how the strategy seemed oblivious to the voices of young mothers themselves. Where it did include the accounts of young mothers, the reliability and validity of such evidence have been questioned as it appeared that quotations from young mothers had been selected carefully in order to support a pre-set policy agenda. The TPS failed to provide a balanced account of the experience of teenage pregnancy and motherhood, consequently missing a vital insight into the meanings attached to pregnancy and young women's decision making. One study argued that policy was misdirected in its aims, used inappropriate instruments, and was unhelpful to many teenage parents (Duncan et al., 2010: 20).

A common complaint about the TPS is the lack of attention it paid to the social and cultural explanations of teenage pregnancy and parenthood. In communities where pregnancy is regarded as an achievement to be celebrated rather than a calamity, the provision of better sex education is unlikely to have a significant impact on the decision-making processes of young women. By focusing on the individual at the expense of looking at wider community and societal factors that influence teenage pregnancy, it has been argued that the real inequalities that exist amongst young people were neglected.

Alongside the development of the TPS, qualitative research sought to investigate, through the accounts of young mothers, the experience of teenage pregnancy and parenthood (Arai, 2003; Cater and Coleman, 2006; Mitchell and Greene, 2002). By exploring the meanings, feelings and thoughts attached to such experiences, this research aimed to provide a more nuanced understanding of teenage pregnancy and motherhood. For example, a review of the qualitative research literature showed how teenage mothers expressed positive attitudes towards motherhood, describing how motherhood made them feel stronger, more competent, more connected, and more responsible (Duncan et al., 2010).

These alternative discourses hold real meaning for young mothers, and can help them to challenge and deal with the negative stereotypes and assumptions that they have to negotiate on a day-to-day basis. They can also impact on the lives of young mothers by helping to inform policy so it is more responsive to their needs. This chapter will now turn to exploring these alternative discourses of teenage pregnancy and motherhood.

Alternative discourses – insider accounts

When an alternative perspective to the dominant discourse is adopted, it is possible to reach very different conclusions about the nature and experience of teenage pregnancy and motherhood. By questioning and critiquing the assumptions on which the dominant discourse is based, we can gain a better understanding of the limitations of mainstream research, policy and practice.

Research conducted *with* young mothers (qualitative studies) is often critical of perspectives that regard teenage pregnancy as a 'pathology'. For instance, Arai argues that an important issue that has been neglected is how some young women make decisions about when they will have children – teenage pregnancy is not just caused by ignorance about sex and contraception. Current policy, she argues, fails to recognise that becoming pregnant can be a positive choice for some young women, who may feel it is right for them, regardless of guidance that may be offered and services that may be available to them (Arai, 2003). Arai also argues that young women having children at a young age can be viewed as a sign of maturity, rather than immaturity. Many young mothers have experienced significant adversity even before they became pregnant and have had to grow up quickly because of this.

Arai's qualitative, small-scale research study allowed her to delve deeper into the experience of being pregnant and becoming a young parent. This sort of research can help to provide policy makers, as well as practitioners, with a clearer understanding of teenage pregnancy and parenthood, including how dominant ideas, assumptions and stereotypes shape how young parents are seen and treated. Research has shown that young mothers are subjected to the stigma and prejudice surrounding teenage pregnancy and motherhood (Graham and McDermott, 2005; Whitehead, 2001; Yardley, 2008). Policies that merely problematise teenage parents not only prevent such prejudice being challenged, but actually reinforce it.

Allowing young women to express their own views about their life decisions in their own terms can help create a better understanding of the thinking which lies behind the decision to become a teenage mother:

> 'What can you do when you grow up around here anyway? There's too many kids going to school and then nothing for them to do. There's no decent jobs, and then they wonder why girls get pregnant. For me it was because I wanted to do something – I wasn't gonna do nothing, like, so that's like, that's like my job – being a mum to K (baby son)' (female, aged 17). (Cater and Coleman, 2006: 31)

> 'It has made me more settled in, like, myself, because I have a goal now and I have something to achieve and I have to bring her up the best way I can and give her the best of everything and do what I can to help her grow up and not be like how I am'. (Corlyon and McGuire, 1999: 140)

In direct opposition to the assumptions made within public policy, qualitative research has shown how teenage mothers can express positive attitudes towards motherhood. It also indicates that, for many young mothers, parenting can provide the impetus to change direction or build on existing resources, so as to take up education, training and employment (Duncan, 2007; Duncan et al., 2010).

Such alternative perspectives offer important insights and ways of thinking about teenage pregnancy and parenthood. As well as giving a voice to young mothers, they help to provide a different understanding of issues relating to teenage pregnancy and parenthood, including how young women respond to becoming and being mothers, and the impact young motherhood has on their lives. Qualitative research can help us to critique the assumptions about teenage pregnancy and parenthood that usually inform policy and help us to retain a focus on young people's experiences and choices.

Implications for policy and practice

Teenage pregnancy and parenthood has received a huge amount of policy interest, most notably through new Labour's TPS that spanned a 10-year period. If we look at the impact of this policy, real tensions become apparent. On the one hand, we can see how policy based on assumptions that young parents are a problem can lead to them being and feeling stigmatised, which is harmful. On the other hand, it can be argued that, delivered in the right way (non-judgementally and respectfully), targeted provision can provide critical support at times of need (Smithbattle, 2003; Wenham, 2011). For example, research has shown that professionals played an important role in reassuring young women they were indeed 'good' mothers (Wenham, 2011).

A tension exists between policies that can be seen to be empowering or disempowering. Whether you are a researcher or practitioner actively trying to dispel myths surrounding teenage pregnancy, it can be difficult to resolve these tensions. Policy is often formed and resourced as a consequence of dealing with what are presented as social problems. Whilst the popular discourse surrounding teenage parenthood is stigmatising and harmful, I would argue that policy that has been developed in response can be received as positive and even 'life changing', and that we can learn from policy implementation that has successfully supported young parents. Key to successful support is the relationships that professionals and other workers can form with the young women they are working with. Such discussions raise important questions about the role of the practitioner in the lives of marginalised groups of young people. Increasingly we are witnessing the surveillance and regulation of young people (Coburn, 2011; Davies, 2010) and 'problem' parents (Gillies, 2007). Consequently, practitioners increasingly have to work within a professional capacity that is at best restrictive, and at worst oppressive. This ultimately leads to the question: are those who find themselves working with marginalised young mothers agents of change, or agents of the state?

What next for teenage parents?

The social policy landscape for young people has altered considerably following a change of government in 2010. The Conservative-led coalition government has introduced an array of far-reaching reforms that present a number of challenges for young people and for young mothers in particular. Of particular importance is the ongoing economic uncertainty. At the time of writing this chapter the UK is still in deep recession, with very little sign that it is going to emerge from this in the near future (Giles, 2012). Government has responded with substantial cuts to spending and increases in taxation. There is also likely to be a further £15 billion round of cuts and/or tax increases beyond the current spending round in 2015 and it is expected that £10 billion of this will have to come from social security benefit expenditure.

Such developments are taking place at a time when we are witnessing a record high number of unemployed young people. For example, between June and August 2012 the youth unemployment rate hit 20.5 per cent, the highest figure since records began in 1992 (Evans, 2013). For young people as a whole, cutbacks to public services are going to affect avenues of social support, whether this is through the closure of youth clubs, Connexions support for young people or the ending of 'The Future Jobs Fund', to take a few examples. The ending of the Educational Maintenance Allowance (EMA) has also been heavily criticised for impacting upon the most vulnerable young people in society (Coles, 2011: 23–25). With one of the greatest risk factors correlated with teenage pregnancy and parenthood being poverty and deprivation, young parents, and future young parents, are likely to be particularly vulnerable to cuts in public spending and public services.

In response to the Comprehensive Spending Review in 2010, the Social Policy Association (SPA) produced a report entitled *In Defence of Welfare* (Yeates et al., 2011). The report highlighted how we are witnessing the biggest single set of spending cuts since the Second World War – £81 billion in total. It also warned of the repercussions of planned reforms and spending cuts for specific groups of people. It concluded that planned cuts in benefits and services are likely to impact most heavily on people on low incomes and on women and children.

Further concerns have been raised that the restructuring of public services, alongside local authority cutbacks, will lead to a fragmentation of services, with piecemeal provision being provided by a wide variety of service providers and the private sector playing a more prominent role. Reforms outlined under the localism agenda are also likely to generate variations in scope, range and standards in provision in different areas (Taylor-Gooby and Stoker, 2011). Such concerns indicate that provision for young parents is likely to be varied and dependent upon geographic locality.

Many of the changes outlined will have a disproportionate impact on young mothers, given the changing youth policy landscape discussed earlier but also the distinctive gendered dimension to cuts. Figures produced by Taylor-Gooby and Stoker suggest that women will bear 72 per cent of the cutbacks through tax and benefit changes. Cuts to child benefit, lone parents' benefits, Sure Start maternity benefit, Tax Credit, housing benefits and pension credit are borne disproportionately by women (Taylor-Gooby and Stoker, 2011: 8). The abolition of the Health in Pregnancy Grant, the baby element of the Child Tax Credit (which doubled a family's income in the first year), and Community Care Grants (as well as most aspects of crisis loans), are likely to profoundly impact upon young parents in particular. At the time of writing, the introduction of Universal Credit in 2013 fails to differentiate between under-25s with or without children. Under-25s will receive the lower rate of benefits under the new system – regardless of whether they have children or not. This will result in out-of-work single parents between the ages of 18 and 25 receiving £780 a year less than they would under the current system.

Young mothers, through their dual status as 'adults' within their parental role, and 'young' people due to their age, receive what is effectively a double blow. Considering the often stated correlation between teenage pregnancy and deprivation, the impact of cuts in spending and services is likely to only further entrench poverty and disadvantage for teenage mothers and their children.

Conclusion

The discourse of early childbearing as 'problematic' continues to hold strong. In the run-up to the 2010 election, David Cameron made his feelings on the topic of 'young girls having children' very clear, just as Tony Blair did before him:

> When you are paid more not to work than to work, when you are better off leaving your children rather than nurturing them, when our welfare system tells young girls

that having children before finding the security of work and a loving relationship means home and cash now ... is it any wonder that our society is broken? (Cameron, 2009: 6)

Young mothers are likely to endure stigmatisation as a result of the sorts of views being expressed here. The circumstances of young mothers are only likely to really improve if, instead of vilifying them, we begin to understand their experiences and listen to what they have to say. Providing opportunities for young parents to have a voice, including through research, can help to address some of the power imbalances that are present and open up alternative perspectives and policy responses.

This chapter has highlighted the different ways in which teenage pregnancy can be explored, explained and understood. It can be looked at 'factually', through research based on an examination of statistics, trends and correlations; it is also possible to explore teenage pregnancy and parenthood through qualitative research that highlights the complexity of teenage pregnancy and motherhood through the accounts of young mothers themselves. While I would not dispute that large-scale studies have real value, I would suggest that we need to be very cautious when interpreting the lives of young mothers through them. The accounts of young parents have shown the complexities of teenage pregnancy and motherhood, including how for some young women it can provide a positive and valued identity. The changing social context for young people is also significant, and any discussion of young people making the transition to adulthood needs to appreciate young people's varied experiences of this journey and more importantly how these transitions are regarded as meaningful.

An aim of this chapter was to go beyond providing a descriptive account of 'good' versus 'bad' evidence/research, but instead to explore the underlying influences that often get overlooked or overshadowed. Researchers, as well as practitioners working with young parents, approach their work from particular perspectives, some of which can be conflicting. It is important to remember that we are not passively observing teenage pregnancy and motherhood but we are interpreting it – as are the teenage mothers themselves. This is key; different norms and values will shape our understandings and interpretations and influence our actions. We need to be able to critically explore dominant ideas about teenage pregnancy, and the prejudices and stereotypes that inform these ideas, as a basis for understanding our own position and perspectives. Ensuring the best interests of individual parents is placed at the heart of any intervention, regardless of professional or personal viewpoint, is integral to any meaningful intervention. It is therefore important to remember that professional workers do not operate within a vacuum – there are huge difficulties in challenging professional attitudes as well as public misconceptions surrounding teenage pregnancy and parenthood that need to be overcome.

This highlights that whilst work with young parents is likely to continue, the form it takes in practice is likely to change. As youth services are decimated in many parts of the UK, and austerity measures impact on the most vulnerable and disadvantaged in society, the work with young parents that does remain will increasingly take place within a range of new, and rather prescriptive, initiatives. Only time will tell how prescriptive or pathologising these strategies turn out to be. One thing is for certain though – like much policy that has gone before, the impetus behind intervention is based on a stereotypical view of the teenage parent or pregnancy as inherently problematic or troublesome. Despite research telling us that young parents dispute such claims, these assumptions continue to be pronounced within policy frameworks. The voices of young parents, once again, have disappeared into the background.

References

Alexander, C., Duncan, S. and Edwards, R. (2010) '"Just a mum or dad": experiencing teenage parenting and work–life balance'. In Duncan, S., Edwards, R. and Alexander, C. (eds) *Teenage Parenthood: What's the Problem?* London: Tuffnell Press.

Arai, L. (2003) 'Low expectations, sexual attitudes and knowledge: explaining teenage pregnancy and fertility in English communities. Insights from qualitative research', *Sociological Review* 51: 199–217.

Arai, L. (2009) *Teenage Pregnancy: the Making and Unmaking of a Problem*. Bristol: Policy.

Cameron, D. (2009) 'The big society', Hugo Young Lecture, 10 November. Available at: www. conservatives.com/News/Speeches/2009/11/David_Cameron_The_Big_Society.aspx

Cater, S. and Coleman, L. (2006) *'Planned' Teenage Pregnancy: Perspectives of Young Parents from Disadvantaged Backgrounds*. Bristol: Joseph Rowntree Foundation, Policy Press.

Coburn, A. (2011) 'Liberation or containment: paradoxes in youth work as a catalyst for powerful learning', *Youth & Policy* No. 106.

Coles, B. (2011) 'Youth'. In Yeates, N., Haux, T., Jawad, R. and Kilkey, M. (eds) *In Defence of Welfare: The Impacts of the Spending Review*. Social Policy Association.

Corlyon, J. and McGuire, C. (1999) *Pregnancy and Parenthood: The Views and Experiences of Young People in Public Care*. London: National Children's Bureau.

Davies, B. (2010) 'Straws in the wind: the state of youth work in a changing policy environment', *Youth & Policy* No. 105.

Dennison, C. (2004) *Teenage Pregnancy: An Overview of the Research Evidence*. Wetherby: Health Development Agency.

Department for Education (DfE) (2011) 'Teenage conception statistics for England 1998–2009'. Available at: http://media.education.gov.uk/assets/files/pdf/e/england%20under%2018%20and%20under%2016%20conception%20statistics%201998-2009%20feb%202011.pdf

Department for Education and Skills (DfES) (2006) *Teenage Pregnancy Next Steps: Guidance for Local Authorities and Primary Care Trusts on Effective Delivery of Local Strategies*. Department for Education and Skills.

Department for Education and Skills (DfES) (2007) *Multi-agency Working to Support Teenage Parents: A Midwifery Guide to Partnership Working with Connexions and other Agencies*. Department for Education and Skills.

Duncan, S. (2007), 'What's the problem with teenage parents? And what's the problem with policy?', *Critical Social Policy* 27: 307–334.

Duncan, S., Edwards, R. and Alexander, C. (eds) (2010) *Teenage Parenthood: What's the Problem?* London: Tuffnell Press.

Ermisch, J. and Pevalin, D. (2003) 'Does a "teen-birth" have longer-term impacts on the mother? Evidence from the 1970 British Cohort Study', Working Papers of the Institute for Social and Economic Research, paper 2003–28. Colchester: University of Essex.

Evans, J. (2013) Youth Employment Statistics, SN/EP/5871, London: House of Commons Library. Available at: www.parliament.uk/briefing-papers/sn05871

Giles, C. (2012) 'Osbourne's hard road is still winding on', *The Financial Times*, 4 October.

Gillies, V. (2007) *Marginalised Mothers: Exploring Working-Class Experiences of Parenting*. Milton Park: Routledge.

Graham, H. and McDermott, E. (2005) 'Qualitative research and the evidence base of policy: insights from studies of teenage mothers in the UK', *Journal of Social Policy* 35(1): 21–37.

Hawkes, D. (2010) 'Just what difference does teenage motherhood make? Evidence from the Millennium Cohort Study'. In Duncan, S., Edwards, R. and Alexander, C. (eds) *Teenage Parenthood: What's the Problem?* London: Tuffnell Press.

Hobcraft, J. and Kiernan, K. (2001) 'Childhood poverty, early motherhood and adult social exclusion', *British Journal of Sociology* 52(3): 495–517.

Mitchell, W. and Greene, E. (2002) '"I don't know what I'd do without our mam": motherhood, identity and support networks', *Sociological Review* 50(1): 1–22.

Smithbattle, L. (2003) 'Displacing the "rule book" in caring for teen mothers', *Public Health Nursing* 20(5): 369–376.

Social Exclusion Unit (SEU) (1999) *Teenage Pregnancy*. London: The Stationery Office.

Taylor-Gooby, P. and Stoker, G. (2011) 'The coalition programme: a new vision for Britain or politics as usual?', *The Political Quarterly* 82(1): 4–15.

Teenage Pregnancy Independent Advisory Group (TPIAG) (2010) *Teenage Pregnancy Independent Advisory Group Final Report. Teenage Pregnancy: Past Successes – Future Challenges*. London: Teenage Pregnancy Unit.

UNICEF (2001) 'A league table of teenage births in rich nations', Innocenti Report Card, Issue no. 3. Florence, Italy: UNICEF.

Wenham, A. (2011) 'Mothers in the making: a qualitative longitudinal study exploring the journey of becoming and being a teenage mother', unpublished PhD thesis, University of York.

Whitehead, E. (2001) 'Teenage pregnancy: on the road to social death', *International Journal of Nursing Studies* 38: 437–446.

Yardley, E. (2008) 'Teenage mothers' experiences of stigma', *Journal of Youth Studies* 11(6): 671–684.

Yeates, N., Haux, T., Jawad, R. and Kilkey, M. (eds) (2011) *In Defence of Welfare: The Impacts of the Spending Review*. Social Policy Association.

5

What Does the 'Teen Brain' Research Say, and What Does it Mean for Practitioners?

Howard Sercombe and Tomas Paus

Recent advances in neuroscience have enabled the structure and functioning of the living, working brain to be studied as never before, and much has been learnt about the way the brain develops during the teenage years. However, the interpretation of these findings remains controversial. Too often they have been understood in terms of old prejudices and negative stereotypes of teenagers. A more positive picture emerges from considering the neuroscientific findings alongside what was already known about young people, from the established academic disciplines of psychology and sociology, and from the practical experience of those who work with them.

Throughout the last five years an avalanche of writing in the academic and popular press has been talking about 'the teen brain' (Epstein, 2007a, 2007b; Strauch, 2004; Wallis et al., 2004). A new generation of tools and techniques has not only allowed scientists to see the internal structure of the brain in exquisite detail while the person is alive, but to study brain function when they are awake and working. These studies have indicated some differences between young people and adult members of the population: but what do these observed differences in structure and function mean for our understanding of young people?

Adapted from Sercombe, H. and Paus, T. (2009) 'The teen brain research: implications for practitioners'. *Youth and Policy* No. 103, Summer, pp. 25–38 and Sercombe, H. (2010) 'The teen brain research: critical perspectives', *Youth and Policy* No. 105, pp. 71–80.

The technology

At the forefront of the new brain research has been an exponential improvement in the tools available to study the brain. Thirty years ago most of what was known about the brain came from brain injury, dead people or EEG (electro-encephalogram) examinations that record brain impulses across a handful of electrodes placed on the scalp. In the last 20 years a range of new techniques have allowed us to see what is happening to the brain structurally over time, and functionally in real time, while the brain is actually working. The resolution of images has improved massively in that time also. Think about what has happened with digital camera or mobile phone technology in the last 20 years and you'll have an idea of how things have progressed.

At the forefront of this development has been the Magnetic Resonance Imaging (MRI) scanner. There are lots of ways the scanner can be used, but the two most common applications are:

- *Structural MRI (sMRI)*. The scanner can take cross-sectional images of the brain that are like a black and white photo. These can now show sharp detail: still a long way from the microscopic level needed to show actual circuits but it can certainly show the fine structure of brain architecture, and allow comparison between different people's brains.
- *Functional MRI (fMRI)*. Functional MRI works a little differently, though still using the same MRI scanner. Brains get their energy from the oxidation of sugars in the bloodstream. If a part of the brain is active, blood containing oxygen will flow to that part of the brain, and as the oxygen is used, the oxygen in the blood in that part of the brain will drop. An MRI scanner will pick that up, giving a clear picture of the parts of the brain that are using most oxygen: all while the person is awake and active, albeit lying quite still in the scanner. A person can be shown pictures or videos, and asked to think about certain things or do mental tasks, and we can see what parts of the brain are working while they do that.

We need to be aware, though, that these are not photos of people's brains. They are computer-generated images, using particular kinds of magnetic pulses which are picked up by receptors and heavily processed. Especially with fMRI, scientists will themselves make lots of decisions about what is going to be included and excluded, what level of activity is significant, and where to look. Functional MRI is still highly experimental. And, it has to be said, at this stage, not sufficient as the only method for understanding human behaviour. The MRI scanner might generate an image with parts of the brain lit up with bright colours, but what does that mean? We are still working that out. In the meantime, anything you read about a study using fMRI, take it with a grain of salt.

More technologies are emerging all the time which improve both the way we see into the body, and the way computers are able to recreate a reality from the sensors. However, the technology is expensive, and experiments have to be painstakingly carried out. A lot of work (and money) goes into finding each fragment of new data but there are some interesting and exciting findings.

Structure and function

For a long time in the human sciences (especially psychology), debate has raged about the extent to which human behaviour is determined by genes, and to what extent by experience and environment – the so-called 'nature–nurture debate'. One of the most important findings of brain science research is that *experience actually shapes physical structures in the brain*. The theory isn't new. Sixty years ago, Donald Hebb wrote:

> When one cell repeatedly assists in firing another, the axon of the first cell develops synaptic knobs (or enlarges them if they already exist) in contact with the soma of the second cell. ... The general idea is an old one, that any two cells or systems of cells that are repeatedly active at the same time will tend to become 'associated', so that activity in one facilitates activity in the other. (Hebb, 1949: 63, 70)

Or, put more simply, 'neurons that fire together, wire together'. Several studies have confirmed that when a particular neural circuit is engaged repeatedly it leads to changes in brain structure. This has been tried across populations as diverse as musicians (Gaser & Schlaug, 2003; Sluming et al., 2002), London taxi drivers (Maguire et al., 2000) and people who are bilingual (Mechelli et al., 2004). You can actually see, using an MRI scanner, the bit of their brains that is different.

Brains are formed of a massive number of networks of neurons: spindly, branching cells looking like plant roots that transmit electrical currents along their length, like circuits in a computer. With every experience you have, something happens to a neuron somewhere. It might be a new connection, or an extension of an existing connection, or a new branch. The brain cannot develop without experiences. It is as useless as a computer without software. While the theory is not new, the scanners are now so good that we can *see* the differences in brain structure and function that result from different experiences. Genes are important as well, of course. The brain develops according to a genetic programme as well, and these two elements work in constant interaction with each other. The expression of genes – whether they 'switch on' and when – is also in many cases environment-dependent. The timing of the onset of puberty may be a good example of that.

In studies of the brain and behaviour, it is difficult to manage the way that all these factors influence each other. It is not possible to hold one still while you see what happens with the other one, because the first doesn't hold still. What we do know is that the human brain as a structure is highly 'plastic': it is flexible, responsive and by no means determined at birth.

There are a number of important implications of this discovery. The first is that *the nature–nurture debate is obsolete*. Neither genes nor experience determine behaviour. Both do, in a complex dance which includes the person's own brain as a structure. It makes no more sense to talk about which is determining behaviour than it does to talk about a coin only having one side. Neither variable is independent. In addition, human agency is a third element in the dance. The individual themselves is making decisions about their own behaviour. All of this is dynamic: none of it stays still.

The second results from the fact that the process of circuit-building is not linear throughout life. There is a massive proliferation of circuits, for example, in the first two years of life, and another just before puberty. If the environment is poor, cruel or chaotic during these periods, that may determine many of the circuits that are laid down, if not the way they are laid down. This is already having an impact on policy around the care and education of infants.

The same attention is not yet being paid to school-age children and young people. If you want good circuits to use as an adult, you need good things in your environment when you are young. Notwithstanding this, no matter how poor, cruel or chaotic the environment, some good things happen to children – some good experiences, some good relationships. Some people seem to be able to foreground these experiences, regardless of how few they have had. On the other hand, others seem to foreground bad experiences, no matter how privileged, kind and ordered their environment has been. This can change. It is likely that the more poverty, cruelty or chaos you have had while the circuits are being built, the more difficult it is to foreground the helpful ones. One of the things we do in practice is to try to help young people foreground what is helpful in their experience, and sideline the circuits that make them smaller and meaner.

'Pruning' and the changing balance of grey and white matter

Over the past 20 years MRI has provided new opportunities to assess brain development in large numbers of healthy children and adolescents. It is now clear from a number of studies that the human brain continues to change during adolescence (Blakemore & Choudhury, 2006; Lenroot & Giedd, 2006; Paus et al., 2008). One of the key changes is in the balance between grey matter and white matter. Using a computer analogy, the grey matter is the circuits and processors. The white matter is the wires between them, with insulation wrapped around them. It is called white matter because a major component is myelin, a white fatty substance that insulates the wires, making the transfer of electrical pulses or 'messages' faster and more efficient.

Another useful analogy is that of roads. When an area is first being settled, if someone wants to go somewhere they point their cart in the direction they think they want to go and off they go. Others might follow their track, and as they do a road forms. Or they might go another way that they thought was quicker or easier, and make another road. Over time, if the road was used a lot the Council might grade it and lay gravel, and eventually seal it with asphalt or tarmac. Once the road is sealed, everyone goes along the sealed road, and the little dirt roads become overgrown. They rarely disappear completely, but going along them is hard work and they mostly end nowhere.

Childhood is a process of creating little dirt roads all over the place, learning so fast, learning or inventing a hundred ways to do things, and learning a hundred things to do every day. Children's grey matter is just blossoming. In adults it is much harder to see all these little dirt roads. Instead there is a network of sealed highways:

serious, efficient, fast. All the roads that don't go anywhere, or aren't the fastest or safest ways to get there, have been left to grow over.

The amount of grey matter appears to reach a maximum in the teenage years. After that there appears to be a decrease in grey matter and an increase in white matter. A common way to describe this change is 'synaptic pruning' (Thompson et al., 2000). In this metaphor unwanted circuits are pruned away, leaving the circuits that are most efficient or most useful for survival. To use our other analogy there is a serious road-building programme going on here, starting with the areas that are more fundamental to survival, and moving on to areas that are more concerned with conscious thought. The process is generally called plasticity – and myelination is part of it. Myelinating a circuit in the brain is like sealing a dirt road.

Implications of plasticity

We assume that the human organism will make decisions about which circuits will be maintained and/or enhanced according to the imperatives of its environment. These are presumably part of a survival process. *The environment in which young people live while these decisions are made is critical in determining the mind-set of the adult.* If young people live in an environment of suspicion and repression, the circuits that are confirmed during the teenage years will be those that are most appropriate to survival in such an environment. If this was to be taken seriously, it is doubtful that what passes for youth policy would have quite the shape that it does at the moment.

At the level of practice our work is often about helping young people find other ways to do things. They may have strengthened a circuit in a context where their life was full of threat and violence and where there were few real options. In counselling situations, helping young people connect with the relationships or experiences in their past that worked and nourished them can help them find a different way of being in the present. So asking questions like, 'So who liked you as you were growing up? What teachers respected you? What was that like?' or 'When have you been at your best with this stuff? When has it worked? What was going on for you then?' or 'How would you like to be? What are you like when you are at your best?' might help.

In practice this approach is very useful in working with young people, especially young men, around a range of issues including violence and drug use. The mechanics of how the brain works often makes real sense to them, helping them understand why they react the way they do, and empowering them to take charge of the way they want their brain to work. We don't know enough to be prescriptive about this, or even to design 'brain-based' interventions, but we do know that the brain is highly flexible and adaptable, and change is possible.

This can also help inform the logic of activity work with young people. Young people from impoverished backgrounds often have a limited range of experiences, and their environment can be highly conservative in its own way. New experiences can force the development of different connections and new circuits, creating opportunities for young people to do things a little differently and see other possibilities while still respecting the integrity of their lives and the choices they make.

The teenage brain versus the adult brain

The brains of young people are not radically different from adults in structure. There is no great difference in capacity between young people and adults. There is a difference, however, in the degree of plasticity, which makes brains more reliable and efficient in their reactions and responses but less flexible and less available for new learning.

The primary difference between a teenager's brain and an older person's brain then is not a difference in capacity but in the *selection of capacities:* that is, which of the brain's capacities are to be foregrounded and used and which are to be side-lined and fall into disuse. This is an active process in which young people are consciously or unconsciously selecting preferred pathways for action and response, confirming favoured templates for life from the smorgasbord of ways of being generated through the process of childhood. Young people are not passive victims of brains that are out of control. They are active agents in the design of an adulthood that meets their needs and enables them to survive within their environment and make sense of their experience.

Youth is not separate from adulthood. It is the emergence of adulthood. There is no 'next stage' of adulthood, which is qualitatively different from being a young person (Moshman, 2011), and adulthood is not itself a destination. You don't learn what you need for adulthood by being excluded from it until you can demonstrate that you have got the right circuits. A smart society would engage young people progressively in adult processes as they demonstrate their readiness. Our society does this a little but mostly we exclude young people until a certain arbitrary age is reached and then bestow the right to participate – mostly without guidance and support (Epstein, 2007a, 2007b). It should be no surprise that it does not work too well. We respond to this failure usually by increasing the age at which responsibility will be granted. Folly, as Barbara Tuchman tells us, is the pursuit of a failing strategy by prescribing ever-increasing amounts of the same (Tuchman, 1984).

Different locations for processing information

Functional MRI (fMRI) provides yet another avenue for exploring brain–behaviour relationships in the maturing human brain. Functional MRI allows researchers to see what parts of the brain 'light up' when subjects are asked to respond to different situations or perform different kinds of mental activity. It is difficult work: it can be hard to pinpoint exactly what is being measured, for example whether the person is actually thinking about the activity or something else, or whether a difference in the way that the brain works is about age, or something else like intelligence or performance. Some of these things can be controlled for, some cannot, and some the researcher may not have thought of yet. But the possibility of seeing how the brain is working while tasks are being performed is ground-breaking.

An area that has received a lot of attention is the study of risk-taking behaviour. These fMRI studies usually involve the subject being scanned while engaged in a simulation of risk-taking behaviour: typically playing a computer game that offers varying rewards according to the risk taken within the game. In reported studies, this work shows that young people have a different response to either children or people over 25. The theory is that as the adolescent brain develops over the teenage years into its adult configuration, the reward centres of the brain develop before the areas responsible for executive function, including rational consideration and judgment (the pre-frontal cortex) (Casey et al., 2011; Galvan et al., 2007). This disconnect results in an increased tendency for young people to take risks. This has been expressed metaphorically in the literature as 'all gas and no brakes' (Casey et al., 2011; Payne, 2012).

However, fMRI-based research is inherently less objective than structural MRI. The results are also more controversial, and data emerging from Magnetic Resonance Imaging (MRI) scanners are frequently interpreted within frameworks for thinking about young people which see adolescence pathologically. For example, a *Time* magazine feature article suggested that, 'Increasingly, psychologists … are trying to connect the familiar patterns of adolescents' wacky behavior to the new findings about their evolving brain structure' (Wallis et al., 2004).

The academic literature is often (but not always) more careful than this and, at its best, is overt about how little we yet know about brains at any age, the complex interplay of variables, and the dangers of over-interpreting the data. However, often poor causal arguments are built from premises about what the data 'might' mean to much more solid conclusions about the inadequacy of teenage brains. On this basis recommendations are made for the development of law and policy relating to the protection and control of young people. In the following section, we consider some criticisms of the 'teen brain' research.

Sampling

There are a number of difficulties which are endemic to the teen brain research field. The equipment is expensive, so any research can only work with limited numbers of people. This is improving, as more scanners come online and the costs per scan fall. In some areas of study, especially MRI scans which look at brain *structure*, researchers are not limited to the scans they do themselves: they consult libraries of scans in other laboratories giving access to data from hundreds of individuals. There is a bigger problem in *functional* MRI research that looks at how the brain works while a person is thinking. These studies will often look at tens of individuals. You can't generalise from these kinds of numbers. The results might be interesting, but they don't prove anything.

If brain structure is partly a product of experience, the background of research participants is important. For example, if the sample only includes middle-class teenagers, or teenagers in school, or boys, and something interesting is discovered, it may well be that the salient feature is about them being middle class or in school or male, rather than about them being teenagers. To be confident about results, large numbers, and preferably repeated scans over time are needed, so that these extraneous factors can be excluded. The smaller the sample, the higher the risk that a researcher is not measuring what they think they are measuring. The work is still important, but there needs to be caution about the significance claimed for the results.

There is also a broad developmental range even within the categories identified as 'teenagers', 'young people' and 'adolescents'. Studies frequently select their participants by age: but age is an imprecise measure of development. Very few studies measure brain development even by pubertal stage. While the number of longitudinal studies is increasing, and more 16- and 17-year-olds are being included, many have worked with 10–13-year-olds (Baird et al., 1999; Whittle et al., 2008). Whether these are all studies of 'youth' or even 'adolescence' can be contested.

Design

Research design is especially important in functional Magnetic Resonance Imaging (fMRI) studies. Functional MRI has huge potential for understanding what parts of the brain are employed for different mental processes. A limitation of fMRI studies is that the person has to be completely still to obtain reasonable pictures. It is possible to talk to the subject while they are in the scanner and to show them pictures or have them play video games. However, this is not 'real life': it is a *simulation*. We presume that this tells us something about how it reacts to real situations, but it might be that we are just measuring responses to simulations. Because young people are going to school, and most school work deals with simulations, they work with simulations all day every day. Add to that their experience with the media, video games and the internet, and it is clear there are *also generational differences in the experience of simulations*.

Especially in fMRI research, extreme caution needs to be taken about the implications of this kind of difference. This is a science which is still in its infancy. Brain research needs to be pulled alongside other cognitive and sociological research, rather than common prejudice, in the interpretation of the data. This is becoming more common, but is still absent from the literature reviews of most scientific articles in this field.

There is also a *bias* in interpretation that privileges the age, class and cultural position of the researcher. Myelination has it advantages and disadvantages. The increase in efficiency is at the cost of flexibility and availability for new learning. Older adults can do things they know how to do better than young people, as a rule. But they find it harder to learn things they don't know how to do. Researchers celebrate the increasing 'maturity' of the brain towards the end of the twenties, without grieving for the loss of flexibility in processing information that this inevitably involves.

Conclusion

Brain architecture research represents exciting and fertile ground for understanding more about young people: about the nature of youth and adolescence, about its potentialities, and the continuities and differences between youth and adulthood. It pushes us to develop concepts and theories beyond old and unproductive dualisms such as nature/nurture. It may help us to correct social policies which are harmful to development, and which produce populations that are fearful, constricted and conservative.

However, interpretations of the data remain locked into the dominant, hundred-year-old framework for understanding youth in terms of a qualitatively different stage of human development characterised by trouble (Bessant et al., 1998; Epstein, 2007b). Alternative conceptions struggle for traction, and experimental work which seeks to discover the capacities of young people, rather than their deficits, struggles for funding. Notions of adolescence which conceive the teenage years in terms of a blossoming, emergent adulthood (rather than a turbulent compartment of the human experience to be contained and controlled) are pushed aside by media representations of the science which amount to little more than 'hate speech' about young people.

Yet social scientists and youth practitioners can be reactive and alarmist about the brain research. Understanding of this field is often poor, and it is easy to slip into inaccuracies and misconceptions. The development of collaborative liaisons between disciplines has never been more important. While much of the science is beautiful, it needs the complementary intelligence of psychology, sociology and practice knowledge to avoid interpretations which just confirm common sense. Common sense is too often merely old prejudice. More than ever, this field of work needs people to be communicating across the divide between the life sciences and the social sciences.

We already knew a lot about what makes young people tick, long before the first MRI scan: in psychology, sociology and in the range of professions, including youth work, that have attended to young people as thinking subjects. If the teen brain research is pursued in ignorance of this work, it is in danger of retracing earlier problematic discourses about young people and making claims which have long been disproved in other disciplines. What we know already about the effect of social factors such as poverty will be passed over. At the same time, there is potential for a cascade of new insights about young people from cognitive neuroscience. Partnerships between social scientists, psychologists and cognitive neuroscientists as well as youth workers and other practitioners might make for some fascinating new perspectives on how to think about young people, as well as how young people think.

References

Baird, A. A., Gruber, S. A., Fein, D. A., Maas, L. C., Steingard, R. J., Renshaw, P. F., et al. (1999). 'Functional magnetic resonance imaging of facial affect recognition in children and adolescents.' *Journal of the American Academy of Child & Adolescent Psychiatry*, 38, 195–199.

Bessant, J., Sercombe, H., & Watts, R. (1998). *Youth Studies: an Australian Perspective*. Melbourne: Addison Wesley Longman.

Blakemore, S. J. & Choudhury, S. (2006). 'Development of the adolescent brain: implications for executive domain and social cognition.' *Journal of Child Psychology and Psychiatry*, 47, 296–312

Casey, B., Jones, R. M., & Somerville, L. H. (2011). 'Braking and accelerating of the adolescent brain.' *Journal of Research on Adolescence*, 21(1), 21–33.

Epstein, R. (2007a). 'The myth of the teen brain.' *Scientific American Mind*, 57–63.

Epstein, R. (2007b). *The Case Against Adolescence: Rediscovering the Adult in Every Teen.* Sanger, CA: Quill Driver Books.

Galvan, A., Hare, T., Voss, H., Glover, G., & Casey, B. J. (2006). 'Risk-taking and the adolescent brain: who is at risk?' *Developmental Science*, 10(2), 8–14.

Gaser, C. and Schlaug, G. (2003). 'Brain structures differ between musicians and non-musicians.' *Journal of Neuroscience*, 23, 9240–9245.

Hebb, D. O. (1949). *The Organization of Behavior.* New York: Wiley.

Lenroot, R. K. and Giedd, J. N. (2006) 'Brain development in children and adolescents: insights from anatomical magnetic resonance imaging.' *Neuroscience and Biobehavioural Reviews*, 30: 718–729.

Maguire, E. A., Gadian, D. G., Johnsrude, I. S., Good, C. D., Ashburner, J., Frackowiak, R. S., et al. (2000). 'Navigation-related structural change in the hippocampi of taxi drivers.' *Proceedings of the National Academy of Sciences USA*, 97, 4398–4403.

Mechelli, A., Crinion, J. T., Noppeney, U., O'Doherty, J., Ashburner, J., Frackowiak, R. S., et al. (2004). 'Neurolinguistics: structural plasticity in the bilingual brain.' *Nature*, 431, 757.

Moshman, D. (2011). 'Adolescents are young adults, not immature brains.' *Applied Developmental Science*, 15(4), 171–174.

Paus, T., Keshavan, M., & Giedd, J. N. (2008). 'Why do many psychiatric disorders emerge during adolescence?' *Nature Reviews Neuroscience*, 9, 947–957.

Payne, M. A. (2012). '"All gas and no brakes!" Helpful metaphor or harmful stereotype?', *Journal of Adolescent Research*, 27(1), 3–17.

Sluming, V., Barrick, T., Howard, M., Cezayirli, E., Mayes, A., & Roberts, N. (2002). 'Voxel-based morphometry reveals increased gray matter density in Broca's area in male symphony orchestra musicians.' *Neuroimage*, 17, 1613–1622.

Steinberg, L. (2007). 'Risk taking in adolescence: new perspectives from brain and behavioral science.' *Current Directions in Psychological Science*, 16(2), 55–59.

Strauch, B. (2004). *The Primal Teen: What the New Discoveries about the Teenage Brain Tell Us about Our Kids.* New York: Doubleday.

Thompson, P. M., Giedd, J. N., Woods, R. P., MacDonald, D., Evans, A. C., & Toga, A. W. (2000). 'Growth patterns in the developing brain detected by using continuum mechanical tensor maps.' *Nature*, 404, 190–193.

Tuchman, B. (1984). *The March of Folly: from Troy to Vietnam.* New York: Random House.

Wallis, C., Dell, K., & Park, A. (2004) 'Secrets of the teen brain.' *TIME* Magazine, May 10, pp. 56–65.

Whittle, S., Yap, M. B. H., Yucel, M., Fornito, A., Simmons, J. G., Barrett, A., et al. (2008) 'Prefrontal and amygdala volumes are related to adolescents' affective behaviours during parent–adolescent interactions.' *Proceedings of the National Academy of Sciences USA*, 105(9), 3652–3657.

6

Youth Work in a Cold Climate

Tom Wylie

Work with young people is currently taking place in a context where youth unemployment is rising, and where public funding for youth services is being cut. This chapter considers the challenges that this context presents for young people, particularly young people growing up in the most disadvantaged communities, and the challenges that it also presents for youth workers. It highlights the importance of continuing to make the case for investment in youth work, and of demonstrating how youth work can benefit individuals, communities and society as a whole.

Introduction

Youth work has rarely marched with the wind at its back and the warming rays of the sun on its face. There have been brief periods when its contribution to social policy was appreciated and relatively substantial finance, by youth work standards, flowed into the work. These periods included a few years in the 1960s after the Albemarle Report and again in the first decade of the 21st century with 'Resourcing Excellent Youth Services' and 'Aiming High'.[1] But most of the time it has been a case of 'make do and mend': capital to replace outworn buildings was not made available and, with no agreed national standards for neighbourhood provision, recurrent spending drifted towards capricious decision-making by local authorities mixed with voluntary endeavour and charitable fund-raising. From the late 1990s the National Lottery made an ad hoc input to different themes concerned with young people, but this source diminished with the demands of the 2012 Olympic Games extravaganza in London (though the hoped-for benefits in participation by young people in sport have yet to be achieved).

This is a revised and updated version of an article which appeared in *Youth and Policy*, No. 105, in 2010.

As a nation, and as a sector devoted to improving the condition of the young, we are living once more in wintry and troubled times. The crisis in financial services pulled the whole economy into recession, not just in the UK but also in much of Europe, with uncertain outcomes for employment in the long term. The private sector may struggle to create a high volume of secure, new jobs while reductions in public service employment are likely to last for years. By 2012 one in five young adults in the UK was out of work. The consequences for the young trying to enter the labour market will be particularly hard as the experience of being unemployed during young adulthood is immediately discouraging and has also been shown to have severe consequences in terms of their long-term health, future income and blighted lives. Jobs available for young adults are often low-paid, casual or part-time. The scars will be particularly marked in those areas from which public and private capital fled during earlier economic re-structuring and recessions; these have become communities of the left behind with horizons narrowed, hopes thwarted and aspirations diminished.

Many in the youth cohort also sit inside a population of some 13 million in the UK who are living in poverty. The gulf is widening, both geographically and in human and social capital, between those who are doing well, those getting by and those going nowhere. Social mobility has stalled and the constraining contours of wealth, class and privilege are evident. Divided, unequal nations become under-achieving societies in which the more vulnerable are prey to extremism or tempted into acquisitive crime or self-medication through alcohol or drug misuse. Although some economic remedial initiatives have been introduced, for example on infra-structure projects or to employ apprentices, spending on supportive public services and on social security will be constrained for years to come. Living with debt and family poverty and thus having limited opportunities for new, imaginative experi-ences, coupled with anxiety about educational achievement and precarious future employment, mean that for many young people it will not be a good time in which to grow up. Their natural exuberance will often morph into a sullen passivity; their peer loyalties imprison some in anti-social gang cultures.

Cuts in public spending are having a devastating effect on what is offered to young people in their leisure time by the local authority and voluntary sectors alike. A service such as youth work with a weak statutory base is always vulnerable dur-ing times of economic difficulty. In consequence, advocacy for young people and for youth work has to be re-thought and re-fought.

Policy responses

History will eventually judge how successful the Labour government of 1997–2010 was in managing the UK economy in the face of globalisation; in its approach to reforming public services, often through the use of top-down targets; and in its funding of social provision including hospitals and schools. Despite occasional bursts of financial sunshine and sporadic policy interest, it missed the opportunity to develop a vibrant youth work sector which would have the resilience provided by a robust infrastructure to ride out an ice storm. There was a little new capital to improve the building stock; a few, short-term innovative programmes; a marginal improvement to the legal basis for youth work; and some attention to strengthening the voice of young people in decision-making. But many of those who work in the sector felt diminished by the absence of consistent policy support for their values and approaches, by unpredictable funding and by the endless re-structuring of services, especially for work with those aged over 16. Labour's eventual configuration of local Children's Services followed the botched design and clumsy implementation of its previous Connexions fiasco, which even sought to suppress the very name 'youth worker'. Despite good intentions, the all-encompassing concept of Children's Services served to marginalise the place of young people as distinct from children, of personal development as distinct from safeguarding, and of youth work as a profession which can complement others and not be subsumed by them. Instead, this structure reflected a continuing search for the holy grail of joined-up services, with a good deal of vagueness about what this meant in practice for local youth provision, for support to voluntary bodies, and for the roles of those in the workforce.

Despite their rhetoric, modern general elections rarely provide a critical break between the approaches of different administrations but the Conservative-led coalition, elected in 2010, introduced severe levels of cuts on youth and other public services and adopted three underpinning themes in its approach to young people (as exemplified, for instance, in its 'Positive for Youth' policy statement in 2011 (DfE, 2011)). First, encouragement of high levels of individual (and family) responsibility; young people are to become the authors of their own lives and thus take increasing responsibility for establishing and following individual career paths and managing their lifestyles, including their health. Deep-rooted social problems are seen as an expression of individual dysfunction, rather than vice versa. Young adults who can't fend for themselves are to live for as long as possible in the family home and to be inculcated at the age of 16 into civic responsibilities through a scheme of National Citizens Service. Second, as a matter of principle not just of financial constraint, the role of the state towards providing wide-ranging local opportunities for the personal and social development of the young has been reduced. Instead, national government follows the precept of subsidiarity and emphasises the need for local decisions rather than national direction or standard setting. Third, within a rather nebulous concept of the 'Big Society', the private, philanthropic and voluntary sectors are expected to fill the gap left by the withdrawal of the state; indeed, they are encouraged to do so by devices such as 'payment by results'. Since few voluntary bodies have the financial capacity to operate to any scale while awaiting payments for their services, they are tempted into acting as 'bid candy' to enable larger, profit-making companies to win any government contracts. In this new world there is little accountability and even less equality. There is not an adequate blend of the responsibilities to be carried by individuals and those to be discharged by the state: representing, in sociological terms, the interplay between (personal) 'agency' and (social) 'structure'.

Ofsted reports describe the effective contribution youth work makes to young people's lives but the sector is not well-equipped to face harsh economic winds. In an environment where financial resources are constrained, and cuts are being made to public services, how is youth work to argue its case in competition with cancer screening or care for the elderly? Or even with other parts of the wider children's and young people's sector including early years, sport, youth justice and the ever-open maw of schools? Can it handle the process of being commissioned against outcomes? Making the case for investment in youth work has rarely been more important. Or more difficult.

Three traditions of advocacy

Three different traditions of advocacy for youth work have long been evident. First, the romantics. These adhere to 'the old-time religion' of youth work (though without the rousing gospel hymns): heart-warming tales are told of young brands plucked from the fire, of lives turned around. Some of these accounts are even true: many youth workers have good stories to tell of supporting individuals in difficult circumstances, of helping them to put their lives back on track, of offering them new experiences in order to escape the limiting contours and low expectations of their own neighbourhoods. Some romantic purists would stop there. Tell the stories. Describe youth work in its own terms. Avoid acknowledgment of any government targets. Instead, assert the enduring truths of the voluntary relationship and the convivial conversation round the pool table.

But consider for a moment the politics of appearing to imply that youth workers don't need to be accountable to those who are paying or to offer any metrics which demonstrate successful intervention. Tales of personal triumphs with individuals can add colour to a narrative but they don't convince even sympathetic politicians in good times. Especially not when the tone adopted is one which suggests a measure of victimhood in the profession.

The second kind of approach – the technocratic – goes along with whatever new managerialist ideology triumphs as local services emerge from another round of re-structuring and financial stringency. Under pressure to demonstrate early success for new structures, the technocrat accepts meaningless, de-contextualised targets and fashionable mantras about 'ending silo working', 'radical workforce transformation' and much more, articulated – if that is not too generous a term – by careerists who have little knowledge of how youth work actually engages with the young and their communities. The term 'Integrated Youth Support' is a case in point; each word is problematic: what actually is to be understood by 'integrated', at what age does 'youth' begin and end, what features constitute 'support'? The consultants and officials who coin such vague jargon see any challenge as unwelcome dissent and don't appear to read the evaluations before they move on to the next vogueish idea.

The third group – in which this writer places himself – is of principled pragmatists. We draw from the deep well of youth work values, we know that many youth workers don't need to be set national targets to make contact, develop relationships, negotiate a shared curriculum and encourage young people to make progress towards achieving important outcomes (the terms 'curriculum' and 'outcomes' don't find much favour with the romantics). But we believe also that youth projects, and youth services in general, need to be able to express cogently their contribution to the broader goals of contemporary social policy, such as developing skills for employability and for life, preventing offending, promoting emotional well-being, and encouraging democratic involvement. The task of articulating such outcomes can carry its own dangers. It is important to be positive about youth work's virtues but some advocates claim too much by suggesting that it can remedy all manner of social ills. Such advocacy can also split the sector, with some voluntary bodies quick to claim that they can go faster and fly higher (and more cheaply) than the agents of the state. They are seduced by talk of a 'big society', ignoring the part that a state-regulated framework and financial support plays in making it possible. Some apply the 'Easyjet philosophy': pay only for the most basic service, never mind the quality. Some political ideologues, and their voluntary sector fellow-travellers, would gladly 'shrink the state', though they are not so keen on picking up the bill when the consequences eventually arrive by way of poor health, crime or unemployment. Passing responsibility for community services to volunteers may work in some places but is not a solution for the more intractable social issues and problematic localities.

Youth work needs to make a convincing case for proper investment and show, in figures not just in stories, how individuals, communities and society benefit. It is not unreasonable, surely, for youth workers to be able to say: 'with this level of resource we will be able to reach this number of young people, we will be able to offer this range of experiences, help more of them to decide things for themselves and take responsibility for this or that activity; and for a percentage of them to make progress in acquiring new skills which are robust enough to be accredited by an external body, if they choose'? Properly aggregated, and backed by good research on beneficial impact, such an approach would show convincingly how youth work contributes to individual well-being and social capital alike.[2]

Not all managerial practices or approaches to target-setting in previous decades have been either wise or feasible. We should consider what kinds of outcomes are now relevant and what accreditation systems best capture personal and social development when such accreditation is needed. But we should not see the absence of specific targets as some form of liberation. On the contrary, it may mean that youth services are not worth funding since they can't, or won't, demonstrate what they achieve. Youth work exists to benefit the young. If it is to flourish, perhaps even survive, in chilly times, it needs to be better able to demonstrate how these benefits are realised. It has to be able to answer cogently these three questions:

- How much did we do?
- How well did we do it?
- Who is better off?

Priorities

The question of beneficiaries, as well as the pressure of contemporary structural fads such as 'targeted youth support', opens up the contentious issue of priorities. Youth work has always aspired to be a 'universal' service, open to all young people; it has usually resisted any suggestion that it should focus, or target, its activities on those disaffected with life or in trouble with society's institutions. Moreover, it is well known that services for the poor often become poor services. One of the explanations for the weak funding of local authority youth services may be the lack of engagement by middle-class parents on behalf of their children who would enjoy youth activities but have not been encouraged to participate in council-run provision. Whatever the explanation, the money has never been there for youth work to be established as a universal service similar to schooling and, in practice, local authority youth services, and some voluntary sector projects, have tended to concentrate in areas of socio-economic disadvantage. It can be argued that this is a wise and socially just allocation of limited public resources, based on an approach described as 'progressive universalism', or what theologians call 'the preferential option for the poor'. Surely we want the benefits of youth work to be available to those most in need? Moreover, such an approach is not in itself in breach of the desire to offer open access provision for all alongside, or as a gateway to, more deliberate, structured programmes designed and differentiated to meet particular needs. Such programmes could include, for example, the specific personal and social development needed by those young people who have difficulties keeping a job or moving into independent living or managing money or relationships with family or peer groups. This is exactly the kind of ground on which youth work engages but it rarely explains exactly how it goes about helping young people to make those changes and take those chances which are within their reach, rather than simply lamenting the impossibility of grappling with major social and economic forces. It would also include encouraging young people, as individuals and in peer groups, to access cultural experiences such as theatres or museums and to build their skills and confidence in participating fully in environments that may not be familiar. We want to encourage all young people to have a sense of belonging and of purpose. The years of austerity will require youth workers to be even more focused on the needs of the disadvantaged young: to build their resilience, respect for others and capability, to be creative and, despite everything, ambitious and hopeful. In Gramsci's famous phrase: they will need to demonstrate 'pessimism of the intellect, optimism of the will'.

Good youth work practice

It is not just the wider politics, policies and structures with which we need to be concerned. It is also a matter of how to secure good practice in everyday encounters with the young. At the heart of excellent performance is dialogue and reciprocity with the young. Here is youth work's core task: the fine grain of building and sustaining relationships with individuals and groups. Conversation, yes, but conversation with a purpose. A voluntary relationship, yes, but one which looks towards growth and development. The ability to offer young people space for reflection, new experiences, even moments of joy – for youth work is concerned about young people's lives in the present, not only with what they may become. It requires workers who can seize encounters 'on the wing', not just in structured programmes. Who will stick by troubled young people who may have few continuing, supportive relationships with adults? A key activity will be that of building partnerships and working with others for changes which will improve the lives of young people in their communities and in those institutions, such as schools, which are meant to serve them. Such tasks, and assessment, curriculum design and evaluation in non-formal settings, have always demanded a high level of skill from youth workers. So the development of a competent, idealistic workforce, both voluntary and professional, has to be at the heart of the action. Regrettably, there are still voices in the sector which resist the creation of a proper 'licence to practise' for youth work as the foundation on which a fully successful workforce can be built. In this resistance there is often an unholy alliance between the romantics and the technocrats. The former resist because they believe that 'convivial conversation' needs no particular skill or that, if it does, it is not for the state to determine what it is. The technocrats resist because they wish to blur the boundaries between professions and to keep costs down. We need youth work organisations, in all their rich diversity, to establish an appropriate 'fit and proper person' test for all staff appointments and for the training system nationwide to make available a range of qualifications to meet the needs of individuals in different roles; a detached youth worker needs different skills to those of a scout leader, even if they share a value base. And both are different in principle to nursery teachers or sports coaches. Youth work is offered in a range of settings, not just by designated youth work bodies. The use of the term 'youth work', however, signifies the presence of three distinguishing features: a focus on the personal and social development of young people; the use of experiential learning especially in groups; and the conscious presence in the worker of a particular value base. Good workers think about their practice and take responsibility for becoming better at it; the stories of youth work can have impact if they are shared and analysed by practitioners themselves for the nuances of how they contact and work with young people. All youth workers need continued professional development if they are to keep their skills and knowledge up to date. They have to learn how to apply their approaches and values in changing circumstances, for example in handling potentially confidential disclosure, in working with gangs or dealing with embryonic political extremism. Such continuing professional development should be an element in renewing any licence to practise.

Individual workers and the sector overall need to be responsive to new needs and to learn from different forms of work, including in other countries (the absence of serious engagement in European youth policy and practice is a particular British blind spot). Youth workers need easier access to research, to cogent interpretation and critical analysis of policy, to stimulating journals, to reasonably priced seminars and conferences shaped to promote debate not conformity. Much learning and support can be achieved at low cost through networks of practitioners in different settings such as schools or detached work but these require modest infrastructural support. Not least, the sector needs champions – bodies and alliances which will help youth work better express its role, establish clear national standards, inform and lobby parliamentarians, celebrate young people's achievement, and challenge not only policy-makers but also the sector itself. On a technical note, the sector needs to assemble evidence for each successive national Spending Review which shapes the government's departmental budgets for years ahead. Perhaps reflecting a general distaste for quantitative approaches, the youth sector is not good at building a cogent economic case or even at understanding how public finance operates.

The public mind

Recent years have seen a growing caution in the minds of many adults about their relationships with young people. For some, this has extended to a more overt suspicion, even hostility, and these attitudes have been amplified by parts of the media and by politicians anxious to use surveillance, or financial stringency in welfare provision, as devices to control all manner of undesirable behaviour. It is hard to build active citizenship when the focus is on moral deficiencies or 'broken Britain' rather than on an individual's or a community's assets. One looks forward to the day when a Secretary of State, or shadow, will announce a commitment to increase the number of youth workers, not police officers. Negative public attitudes about young people, when taken with doubts about the efficacy of youth work as an intervention, make it increasingly hard to argue the case for developmental services for the young. Given these challenges, it is vital to further extend those structures and processes which enable young people, individually and collectively, to give their own testimony about their needs; to be involved in local budget-setting; and to learn how to make decisions by creating and running more projects for themselves.

There are important tasks also for those in management in both the local authority and voluntary parts of the sector. New hybrid structures may well arise from the years of austerity and these in turn will be reviewing local priorities, re-allocating resources and selecting, supporting and supervising personnel. Financial pressures make all these tasks of performance management harder. Careful consideration is required as to where youth work should position itself alongside other services for the young, notably schools and colleges, but also the neglected arena of the arts, especially theatre, music, film and the social media. At its best, youth work has been a service shaped by local imperatives so, as a national drive to offer direction diminishes, the consideration has to be how it can establish its place within varied, local structures which identify needs and determine, plan and fund the shape of provision for young people. The case needs to be made for youth work as a locally co-ordinated, preventative service, an early intervention before problems become deep-seated. It is timely also to consider merging some voluntary bodies, the better to consolidate skills and focus effort. Of course, a reasonable level of diversity is essential in order to maintain local choices for young people, but there is so little actual differentiation in what some bodies offer that administrative and other costs could be reduced by a judicious coming together of organisations and by the development of social enterprises or mutually owned community organisations. Such efficiency gains can free up resources for what is now usually described as the 'front line' (though one hesitates to use the military metaphor in speaking of work with young people).

Conclusion

Arguments sometimes occur within the profession about arcane aspects of youth work's theology, for example on what constitutes a voluntary relationship with young people or what the exact balance should be between open access and targeted work. This 'narcissism of minor differences' will not advance the case, especially if these are the only tunes coming from the sector which are heard by politicians and their officials. A bolder, more vibrant approach should be adopted, backed up by strong evidence of impact. This would re-assert the central moral purpose of youth work: the exploration with the young of the question 'what kind of person do I want to be?' and demonstrate how the sector achieves that end. In a chilling landscape where the language of the utilitarian marketplace often holds sway, we need to advocate the politics of the common good and demonstrate, in numbers as well as stories, how good youth work achieves it. All the while keeping a clear-eyed idealism. To adapt some words of Robert Kennedy, it is the great task of youth work: to see pain and try to end it; see prejudice and strive to overcome it; see potential and seek to nurture it.

The changing seasons alter the landscape and we are likely to remain for some years in a deep winter of funding constraint. Despite the best efforts of families, schools and voluntary groups, little is likely to change for the better in many young people's lives, or in what youth work can do to support them, until central and local government re-discover their enabling and leadership roles in communities. Unless they do, an impoverished, laissez-faire state will fail to chart the way forward for youth work in an environment of fragmented local structures. Even if central government becomes more active, it will have little money to invest and few levers to pull to improve the levels and quality of youth provision. But young people and their needs will still endure. The future for many of them now depends on the skilful actions of those in local youth work.

Notes

1 Policy documents referred to in this chapter are primarily concerned with England. Policy in the other UK jurisdictions did not have such frenetic features in the period being reviewed though it grapples with similar issues.
2 As expressed, for example, in *The Benefits of Youth Work* by Viv Mckee et al., published by Unite/Lifelong Learning UK in 2010 and *Hunch: A Vision for Youth in Post-austerity Britain*, published by London Youth in 2011.

References

Department for Education (DfE) (2011) *Positive for Youth: A new approach to cross-government policy for young people aged 13–19* [online] www.gov.uk/government/publications/positive-for-youth-a-new-approach-to-cross-government-policy-for-young-people-aged-13-to-19.

Part 2

The Nature of Work with Young People

7

Defining Good Youth Work

Gina Ingram and Jean Harris

> Few people know what youth workers do and youth workers are bad at explaining it. This is partly because workers are often unaware of the skills they use, and partly because the work is so diverse and workers sometimes regard the kinds of work they themselves do as superior to other kinds. Youth workers need to appreciate the entire range of the work and to learn to describe the skills they use. Particularly important is to explain the way youth workers start from individual young people's learning needs, and form good relationships with them.

There is a story that may or may not have its origins in truth:

> Matt had been going to the local youth centre for six months. His mother decided that she ought to go and see what they did there. She called at about 8.30 p.m. It was a busy night. Two young people welcomed her and took her to see George, the full-time worker in charge. She explained why she had come and George asked two young people to show her around. They took her through the coffee bar where a group was planning a visit to Hungary. They pointed out the murals done by members over a number of years. She saw the arts and craft room where the women's group were working on entertainment for a local hospital. In the yard she saw where the young men and women had set out an outdoor training circuit. She returned via the counselling room: she couldn't enter of course, but her guides explained to her about the help-line that the youth council had established. The young people returned her to George who was in the office talking to a young woman about her portfolio for her Youth Achievement Award. The mother's comment was 'What an interesting hobby you have George but what's your real job?'

Obviously the joke has its origins in the fact that few people actually know what youth workers do and youth workers are bad at explaining this. If you asked people what youth workers do, the general view is often that:

This is a revised version of the original text which appeared as Chapter 4 in *Delivering Good Youth Work* by Gina Ingram and Jean Harris. First published in 2001 by Russell House Publishing.

- A youth worker is a type of social worker who gets on well with young people.
- They keep them out of trouble by doing things with them and often work with difficult young people whom no one else wants to know.
- Some do it voluntarily, like guides and scouts. A few are paid, but why that is, people are unsure. They do a bit of training to make sure they do things safely.

In most groups of adults, there are those who have had experience of youth clubs, projects or voluntary organisations. They tend to speak warmly of the youth workers and say how a youth worker helped them and was good to them, but they seldom specify what the youth worker actually did.

When asked to describe their job, youth workers often rely on words and phrases that mean little to the general public:

We work to empower young people; to help them take control of their lives.

Youth workers build relationships with young people ... and help them to become effective adults.

We offer them learning opportunities through which they grow and develop.

We help young people do what they want to do.

Alternatively, youth workers offer a long explanation:

Well, it's hard to explain in a sentence; can I give you an example? We were working with Mike (that's not his real name, I can't tell you that because of confidentiality, you might recognise him from what I say). Mike had this problem ...

No wonder workers can sometimes be seen as being woolly-minded! There are a number of difficulties in describing youth work.

Identifying the skills

The first problem is that although the delivery of youth work is very highly skilled, youth workers are not always aware of the skills they are using. When they can describe their skills, they can accurately communicate what they are doing. Then, instead of saying things like:

Well, I just do it; I don't really know why it works, it just does.

they would be able to say:

I begin by making young people feel safe; no one can learn if they don't feel safe. I make opportunities for young people to talk to me about things that matter to them: for them to tell me their story. If a young person is a bit shy, I always try to ... etc.

When people understand what youth workers do, and why they do it, they tend to be more sympathetic and supportive. It can also help people to be more aware of the difficulties that young people face.

The wide range of youth work

The second difficulty about offering an explanation is that youth work takes place in a very wide range of settings using a diverse set of activities. These include:

- Detached or outreach work and work in mobile centres.
- Clubs that may operate every night of the week in large urban centres, or once a week in rural areas.
- Specific project work, such as the Duke of Edinburgh's Award, youth theatres, adventure clubs.
- Work in units based on the identity of the young people (young women's groups, groups of black young people, PHAB groups [Physically Handicapped and Able Bodied], groups for young people who are lesbian, gay or bisexual).
- In specialist projects based around such issues as health or prostitution.
- There are information services, one-stop information shops and centres that offer counselling.

Youth workers may work in a wide range of other settings: colleges, schools, health centres, social service units as well as in multi-agency projects such as Connexions, Youth Offending Teams and social inclusion units.

This is a complex situation, difficult to explain to people quickly. It can be put like this:

> Youth workers work wherever young people are: in clubs, on the streets, in schools. The work is the same; it just takes place in a range of settings.

Competition between different settings for youth work

Some workers often see the work in their setting as being more relevant and appropriate than work in another setting. For example, workers say:

> Detached work is where it's at. We work with young people on their territory. This gives them power ... they don't see us as an institution like building-based work.

> I work in a youth club; everyone says we are irrelevant and old-fashioned but where else is work so embedded in the community? The workers are off the estate: many were members themselves. Young people hear about the club from their parents, we're part of their scene ... each generation makes the club their own.

> The Duke of Edinburgh's Award is fantastic. OK, so we do appeal to lots of kids who achieve more, they've got needs too, but we also run groups aimed at including disaffected young people. Our young people get a tremendous sense of achievement; a nationally recognised qualification ...

There is a need for youth workers to celebrate that they work in a range of different ways. This level of differentiation means that a wide range of young people have their needs met. Additionally, they can move on to different things as their needs change. Youth workers offer a highly accessible and differentiated service. Working in different ways requires different skills. Youth workers are multi-talented.

Why working with the individual is important

We need to tell people that youth workers are not specialists; they are the last of the generalists and they should be proud of this. Educational establishments such as schools, colleges and universities offer a fixed curriculum and a system that takes the learners through it. Youth work is different; youth work starts where young people are, not from where we would like them to be. We identify their learning needs and design a learning pathway through which individuals and groups can have their needs met. It follows that because the learning pathway is based on the age, experience, needs and interests of individuals and groups of young people, the activities that make up the pathway are very wide-ranging.

In summary:

- Schools and colleges work on fixed programmes of learning. Youth workers are different: they base their work on the young people's needs and interests.
- We use this as a starting point to offer young people learning that is relevant to their lives and appropriate to their age, experience and interests.
- We offer a tailor-made service of individual learning pathways.

Why making a relationship is paramount

Finally, youth workers are justifiably proud of offering learning through the caring, equal, relationships that they make with young people. People often do not understand how important this is. From their point of view:

> Why do you need a relationship to do what you do? Why don't you just get on with it and set things up for them?

When people say this, we need to explain that many young people do not have good experiences of adult relationships. It is important that they develop a good relationship with someone, to help them to become skilled parents, or good working colleagues, or friends. Youth workers act as role models so young people can learn and develop skills such as:

- caring and being cared for
- disagreeing and remaining friends
- negotiation and compromise
- building relationships that are open, honest and based in trust.

The skills of describing our work to others in ways that they can understand and sympathise with are vital. These descriptions, however, must not betray the work. This is the platform from which we can obtain wide support for the work.

8

Every Day is Different

Jean Spence and Carol Devanney

This is an edited version of a chapter which originally appeared in J. Spence and C. Devanney (2006) *Youth Work: Voices of Practice. A Research Report by Durham University and Weston Spirit,* and which was published by the National Youth Agency. It presents the findings of a research project which set out to explore the 'real' nature of youth work and the experiences of young people and youth workers in different practice settings. This involved the researchers participating in the everyday life of a range of youth projects and organisations, and included focus groups and interviews with young people and youth workers in which they described and reflected on their experiences and understanding of youth work.

   The chapter examines the realities of day-to-day youth work practice from the perspectives of practitioners and young people. It looks at some of the challenges that practitioners experience as they seek to be responsive to young people and their everyday lives, alongside responding to externally determined agendas and organisational priorities and requirements, which may not always be the same.

Behind the scenes

Exploration of the everyday world of youth work spending time in youth projects, talking and listening to youth workers and young people and looking 'behind the scenes', beyond the public narratives of practice. As well as looking at everyday interactions, the research also examined the processes leading to 'extraordinary' events such as residentials, which might be the culmination of many weeks, if not months, of preparation and development, as well as the event itself.

   The voluntary participation of young people presents opportunities for creative and spontaneous youth work interventions which can lead to developmental and

---

This chapter is edited from Spence, Jean and Devanney, Carol (2006) 'Every Day is Different' Chapter 3 in *Youth Work: Voices of Practice – Research Report by Durham University and Weston Spirit,* Leicester: National Youth Agency. Republished by kind permission of Jean Spence and Carol Devanney.

structured work. However, voluntary participation also makes the everyday unpredictable. Regardless of the planning of programmes, organisation of events and the regularity of groups and opening hours of buildings, the underlying rhythm of practice is subject to the rhythms of the everyday lives of young people and needs to be responsive to those lives. Youth work is only one feature of a young person's social landscape. Other institutions such as family and school dominate and different formal and informal relationships impact on their actions and emotions. Thus the circumstances and conditions of young people's contact with youth projects are regularly subject to events 'off stage'.

The fact that there is no such thing as a typical day was seen by many youth workers as one of the attractions of the job: 'I love it because my days are so different every day' (youth worker). Workers are adept at dealing with changes of tempo and mood. They are able to respond to crises and to create form and shape from mundane or volatile situations. This adaptability is a feature of their professional creativity which workers understand as crucial to their ability to respond to and affect the lives of young people. Not surprisingly therefore, the workers experience tensions between this and pre-determined agendas which they often discussed with the researchers, and which was observed to take the form of a struggle between the realities of face-to-face practice and the abstractions of bureaucratic requirements.

Responding to young people

The willingness of young people to access youth projects is responsive to what is on offer and how far this meets their needs and interests. Even when young people are referred and their participation is not voluntary, as Merton et al. (2004) imply, youth workers adapt and work in such a way as to encourage voluntary engagement. A number of instances were observed when it was apparent that despite their voluntary presence in a building, young people were refusing any meaningful communication with a youth worker.

By the same token, there were other occasions when despite having been referred to the agency, the young people reacted positively to the sympathetic approach of youth workers. These observations do not undermine the argument for the voluntary principle but rather suggest that the terms in which it is generally discussed are too simple. What is significant about the ideal of voluntarism is that youth work can only proceed effectively if the young people choose to participate and if they take some responsibility for the relational elements of the youth work process.

It could be argued that such active participation is necessary to satisfactory outcomes in any person-centred service and what is true of youth workers in terms of the need to 'win' young people to the process is also true for teachers, for example. However, youth work takes place in a different environment from that of compulsory institutions such as schools, and predominantly in time and space which young people identify as their own. The youth project must therefore hold some attraction. Even when young people are present as a result of referral, it is essential that they experience something different from and better than the alternatives on offer if they are to cooperate.

Responding to young people in their own time and space

The motivating idea of the universalism which has traditionally characterised youth work is that young people in general have leisure time needs and interests specific to their youthfulness which ought to be met at a collective, public level. However, a range of social factors, including finite resources in the public sector, the recognition of specific social needs in specific locations and the exercise of political power at a local as well as a national level means that in reality, local provision has always been targeted at those areas and those groups of young people seen to have the greatest needs. Put simply, youth projects are much more likely to be found in poor than in affluent areas, a larger concentration of resources is to be found in urban rather than rural areas, and youth work has dealt as much with the social and personal problems of specific groups in specific situations as with the developmental social education of youth per se.

Yet because of the ideal of universalism, it has been possible for youth work to avoid being perceived by young people as simply a 'problem-orientated' institution. If any young person can access youth provision voluntarily in their leisure time and simply for its own sake, then any problems which they bring with them can be contextualised, and dealt with in a manner which is negotiable. Crucially, this avoids labelling the young person as a 'problem' and enables them to control the pace of the discussion.

Many youth workers operate predominantly in locations which are defined by social and economic problems and frequently by a lack of public provision not just for young people, but for anyone. Those who use youth provision in such areas might do so simply for lack of alternatives and might not be seeking anything other than opportunities to spend time in a space which is orientated towards their leisure needs. Youth workers perceive this as a legitimate use of their resources.

Even when young people are simply accessing youth projects as a space in which to conduct their social lives in safety and away from the supervision of more controlling authorities, those projects are providing a social service. In one case, detached youth workers were concerned about the dangers to young women in an area where they were congregating, and issued personal alarms. Often the service offered is understood as a social benefit by outsiders and by young people themselves as 'keeping them off the streets'.

> Without the [project] there would be a lot of unhappy teenagers running about, going mental, smashing things up, and because they don't have anything else to do. (Young woman)

Young people frequently understand the primary meaning of youth projects and the input of youth workers in terms of recreational opportunities:

> Tom: There's not much to do. The only good thing is the [project]. That's why we're here every day.

> Mark: And the football court.

Tom: Yeah and the football court that's the only two good things.

(Young men)

Youth workers acknowledge the importance of recreation to young people and they respond by offering programmes, activities and events which they perceive to be of use and interest to young people in their localities. However, these are seldom ends in themselves for workers, but rather a means towards the development of other aspects of their work.

Programmes and timetables

The art of programming allows for the possibility of recruitment for development work. Young people who get involved in recreational opportunities are encouraged to form a deeper association with projects, including by participating in planning and organising future events and activities. As well as responding to young people's needs and interests, project timetables may also reflect what are considered to be current priorities.

> ... it's always changing and if the young people don't want to do a project it's changing and it has to always be with their needs as well. Like the health and fitness programme that I do it was something that the young people wanted plus it's something that the government's trying to tackle as well with obesity and keeping fit. So if something else comes and young people are interested in that then it's always got to change. (Youth worker)

Creating order and opportunity through timetabling and programmed activities is an integral aspect of professional youth work. Here the expectations of young people, youth workers, managers and politicians might overlap and be achieved. However, it makes a difference whether timetables emerge from the exigencies of face-to-face practice, or from the managerial demands of organisational planning, as this will have an impact on the type of young people who participate and the type of outcomes that are emphasised.

Centring young people

The researchers sometimes observed tensions between the expectations of young people for simple recreation and the anxieties of workers relating to their responsibilities towards educational process and policy expectations. Whilst opportunities can be seized in a recreational situation to introduce organisational and policy agendas, great skill and sensitivity is required to do this successfully. Workers need to know and be comfortable with the young people involved. Learning about young people as people is the crucial underpinning of developmental educational work. As one young woman explained, youth work is different from other services because 'youth workers get to know you', 'go out of their way to help you', and they 'treat you as an individual'. Similarly one young man told the researcher, 'You have as much of a say as them'. He said that this was about having respect for each other and that they 'Don't talk down to you like a teacher', that they are 'friendly'. However, achieving such levels of mutual respect and trust is not always an easy process:

> Malcolm: You can just be chatting and it can just be an attitude change, somebody's taking time to speak to you, asking how you're doing rather ignoring you or giving you some verbal, that's a change, progress ...

> Gary: Sometimes young lads will come in. 'How's it going?' 'Grunt', 'Are you looking for a job?' 'Grunt'. Eventually – if you keep it up. But it's up to you to keep being positive and welcoming ... And maybe that's what's been lacking in some young people's experience up to that date. (Youth workers)

Learning about young people does not always take place in conventional settings. Workers who understand practice as informal education are alert and responsive to opportunities which present themselves in all the everyday situations when they have contact with young people:

> A lot of conversations – serious conversation takes place when the worker is driving. There is less eye contact with the worker – and the young women know that they are not going to stop the car – so they feel they can ask you things. (Youth worker)

In building relationships, it is impossible to force the pace, and although the youth workers in the research were nothing if not persistent and optimistic, they often had to step back as well as forward in order to bring young people to trust them.

> One young woman was talking to the youth workers about what they do as their job and was joking that all they ever seem to do is 'sit around'. She was asking about how they feel when people are sometimes not very nice to them. The worker told a story about how one young person left one day after calling him a dickhead. The following day the young woman came back in and didn't mention it as if she didn't remember saying it. They talked about how they need to treat every day differently. They did not want to bring that issue back up with the young person so they moved on from it. (Youth worker)

Centring the young people themselves is crucial to the process of winning their voluntary engagement. Developmental and educational activities also need to be grounded in their world, with workers ceding some control over the pace and direction of conversation and future planning:

> We're doing a programme. It's about looking at them, and their community and where they are. And some of it's just about sitting down, like last night it was just about telling their story, about their group, where they first met. And we did a road map of where

they went to and what friends left and who came in and who joined and what did they
get up to when they were 13 … And got to now and looked at where they are going,
and we were looking at other stuff like their relationships and next week we're going
to do this thing with sand and Lego and stuff and build their community on the square.
(Youth worker)

Keeping young people at the heart of youth work practice requires constant vigilance,
especially when their culture, expectations and personal attitudes are disharmonious
with the rationality and schedules of organisational life and may be antagonistic to
any expression of adult or official authority. Although many of the young people
who participated in interviews and discussions with the researchers were able to
understand and respond to organisational rhythms and expectations, and 'performed'
well in terms of explicit organisational agendas, not all were and the everyday lives
of youth projects were frequently marked by unpredictability, unreliability, dissent and
sometimes disorder.

Unpredictability

Drop-in and detached sessions are by nature unpredictable – even if the youth
workers themselves have aims and objectives for the session. They do not know
which young people – if any – they will be dealing with and in what combination
and mood. A flavour of this can be gleaned from the research diary relating to a
session in a youth unit attached to a school:

Throughout the morning young people keep popping in … There seems to be a core
group of young people who always come in at break times to talk to the workers.
There is a lot of negotiation with the young people, for example, this may be getting
them to go to their lessons on time because they will get in trouble which then may
jeopardise whether they can come back over the mobile.

One young woman who had come into school to sit an exam came into the mobile to
talk to the worker. He had done one-to-one work with this young woman (she is the
one that they took to a hostel). They talked about lots of different issues, what she was
doing for a job, her plans for college, how things were at home with her mother, her
relationship with her step father, her social activities …

… The group of young people who had put the gig on last week came in. The workers had supported by helping with the arrangements and also going along to supervise
on the evening. They brought a thank you card for the workers for supporting them.
(Extract from research diary)

Whilst timetabled and programmed sessions create a background sense of predictability and help create boundaries, there can be no way of second guessing when
a crisis will erupt or when the immediate needs of young people will impinge on
this ordered framework. Similarly, both workers and young people use timetabled
contact for discussions which sometimes have very little, if any, relationship with

programme context but which are responsive to the developing worker–young person relationship or to a particular issue raised by the young people.

Unreliability

While unpredictability can be and is used constructively by youth workers, the unreliability of some young people can be disheartening. A great deal of work and effort might be put into a particular activity or event, including by the young people themselves, only to have some people fail to show up at designated times and places:

> There had been seventeen young people coming on the trip but seven had dropped out either that morning or the Friday before. Young people had expected others to be there, particularly the young woman who was the only one from her school and didn't know anyone else.

> The martial arts session was cancelled because only two people showed up … The workers decided that it was not worth going ahead with it. One of the young men from yesterday had planned to come but his dad had contacted him at the last minute and so he changed his plans. (Extracts from research diary)

Despite the discouragement which it brings, such unreliability is understood as an intrinsic part of the everyday world of youth work:

> I think it's difficult for youth workers not to be hurt by the fact that sometimes people don't turn up or sometimes do things differently or say things they shouldn't. And I know it sounds quite cold and blunt but you've got to learn to balance that so you've got to see where you're coming from with the young person because a week's a long time in a young person's life … they mightn't turn up because something's happened in their life and they've completely forgot. (Area manager)

Whilst it is undermining to outcome-led work and appears to indicate failure to establish in young people the importance of a particular social rule relevant to employability, what is actually significant in youth work is that the worker does not use unreliability as an excuse to withdraw and thus affirms the importance of the young person apart from their behaviour. This makes an important contribution to winning loyalty which in the long run can affect the young person's attitude towards reliability.

Dissent and disorder

Even when young people do 'turn up', their full participation in programmed activities can never be guaranteed. Expressions of dissent can range from simply 'switching off' to outright aggression.

But you know, if they're not enjoying it, you know because they start speaking through it. And I've got to say to them, 'Right, come on. Listen.' Because it can be quite embarrassing if there is someone doing a bit of a spiel and they start yapping though it, or their mobile phones go off and they start speaking into their mobile phone. And you know right away, that they're not interested in this. (Youth worker)

In the main, workers attempt to manage dissent through negotiation. Although voluntary participation gives young people some power, this is not absolute and there are conditions and responsibilities consequent upon the use of youth facilities. When the dissent is simply related to disinterest in an activity, it is usually possible for workers to use the situation for further conversation about ground rules for social behaviour and also about why particular subjects are of little interest.

However, there are occasions when dissent signals a breakdown in relationships between youth workers and young people. Sometimes it is important for youth workers to admit that they can make no headway with particular groups. Their interventions are not appropriate for all young people at all times. Changing the conditions of provision for young people or ending youth worker support can, on the other hand, provoke dissent because young people perceive this as a betrayal of their trust.

Disorder can occur in a variety of contexts. Sometimes it appears when workers attempt to introduce structured, outcome-led activity with groups who have volatile relationships with each other or who have not yet established settled inter-personal relationships with the workers. It might also erupt when young people are taken out of their normal environment, when they have no pre-knowledge of social rules of behaviour, when they are excited by the new experience, or when they are together in large numbers and in groups where there is no leadership or direction for their behaviour.

Persistent disorder was most noticeable amongst referred groups of young people. For example:

There were a number of behavioural issues while the young people were at the park – one young man got involved in intimidating some skaters (apparently the worker had some strong words about this – I was with another part of the group at this time). Some of the skaters let the young men borrow a skateboard – they had a bit of a go and then tried to steal it. As we were leaving they went on to the basketball court, there were some younger boys on the court who they gave some hassle to, an older bloke came over and intervened telling the young men to 'fuck off' – which didn't go down well. One of the young men got a stone and was going to throw it but didn't. (Extract from research diary)

What was significant here is that in such groups, participating young people were characterised in relation to 'problems'. In open groups there was a mixture of young people and variability in behaviour, with some young people leading and influencing the behaviour of others. In the referred groups, the concentration of behavioural difficulties and the absence of long-standing friendships or even association between the young people involved meant that there were no internal moderating factors. All responsibility for order was thus transferred to workers, whose role began to shift from befriending and advocacy towards policing and controlling, militating against the possibility of gaining the trust and co-operation, and therefore the voluntary engagement of young people. The difficulties of maintaining order observed when youth workers took responsibility for referred groups highlight issues relating to youth work methods which are framed in educational rather than therapeutic or policing terms. Youth work is not the most appropriate approach for all groups of young people and it is important to recognise this in the context of partnership working.

Small steps

A significant role played by youth workers in the research was to act as a bridge between the everyday worlds, irregular lifestyles and insecurities of the young people concerned and those representatives and features of the outside world which were perceived as antagonistic, challenging or threatening or which were simply unknown. This might range from intervening directly to divert young people from dangerous activities, through offering opportunities to participate in events, activities and excursions which might be outside the range of the everyday, to the development of cross-community work in relation to ethnicity or faith, through encouraging those who were alienated from or refusing school back into the classroom:

> The girl … came back over … asking for a letter from the worker to get her out of lessons for the teacher. She was being really negative, looked unhappy and said that she was going to go home. The worker tried to reason with her and encourage her to stay in school, then followed her out of the room to talk to her. (Extract from research diary)

Because of its informality and flexibility, youth work is able to connect with young people who are in danger of exclusion, or are already excluded from more structured social institutions. It can also act as a bridge between institutions and young people:

> Youth workers are, like, in between a teacher and a parent because they're not so official but they're there to kind of help us to take the right paths. A lot of the time when there's older people in positions of power you tend not to listen to them, it's just that rebellious streak I suppose. But when you've got somebody that's informal and they talk to you on your level and give you advice, it's a lot easier to listen to it because you can see that they sympathise – they know where you're coming from and whatever they say really is in your best interests, and not something else. (Young woman)

One of the contributions which seemed to be of most consequence to the young people and their potential for dealing with the wider social world and other institutions was the way in which youth workers were able to recognise and work on the 'little things' which could be major obstacles to young people's confidence and achievement:

The short steps. It's about breaking down barriers that they put in their own way. 'I can't do that because, I can't make a phone call because', and you take the barriers away from them, 'I can't. I don't know how to get a house because I don't know where the housing department is.' 'Well, we'll take you, we'll go with you.' Trying to break down the barriers to make it easier for them. Because sometimes they put up this shield, 'I can't.' There's no such word as 'can't', 'won't' or 'I don't want to'. (Youth worker)

It took us 18 months just to get a young woman to take her coat off. (Youth worker)

Similar accounts of the amount of time it might take to establish trust or to encourage one individual or a group of young people to participate actively in the youth project in order that they might deal more effectively with the wider society can be found in other research and accounts of practice (Brew, 1943; Crimmens et al., 2004; Montagu, 1954). The start of the developmental journey is usually described in terms of pre-history which involves patient and sensitive efforts on the part of workers to listen to the young people concerned and to acknowledge the significance of their fears and difficulties and to encourage them to take small steps forward.

The amount of time taken to achieve a small and almost intangible outcome can be long and tortuous and the efforts of the worker may flounder along the way. Yet, time and again workers spoke of young people contacting the project after absences – sometimes of years – based upon the young person acknowledging a need that the youth project fulfilled, when the workers had never been sure that any significant outcome had been achieved after the initial contact.

The unstructured or partially structured nature of just 'being there' and of being able to be responsive in the moment, is not just an important feature of youth work practice, it is a foundational element of that practice. And it is a feature of the voluntary participation of young people.

Yet it is difficult, if not impossible, to measure the impact of the work longer term or even to recognise that this might be important when monitoring and recording practice. Consequently, a key element of the youth work approach is relegated to its margins in organisational systems. This in turn impacts upon the assessment of youth workers about what is important to managers, funders and policy makers, and in order to 'perform' effectively, they 'talk up' the significance of some aspects of their work and muffle or silence other aspects according to this assessment (Williamson, 2003). Even when organisations might be sympathetic to 'small steps' and everyday achievements, the dominant 'performance' discourse makes it difficult for workers to value their own achievements at this level.

Real life and organisations

The everyday life of youth projects which are responsive to young people, and which are dealing with behaviour patterns which are not necessarily in the control of the youth worker, can never fully correspond with the linear and mechanistic character of organisational rationality which suggests a systematic approach involving predictability, reliability, conformity and order. Managing the tension between reality and organisational demands is therefore an inevitable and inherent part of the youth worker's and youth work manager's responsibility. This task is particularly significant in view of the nature of many of the young people who come to the attention of young people and whom young people seek to influence.

Anderson et al. (2005) have suggested that different groups of young people view and experience time differently in relation to their experiences, security and expectations of life. Those who do not expect any significant change in their social or physical location over their lifetime live much more for the moment than those who have expectations of an improved life in the future, who plan their present lives according to future reference points. Many young people who might be defined as 'socially excluded' and who make the most use of youth projects fall particularly into the former category. They are entirely present-orientated in both time and place, and they often find it difficult to engage with organisations which are future-orientated in their planning processes and requirement for pre-determined outcomes:

> The other aspect to time constraints is that young people ... see time as the here and now. It's not two years down the line, it's not six months down the line. It's what's happening tomorrow, this week, and that's why trying to engage them in a process of funding programmes and long term strategies to develop skate parks and develop youth enquiry centres and music centres and so forth and you're saying this is four years of time at a minimum that you're committing yourself to. I'm not going to be here in four years time, I'm out of here ... I'm going to do something but I'm not going to be here in four years time. (Youth worker)

The dynamic, responsive characteristics of youth work, which is manifested to a large extent in the personalities of workers, does not reflect the static and bureaucratic rationality of organisations, even if the aims of worker and organisational policy are fully in harmony. In order to maintain their ability to work with young people in their everyday realities, youth workers must first deal with the present. They recognise that there are times when young people are at their most productive and engaged, and they recognise the importance of young people being allowed to pursue their interests and desires in a space of time identified by the young people themselves. This accords with one of the principles of youth work identified by Davies (2005) – working with young people as young people rather than as future adults.

Yet youth workers do have responsibilities towards their employing organisations and they are faced with the realities of organisational time and policy. Their own everyday reality includes administration to run programmes and to initiate and follow up on face-to-face work. Working at a face-to-face level and at an organisational level is intrinsic to youth work practice.

Being there

Youth workers are forced in the immediate reality of their work to find ways of coping with different levels of input, with different types of young people, with different expectations of representatives of other professionals, communities and institutions. In addition, they must marry what they perceive to be the competing demands of their employing organisations and the everyday expectations of young people. To deal with this involves a combination of levels of patience, humour and optimism which ultimately might be claimed to be personal rather than professional in provenance.

The data consistently points to the significance of mutuality in the young person–youth worker relationship which involves personal engagement on the part of the worker as well as on the part of the young person. 'Being there' in the broadest sense of the term – being alert and responding at an inter-personal level is equally, if not more important than being able to access resources, plan effectively and keep up-to-date records. Indeed, without the former, the latter becomes irrelevant in everyday practice.

Acknowledging the amount of energy required to 'be there' highlights the importance of there being time not to be there. Time for rest, for personal privacy and reflection are crucial in a work setting which requires the constant use of a 'positive' self in face-to-face work. This involves a consideration of the time and space available within the working week for workers to not only create and sustain relationships and accomplish tasks, but also to think and reflect. It also raises questions about the relationship and boundaries between private time and professional time.

Managing the need to be flexibly available, to provide structured as well as unstructured access, and to create time for paperwork and self-reflection, reading and pursuing information to improve professional practice, requires a high level of awareness, skill and self-confidence from workers.

Centre-based workers are always involved in the management, supervision and maintenance of buildings which may or may not be fit for purpose, which may or may not be controlled by the youth project, which may or may not be in suitable environments, and which may or may not be permanent residences for the project. Questions of health and safety, insurance, disabled access, security and cleaning are nearly always part of the daily administrative load of youth workers.

My job is as a youth and community learning worker and I'm the sole full-time worker for the [name] project. And my roles are numerous [laughs] to say the least, cleaner, admin assistant, youth worker, manager, driver, anything and everything that comes up. And the roles kind of vary really. My role as a day time worker is that I'm the only worker in the project and I see it as split in three ways really. There's a large admin side to the project to keep the project going. That's all the evaluation forms and all the things that we need to do to monitor and record the stuff and all the money aspects. But also we hire the minibus and I have to monitor all that and keep everything up to date … As well as report writing etc., etc. And then the second bit is to be an advice and information worker for the daytime drop-in. And that's being on hand for anyone in the community to come and use, get my expertise or if I haven't got the information then I'll refer them on to a different agency. So that's kind of individual stuff and then it's the other stuff in the day time as a youth worker and managing groups, whether that's a residential group, whatever comes up so it's about that. And then in the evening I become a detached work manager and I manage the detached team which works Mondays to Thursdays on the streets. (Project manager)

Workers are also involved in a network of relationships with other adults which are building related. These adults might be, for example, managers of a community centre, caretakers or local residents and they are not always sympathetic to young people's needs.

Youth workers can become 'building-bound' but usually their activity extends beyond any building which might be associated with the project. For example, they undertake visits to families, accompany young people to clinics, participate in partnership meetings, take young people on trips and stay with them in residential facilities, and of course spend their time on detached sessions. They must be clear about their roles in different spaces if they are to be effective in them and sensitive to different expectations, being prepared to explain themselves and act accordingly.

In the process of adopting and adjusting, or performing different roles for different situations, and of maintaining a constancy of presence in unpredictable situations, youth workers can become buffeted by the expectations of others. This threatens their sense of the centrality of their own personal and professional priorities and points to the importance of maintaining a professional discourse which affirms the principles and reflects the priorities in the realities of everyday practice. Availability of time and resources for workers to communicate regularly, to associate and to organise in terms which derive from practice is essential for the affirmation of professional values and principles.

Every day has meaning

Working at the level of the everyday is volatile and dynamic and is a source of creativity in youth work. However, it can also be mundane and ordinary, subject to marginality or invisibility. Seldom are everyday informal interventions perceived as an outcome or a success story. Sometimes they are not even perceived as particularly interesting. In this sense they cannot be evaluated and they do not become the stuff of narratives explaining youth work in the same way as the extraordinary.

In the apparently unremarkable world of the everyday, there is significant value and meaning to youth workers, young people and their communities in 'the youth work process'. Meaningful youth work practice does not end when a target has been reached – or missed, or when a formal structured session has ended and everyone has appeared to switch off. The everyday of youth work is as much – if not more – of a location of meaning-making, boundary setting and development through listening and dialogue, as are those more readily defined aspects of youth work that attract and respond to formal scrutiny.

References

Anderson, M., Bechhofer, F., McCrone, D., Jamieson, L., Li, Y. and Stewart, R. (2005) 'Timespans and Plans Among Young Adults', *Sociology*, Vol. 39, No. 1, pp. 139–155.

Brew, J. Macalister (1943) *In the Service of Youth: A Practical Manual or Work Among Adolescents*, London, Faber.

Crimmens, D., Factor, F., Jeffs, T., Pitts, J., Pugh, C., Spence, J. and Turner, P. (2004) *Reaching Socially Excluded Young People: A National Study of Street-based Work*, Leicester, Joseph Rowntree Foundation, The National Youth Agency.

Davies, B. (2005) 'Youth Work: A Manifesto for our Times', *Youth and Policy*, No. 88, pp. 5–28.

Merton, B. et al. (with significant contributions by Payne, M. and Smith, D.) (2004) *An Evaluation of the Impact of Youth Work in England*, Department for Education and Skills, Research Report No. 606, Leicester, De Montfort University.

Montagu, L.H. (1954) *My Club and I*, London, Neville Spearman Ltd and Herbert Joseph Ltd.

Williamson, H. (2003) 'Grand Aims Collide with Practical Reality', *Young People Now*, 28 May–3 June, p. 11.

9

Helping: Definitions and Purpose

Hazel L. Reid and Alison J. Fielding

Working on a one-to-one basis is common in many forms of work with young people. This chapter draws on a number of models and theories to explore the nature of client-centred individual helping relationships. It provides a clear description of their purposes, the circumstances in which they might be useful, the stages they follow and the outcomes they are aiming towards.

Introduction

This chapter explores the nature of a professional helping relationship with young people, by considering some fairly fundamental questions: What to we mean by helping? How much helping? How do you structure that work?

Trying to explain the concept of a model for a professional helping relationship is rather like trying to tell someone how to drive a car – instructions are clarified if you are actually in the car. Like driving a car, 'helping' makes much more sense if you are actually involved, though it does seem at times that there is just too much happening at once to be clear about what is going on. We use the word 'helping' to signify a 'professional helping relationship'. In using the term 'professional' we are referring to a formal relationship (i.e. governed by ethical codes of practice) between the helper and the young person, and we are not excluding practitioners who are viewed as para-professionals or volunteers.

A model of helping

Approaches to helping have been informed by a number of theoretical models, however there is a clear emphasis on the humanistic approach in counselling. The work of Rogers

This chapter is edited from Reid, Hazel and Fielding, Alison (2007) 'Helping: Definitions and Purpose', Chapter 2, *Providing Support to Young People*, Routledge. © 2007 Routledge. Reproduced by permission of Taylor & Francis Books UK.

(1951, 1961) and Egan (2002) informs many of the models used in the counselling field. The concepts have been adapted here for the context of working with young people, but are applicable to a wide range of non-therapeutic settings and 'clients'.

Egan uses the term 'The Skilled Helper', and in this chapter we would like to borrow the term. Our aim is to help or enhance practitioners' abilities to become skilled helpers, working alongside the young people that require professional help and support. That help is *goal-orientated* and it is in the *action*, related to agreed goals, that helpers can reach *positive outcomes* in their work with (not for) young people.

The approach to helping in the Single Interaction Model (SIM) is, like many others, based on a 'client-centered' approach, which we will call a 'young person-focused' approach. The approach is neither directive nor non-directive; instead it is 'facilitating' in that the helper, working alongside the young person, acts as a guide to help the young person make their own decisions in the context of their own lives. This collaborative approach, being young person-focused, is non-prescriptive but follows a flexible, yet time-bound, structure.

Applying the model to a range of circumstances

The model of helping explained in this chapter seeks to demonstrate that the principles of effective helping, and the skills and strategies that can be used, apply equally to the wide range of contexts in which professional helpers find themselves operating, such as with colleagues and agencies with whom they network or refer young people to. In effect, the skills and strategies that are outlined in this chapter can apply in any situation where communication and interaction take place. Although this chapter uses the model for one-to-one work, it can also be adapted for work with small groups of young people. The high level of interpersonal skills and knowledge that helpers need has application beyond direct work with young people. Anyone involved in a 'working with people' context, necessarily participates in a wide range of communication activities, which may or may nor be directly involved with 'clients'. Therefore, the model of effective helping is equally appropriate for a variety of other 'purposeful' situations. For instance, it could include the activities of mentoring, coaching and counselling in a range of settings.

Helping relationships: definitions and purpose

We often talk about helping, and assume that the people we are talking to have the same ideas about what this means. However, as with other commonly used terms, we do not check with them that this is the case. A common understanding and definition of a helping relationship is needed to help overcome any confusion that may exist.

Our definition:

> *A helping relationship enables the young person to move towards their personal goals and to strengthen their ability to manage issues or problems in their lives. It is a collaborative relationship characterised by flexibility on the part of the professional helper in identifying and meeting the individual needs of the young person.*

In common with many professions, the skill and the knowledge base of helpers is wide ranging. These will vary according to the context and the purpose of the helping relationship. The helping relationship encompasses a wide range of activities dependent on the specific needs of the young person or group.

A helping relationship should be a learning process that is open and ongoing. The process is reflective as well as outward- and forward-looking. Helping can take place through a wide range of formal and informal situations.

The purpose of the helping relationship

Everyone seeks help at some time, and this usually involves some type of helping relationship. The difference for professional helpers is that we need to be clear about the intention of the helping relationship. Simply building a relationship and 'being there' for young people is not enough. We need to ensure that our help is focused on the needs of the young person and that together we are moving on from the current situation. The young person needs to know what we can, and perhaps more importantly what we cannot, help with; what the expectations are, what the benefits might be and what the possible outcomes are. In short, the professional helper is engaging in a helping relationship with a young person for a purpose – that of 'moving the young person on' so that, ultimately, they no longer require the help of a professional.

By 'moving the person on' we mean helping them to progress, develop or move forward from the place they are when they seek help. That movement involves identifying what the young person views as a meaningful goal. That said, the degree of movement depends on the individual and their circumstances. For some, even after the intervention of the helper, they may not progress at this time, but hopefully will have clarified their thinking and have learnt from the process of engagement. The basis of an effective helping relationship lies in helping young people to recognise their starting points (and these will be different for different young people), to decide on their goals and to move from the first to the second.

One of the most important things about defining the helping relationship is that the definition we use in our work says something about what we, as professional helpers, are aiming to achieve. This in turn leads to our being able to establish whether we are actually providing the service we think we should so that we can evaluate our work against the definition. We can then set out to improve the service we offer in the light of the evaluation, undertaken at the individual and organisational level.

Individual needs

Definition:

> *'Needs' are literally what people need help with. In simple terms, this is what the young person 'presents' to the professional helper (or another helper who may be a friend or relative) to help them to make changes and implement decisions.*

For example:

- The young person might need help with deciding what action to take about some aspect of their life. Thus the need is for decision-making skills.
- The young person may not term their needs in this way and it is likely that they will refer to their needs as wanting advice or simply as getting help, in non-specific ways.
- In addition to needs that the young person has identified, albeit in non-specific terms, they may have needs they are unaware or less aware of.

For instance, in order to make the decision, they may need to think about what they want as a result of the decision made. It may be that they can only do this effectively if they have a certain level of self-awareness. Egan (2002: 243) discusses the helper's role in assisting the client to identify their needs and wants.

'Counsellors help clients answer the following two commonsense but critical questions:

- What do you want?

  and

- What do you have to do to get what you want?'

A 'common sense' approach is particularly attractive to professional helpers, who often have limited time to work with individual young people. Of course, we cannot assume that one person's common sense is the same as another's and, although they cannot guarantee quality, the purpose of ethical codes of practice is to provide guidelines and standards for our work. Perhaps a better way of describing the approach would be to say that the model follows a 'natural' sequence of (a) identifying an issue, (b) exploring the options, and (c) moving from goals to action.

Identifying the individual needs of a young person may involve formal or informal processes, and will require some sort of assessment of the situation for the young person telling you what they think they require help with, and some discussion of this to ensure that you, as the helper, understand what they are saying. It may involve the drawing together of a range of information about the young person to help them understand it, recognizing the implications and agreeing priorities.

In summary, young people have a range of needs, some of which they are aware of, and others which they are not. A young person may bring these to a professional helper, or other adults, with whom they can develop a helping relationship. They seek help (or are 'sent') to identify goals, make decisions and plan and implement action.

The helping process

Definition:

The stages through which the young person progresses so that they can identify and choose appropriate goals in order to manage change in their lives and to make and implement decisions.

As the above definition suggests, professional helping is often an iterative process. Young people may want help over a considerable period of time, and this need may occur and re-occur throughout the time of their contact with professional helpers. The Single Interaction Model (SIM) presented in this chapter is informed by the work of Egan but is adapted for shorter time-bound interventions. Figure 9.1 offers a comparison between Egan's three-stage approach that is developed over a number of sessions, and our adaptation – the Single Interaction Model (SIM) – for use within a single session or where intensive support is not, or is no longer, required. Whether and how the Egan model or SIM is used, is likely to depend on the level of support a young person needs.

The helping process aims to assist a young person moving forward to their next step in relation to the changes they are dealing with. If they do not seek professional help they may rely on informal help; that is, advice from friends, family or other care-givers.

It is important for helpers to recognise and acknowledge that informal help happens, and will continue to happen alongside any assistance they may offer young people in their role as a professional helper. Support offered by practitioners does not operate in isolation from informal help and the processes that this includes. Acknowledging the importance of the social context for the young person is fundamental for effective helping: helping which ignores the 'world view' of the young person is unlikely to make a difference. How a young person constructs meaning in their lives cannot be ignored or dismissed in the rush to find solutions to help them 'move on'. Working collaboratively, alongside the young person, means understanding the client's story and helping them to script a new story (Reid 2002). However, this does mean challenging 'unrealistic' (too high or too low) aspirations, working towards goals and clarifying and taking action, but these are advanced skills that the helper needs to use within a structured process. The ultimate goal of helping is that the young person will learn from the process and be enabled to help themselves.

For some young people, professional helpers will need to advocate on their behalf, but will be mindful that they are trying to develop the young person's ability to act independently. The role of the helper here is to provide the scaffolding to support the young person in the process of learning how to move forward and construct their own future (Bassot 2003).

Egan three-stage model

Stage 1 – current scenario

- Story: the young person explains current situation.
- Blind spots: helping the young person to identify and be clear about problems and issues.
- Leverage: which are the most important issues to focus on when conducting the remainder of the work?

Stage 2 – preferred scenario

- Possibilities: helping the young person to identify what they want and if it is possible.
- Agenda: translating possibilities into realistic goals.
- Commitment: testing out the motivation considering the difficulties and choosing the goals.

Stage 3 – getting here

- Strategies: helping the young person to consider strategies for action.
- Best fit: which strategy is going to be most appropriate for this young person?
- Plan: turning strategies into a concrete plan for action.

Stages completed over a period of time but each interaction has a beginning (Stage 1), middle (Stage 2) and end (Stage 3).

Single Interaction Model

Stage 1 – negotiating the contract and agreeing an agenda

- Introductions are made and the purpose is shared.
- Young person is helped to focus on their current situation and raise issues for discussion.
- Objectives for the interaction are discussed and prioritised.
- An agenda for the interaction is agreed.

Stage 2 – developing issues and identifying goals

- The young person is helped to explore the issues in greater depth.
- Possible options for the future are discussed.
- Through discussion, sharing of information and evaluation of possible options, realistic goals are identified.

Stage 3 – designing, planning and implementing action

- Identifying possible courses of action.
- Discussing and evaluating the benefits of particular courses of action.
- Agreeing specific action to be carried out.

All three stages completed in a single interaction.

Figure 9.1   A comparison of Egan and SIM

The stages of the helping process

We have described the helping process as something that enables the client to move forward in some way. This moving forward necessarily spans a period of time, which may be difficult to specify, but a period of time that will be constrained by the helping contract established between the young person, the helper and the helping agency. Figure 9.2 depicts that process of engagement in a flow chart, to help us think

External agencies   Direct work with young people

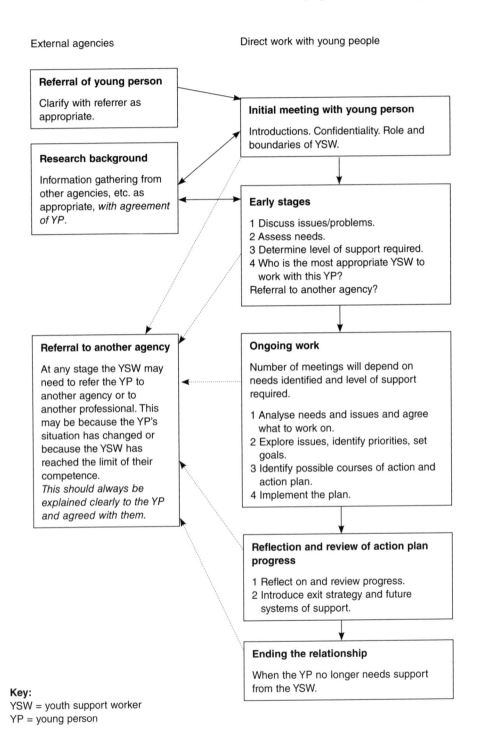

Key:
YSW = youth support worker
YP = young person

Figure 9.2   The process of engagement

about that overall structure for work with a range of young people. But, it is offered as a tool to think with: a guide rather than a 'prescription'.

Practitioners need to be aware of and use these processes of moving forward in order to be effective in the help that they give. That said, the work is not as linear as any structure or flow chart may imply. One of the key things to recognise is that young people seeking help, or 'sent' for help, will be at different stages in the process when they meet an adviser or provider of helping services. Much of the literature on the process of choice and decision making tends to imply that people present themselves at the beginning of the helping process and will, therefore, need help through each stage. In practice people are likely to present themselves at the point at which they are either stuck or confused, or aware of an agency that seems relevant to their needs. Yes, some will present themselves at the beginning in that they have just begun to consider change, or have just been plunged into some sort of crisis or change involuntarily. Equally, a number will present themselves to helpers at a much later stage in an attempt to make sense of any changes, choices and decisions that are affecting them.

An added dimension of the work for professional helpers is that they will be, in many cases, working with young people who are not self-referred. Working alongside young people who may resist the help on offer, can add another layer of difficulty.

Effective helping processes

Returning to the helping process as a series of stages that the young person moves through, we will now move on to identify the different stages that make up the whole process. In the outline of the model that follows we have tried to link the stage that the young person 'is at' together with an outline of where the helper fits into the process.

Stage 1 – current scenario (Egan 2002)
Negotiating the contract an agreeing an agenda
(Single Interaction Model – SIM)

At this opening stage the young person is helped to assess their current situation. This may include an assessment of their current thinking in relation to future plans (these may be educational or vocational or related to other needs). It will include an opportunity for the young person to tell their own story, in other words 'where they are at the moment'.

The practitioner will help the young person to identify their helping needs and consider ways in which these can be met. Depending on where the young person is in their thinking, the practitioner may help with the following as appropriate: self-assessment and awareness; identification of possibilities and options; identifying current knowledge of opportunities and adding to this; decision-making skills; referral and advocacy.

It is important that enough time is given to Stage 1 of the helping process, particularly if the young person is in any way resistant, confused, lacking in knowledge or understanding of the choices available to them, or unrealistic about what they are able to do or achieve. The helper needs to move at the young person's pace and in line with the young person's needs in order to move to Stage 2.

With some young people who require intensive support, it may take several sessions of rapport and trust building to achieve an agenda at the end of Stage 1: an agenda that clarifies the areas for future exploration and action. That said, each meeting will have a structure: a beginning – Stage 1, a middle – Stage 2 and an end – Stage 3 (Culley and Bond 2004).

Stage 2 – preferred scenario (Egan 2002)
Developing issues and identifying goals (SIM)

At this stage in the process the young person is ready to explore and identify possible future goals that are appropriate for them as individuals. Goals are not just what the young person wants to achieve in overall terms. Some goals may be targets of achievement, signposts of specific steps that pave the way for the future large or final goal. For some young people requiring intensive support, achieving small short-term goals can engender a sense of agency, an ability to make a difference in their own lives, and may be all that can be achieved for the present. But, this success is motivating and can provide a 'springboard' where, together, the helper and young person can move towards larger and longer-term goals.

So, in Stage 2 the young person and helper work together to identify the range of possible goals in order to help the young person choose those that are most appropriate and relevant, in relation to their values, abilities, aspirations, resources, context and needs.

Stage 3 – getting there (Egan 2002)
Designing, planning and implementing action (SIM)

This is the stage at which the young person and helper look at what action could be taken, to enable the young person to achieve the goals that have been identified in Stage 2 of the process.

Together they can identify a range of actions that could be taken to get the young person to where they want to be. From this the young person can select the action that seems most appropriate and within their capabilities for the goals (small or large, short-term or long-term) that have been agreed. It is likely that for some young people, who require the helper to advocate on their behalf, some agreed action will also be undertaken by the helper. Together the helper and young person will formulate an action plan, and, depending on the circumstances, this may or may not be written down. The helper may need to assist with and follow up the implementation of the action plan, which might include the identification of further action. This will certainly be the case where a young person needs ongoing help. Figure 9.3 depicts the three stages as diamonds to indicate the process of *opening up* the discussion *then focusing*: moving from *the possible* to *the specific*, at each stage.

Helping is not a linear process

Although the Single Interaction Model is presented in three discrete stages, young people do not necessarily progress through each stage in a linear fashion. If there are a number of issues to be dealt with, or where trust and rapport need to be built over a period of time, a young person might be taken through one or two of these fairly directly. Other issues may stay at Stage 1 for a longer period of time, to be dealt with at a later date.

In addition, the extent to which the whole process is completed will vary from young person to young person. Some may want help with initial exploration and clarification (Stage 1), then feel quite confident to sort out their goal setting and action for themselves, whilst others may present themselves more or less at the goal-setting stage (Stage 2) and need some help with this and action planning. Where you start will depend on the young person's needs and how confident they feel about sorting things out for themselves. The practitioner needs to be ready to help and build confidence for young people who need extra or intensive support. This enabling process may or may not include advocacy, depending on the readiness of the young person to act independently.

The length of time spent on any one stage of the process will depend on the young person's needs and the amount of time the helper is able to commit to the work. The latter will depend on whether the young person requires minimal, additional or intensive support. That assessment of need will be a diagnostic task that takes place before more detailed help can be planned and implemented.

Letting go

Professional helpers must be ready to 'let go' of young people who feel capable and ready to manage things for themselves. We have to remember that we want to enable the young person to act independently and that they have the right to refuse our help. Of course, some young people, despite our very best efforts, may not achieve independence; in these circumstances it is vital that we acknowledge the limits of our ability to help in a time-bound relationship. Such issues need to be brought to supervision to ensure best practice for those that are being helped, as well as to ensure the practitioner's well-being. If the practitioner's well-being is not addressed it is likely that work with 'clients' will not be effective and may even be detrimental (Reid 2006). Having a framework to structure the work can help both

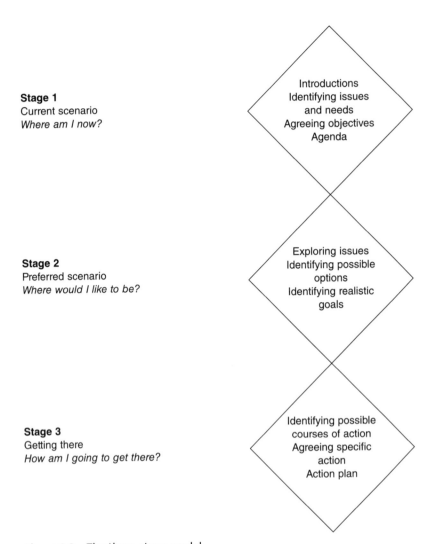

Stage 1
Current scenario
Where am I now?

Introductions
Identifying issues
and needs
Agreeing objectives
Agenda

Stage 2
Preferred scenario
Where would I like to be?

Exploring issues
Identifying possible
options
Identifying realistic
goals

Stage 3
Getting there
How am I going to get there?

Identifying possible
courses of action
Agreeing specific
action
Action plan

Figure 9.3   The three-stage model

the practitioner and the young person to retain a sense of direction and shared purpose, even when the forward movement is minimal or slow.

References

Bassot, B. (2003) 'Towards a situated learning theory for careers education and guidance', *Career Research and Development, The NICEC Journal*, No. 10, Winter, pp. 10–14.

Culley, S. and Bond, T. (2004) *Integrative Counselling Skills in Action*, 2nd edn, London: Sage.

Egan, G. (2002) *The Skilled Helper: A Problem-Management and Opportunity-Development Approach to Helping*, 7th edn, Pacific Grove, California: Brooks/Cole.

Reid, H.L. (2002) 'Are you sitting comfortably? Stories and the usefulness of narrative approaches', in K. Roberts (ed.) *Constructing the Future: Social Inclusion, Policy and Practice*, Stourbridge: Institute of Career Guidance, pp. 51–66.

Reid, H.L. (2006) 'Introduction – constructing the future: transforming career guidance', in H.L. Reid and J. Bimrose (eds) *Constructing the Future: Transforming Career Guidance*, Stourbridge: Institute of Career Guidance.

Rogers, C.R. (1951) *Client-Centred Therapy*, London: Constable.

Rogers, C.R. (1961) *On Becoming a Person*, Boston: Houghton Mifflin.

10

Informal Learning in Youth Work: Times, People and Places

Janet Batsleer

Informal learning is often referred to as the means through which youth and community work operates. This chapter draws on the literature, and on examples of practice, to provide guidance on how informal engagement and conversation can be planned and used to facilitate learning. The author argues that it is by focusing on the lived experience of young people in their own localities, rather than external agendas and targets, that informal learning can be effective in engaging with young people who are often suspicious of adult interventions.

Youth and Community Work is about learning through dialogue and connection, exchange and association. At its centre are conversations and activities which emerge from the time, the people and the places in which they occur, rather than from externally imposed agendas or programmes of learning. The practices of informal learning have been developed through clubs and associations, through street-based projects and through community centres, and now have a systematic body of knowledge, critique and analysis associated with them. They are to be found in Education Departments and in Children's Services, in Local Authority Chief Executive Departments and in Councils of Voluntary Service and Voluntary Action Networks, and their influence can often be seen in political movements and in religious faith communities (Batsleer, 2008; Banks, 2010). The occupational roles through which informal learning is delivered include youth workers, youth and community workers, participation workers, volunteer co-ordinators, mentors and positive activities workers. Most of this work occurs outside the scope of the formal curriculum in schools or the health interventions of clinicians. However, it is often offered in partnership with schools or colleges and increasingly within youth justice contexts and primary health

This chapter is the author's revision of Batsleer, Janet (2008) 'Informal Learning and Informal Education', Chapter 2, *Informal Learning in Youth Work*, Sage.

care networks. Many of the older forms of provision remain, such as youth clubs and detached youth work projects, and new forms and contexts for work are emerging.

Over the last decade there has been extensive restructuring of youth and community work, initially under New Labour to serve particular social policy agendas, and now in the context of the dismantling of public service provision as a result of 'austerity' politics. However, the need for informal education practices which can engage with people who are not necessarily being best served through the existing formal practices of schooling remains urgent, and this chapter draws on a number of examples of youth work in an urban context to show how processes of informal learning can engage with the complexity of pressures and possibilities being exerted in young people's lives.

Processes of informal learning: listening and understanding

Young people are continuously subject to often injurious labelling through social policy and education agendas which need to classify people in order to function. An important way of thinking about injurious labels is to consider the idea of 'discourses' which position and create the identities of populations and places. These discourses exist in public policy, in academic expert knowledges, especially criminology and psychology, but also anthropology and cultural studies, and in the popular media. They exist in part to render the lives of people in a particular area intelligible and legible to the authorities. Consider this extract from the minutes of a Salford Children and Young People's Advisory Group meeting:

> Large groups of young people gathering in Monton and creating a nuisance. Some throwing stones at buses, setting fire to bins and generally intimidating. To look at venues for a youth evening ...

The term 'nuisance' and specifically 'youth nuisance' is routinely used to classify incidents in neighbourhoods. Yet they might be used to support and back up prevailing popular media and political accounts of young people in Longsight, Manchester and Eccles, Salford (especially after the riots of the summer of 2011) as 'at risk of crime', as 'potential terrorists' , as 'low achievers' and 'experiencing multiple deprivation' with 'broken families' and as 'lacking aspiration'.

Examining this process of labelling forms an important part of the listening stage of informal education. One of the first strategies which a youth and community worker will use when beginning a new project will be to undertake a period of listening and questioning about how people 'round here' see themselves and their lives, how they see others and how they are seen by them. This is necessary because the people with whom the informal educator is seeking to engage are always already 'known' in some way that can be injurious to them, and the processes of informal learning are processes which seek to move away from such injuries. The listening is the beginning of a developmental process which starts from a sense of people's strengths and resilience against injury. In Freire's terms, informal learning seeks to achieve generativity, to move in the direction of life and flourishing rather than merely surviving.

Youth workers as informal educators characteristically attempt to *displace* labels and generate starting points for practice from young people's own agendas and to *investigate* the labels, through a process of critical collaborative enquiry. So, for example, trainee youth workers in Longsight are supporting community music making in response to 'grime' and negative 'gansta rap' associations. 'Conscious Hip Hop at Youth on Solid Ground' explicitly rejects the gansta stereotypes which inform much current hip-hop music, both seeking to connect with the language of the streets (rather than simply disavowing it) and moving beyond it. The CSG (Czech/Slovak group) in Eccles, Salford, is working with Roma young people to develop a dance project which also offers them links into education, consciously displacing the negative discourses associated with 'gypsies' and offering access to informal support and learning opportunities. A widely despised group of outsiders are offered a connection with insider networks through youth work.

Starting from where young people are and starting from their strengths – two key youth work traditions – involves starting from an analysis of how young people are affected by the myths which surround their neighbourhoods and communities. By 'myth' I mean a powerful story or belief which shapes people's understanding of the area. Informal learning develops from this starting point; from the acknowledgement of negative labelling and from the affirmation of strengths.

Planning informal learning involves paying attention to the times in which youth work happens, the places it happens in and the relationships it works through. The informality of approach is often what enables engagement. Engagement enables relationship and conversation and facilitates learning. Informality however is not unplanned or unstructured. It has its own structure, grounded in negotiation (Sapin, 2009).

Processes of informal learning: thinking about times

The times of youth work are usually defined as 'young people's own time'. The idea of what is 'young people's own time' has changed and continues to change, so finding out what are 'the right times' to do the work is an essential aspect of planning informal learning. Youth work does not generally take place inside classrooms where national curriculum subjects are being studied by pupils required by law to be there. It is accessed – when it is accessed – by young people in their leisure or free time and as such it competes with commercial opportunities as well as with more formal out-of-school opportunities for learning additional subjects or specialist skills such as those involved in music or sport.

In the past, youth club doors were open to any who wished to attend on most weekday evenings and sometimes over weekends too. Clubs, modelled on 'working-men's clubs', ran after working hours and often had the same pastimes available as the working men's clubs, including darts and snooker/pool. This was the tradition of 'open access' youth work. Detached youth work projects, which are not based in particular centres, always think carefully about the times the worker teams will be out on the streets meeting with young people. Some specialist teams specifically work very late sessions in order to support young people out in town and city centres in the early hours of the morning. Some projects offer 'recovery cafes' for people coming home from a night out. But times have changed and there is no longer a standard structure to the times of work and leisure, even though school hours are still modelled on a notional 'working day' and leisure patterns which revolve around the weekend still persist, rooted in those earlier patterns of working lives.

For many migrant communities, the supplementary schools which offer young people additional cultural opportunities for learning open at weekends and informal opportunities for learning through leisure may be linked to them. For young women who are not encouraged by their families to socialise informally outside of formal education, school or college may be the only place for them to engage in informal opportunities for learning. Festivals and prayer times of all the faith communities are now recognised as structuring time, alongside the 24/7 opportunities to shop (and therefore work) now offered in most cities.

So the times of youth work are changing in response to this new context. Many would still argue strongly for the importance of retaining the traditional times of provision, especially evenings and weekends. One of the consequences of the 'targeting' approach driven by New Labour was for youth work projects to become more computer and office-hours based, limiting the accessibility of informal learning by the 9 to 5 cultures of staff teams. Other public services operated on a 9 to 5 basis, it was argued, so why not youth work?

A second aspect of the 'time' of youth work is the focus on a particular time in the participants' lives – the period of 'youth'. Informal learning can be promoted and encouraged with any age group but the special quality of youth work is that it attends to the time between childhood and adulthood, frequently described as a transitional time, an in-between time. The movement through time called 'growing up' therefore has a particular significance for youth workers, and the notion of accompaniment introduced by Maxine Greene and Chandu Christian (1998) suggests a view of time which is the time of listening. The accompanist takes her cue, her timings from the performer and at the same moment supports the performer by sustaining the various tempi. At any moment we are never simply in the present but also in the past and future, in a mesh of hopes, fears, memories, plans and predictions. Richard Sennett, the sociologist, has likened the relationship between singer and accompanist to the respectful conversations between youth workers and young people: 'Just as Fisher-Dieskau performs respect for his pianist Gerald Moore, so does, I think, the professional youth worker who learns to criticise homeless adolescents without turning them off' (Sennett, 2003: 167). There is a connection here with the acceptance which is discussed in Rogerian therapy as 'unconditional positive regard', but here I want to emphasise the issue of timing and being aware of time as an aspect of the dynamic of informal learning.

The ability to engage in conversation, dialogue and critique takes time and cannot just be summoned up by youth workers on demand. Trust takes time to build and is not easily amenable to six-week or twelve-week projects that come and go. Relationship is at the core of informal education practice, and historically youth workers have expected to have relationships with key groups and individuals over a period of years rather than weeks or months, with professional dilemmas concerning the moments of 'letting go' and 'moving on'. But time in the current global economy has been commodified and monetised, with an emphasis in youth work on gaining accreditation, delivering sessions and offering packages of support or time-limited engagement rather than open-ended projects and opportunities, and this will continue to provide dilemmas and contradictions for professional youth and community workers. In an earlier essay I talked about the current ideal type of 'liquid youth work' (the form most consonant with the current global economy):

> Its characteristic forms are as follows: temporary, short-term project-based work. Relationships are highly individualised and focussed on individual mentoring processes. Recorded achievements and 'quick successes' are important. Projects need to be both constantly repeatable, in order to offer quick success, and re-brandable, in order to show innovation, mobility and flexibility. Like young people, such youth work needs to be 'robust' and 'resilient' to survive in the ever-changing conditions of liquid modernity. (Batsleer, 2010: 160)

This idea of 'liquid youth work' draws on the ideas of Zygmunt Bauman (2000) about 'liquid modernity' and the ways in which the global capitalist economy is shaping all forms of social relationship.

Youth work is, among other things, a form of emotional labour. And emotional labour does not run along clock time:

> Providing emotional support, or looking after children or sick or elderly adults, often requires attention to 'natural' temporal rhythms that cannot appropriately be automated or subjected to considerations of 'time management', but are often necessarily slow and in the present; the processes of feeding, cleaning, dressing and reassurance are repeated over and over again, and their timing is determined at least partly by need rather than the clock (you change the nappy because it is dirty, not because it is four o'clock). Dropping a child off at nursery is not the same as dropping a car off at the garage. (Bryson, 2007: 100)

Whilst youth and community workers do not themselves change nappies all that often, their work is often with people who do; and the rhythms of reassurance and support which Bryson speaks of are the recognisable, oft-repeated rhythms of many youth work conversations.

Finally there is the time of creativity, the wasting of time, hanging out together, chilling, the 'being' as well as the doing ... which is well recognised as a source of creativity. Since such time is no longer scripted or available to most employees during working hours – unless it is present in the formulaic 'hanging out at the water cooler' – and staff who show signs of 'chilling' as part of their working practice are suspected of not having enough to do, it is no surprise that there is a ready market for 'deliverables', off-the-shelf toolkits and other resource packs for hard-pressed practitioners who have no idea what to do in tonight's session and whose managers have long abandoned any sustained process of dialogue with young people as not 'cost-effective'.

Despite this, youth and community workers as informal educators continue to find ways to include their commitment to presence and to the here-and-now of young people's lives within a sense of continuity (there-and-then) and hope (a future orientation).

Processes of informal learning: thinking about places

A room of one's own ... a place of our own ... being with young people in their own places ... places and learning have a powerful connection, and strong messages about what it is possible and desirable to learn are contained in the design of learning places. The early clubs and centres established in the late nineteenth century sometimes took on the architectural prospect of the gentlemen's clubs or Oxford and Cambridge colleges, whilst the centres established after the Albemarle Report in 1960 were often modelled on the new Further Education College Student Unions, with coffee bars and dance floors as well as sports areas and offices. The new buildings associated with the MyPlace Programme in turn have the style of their times, with large sports areas, music areas, computer suites and some rooms for small group work, as well as offices and recreation (rec) areas which still have the staple table tennis and pool tables. The New Labour message that young people need 'Places to Go To. Things to Do. People to Talk To' is depicted in large letters on the walls of The Factory Youth Zone in Harpurhey, Manchester. Places tell their own stories (including stories about the kind of spaces adults think are appropriate for young people) and within this it is possible to find evidence of young people seeking to take ownership of the spaces they occupy as spaces for negotiated relationships and informal learning: at every level, from contributing to architectural plans for new buildings to choosing decor to simply moving the furniture or occupying the Board Room or Committee Rooms through participation projects.

At the same time, many one-night or once-a-week projects have been developed which 'squat' in spaces essentially shared with and belonging to others, with time having to be given at the beginning and end of each session to getting out and putting away equipment and resources. This is classically the case with village (as well as urban) youth clubs held in church halls, but may also be the case with youth projects held on school premises, in sports centres or in colleges. The place is not 'for young people' and young people can easily feel marginal or worse within it.

Detached work projects start from the assumption that, as they are working on the street, in 'young people's own spaces' they have in doing so addressed a fundamental problem about power relationships. There is nothing to stop the young people with whom the detached youth workers hope to build relationships simply moving on and rejecting the offer made by the youth work team. But the question of whose space is the street, and how access to the street is negotiated is never far away for youth workers. The issues of the safety and risk associated with particular places are also very different for different young people: for most the home may well be safer than the park but for others this is not so.

In all the spaces of youth work, the meanings of the space in which practice is occurring cannot be separated from the terms on which the space is used, and how the meanings of the encounter between young people and youth workers are negotiated. There is a popular current view of youth work as a 'border pedagogy' which requires skills in both boundary maintenance and border-crossing: protecting spaces for free association, friendship, informal learning and fun, whilst negotiating with others who work with young people to improve their access to services (Coburn, 2010). In formal contexts, the rules about who does and does not have access to the learning spaces and the roles of teachers and learners within them are usually clearly differentiated. In youth work, the establishment of boundaries and roles is something which has to be negotiated from the beginning and young people always have some say in how the spaces of encounter and of relationship are defined. The power to draw boundaries against young people is also something that is strongly contested by youth workers in alliance with the young people they work with. Good boundaries can create safe-enough spaces for learning and in informal learning contexts these are created in part by the existing social relationships among young people in a particular neighbourhood and in part by the ways in which the youth and community workers create a sense of the norms and negotiate what is and is not acceptable, what is and is not possible in a group. The norms in a youth work/informal learning group may well be different from those experienced elsewhere, with more attention being paid to mitigating the effects of inequality and creating a sense of respect and self-respect.

Urban multi-culture contains a constant negotiation about who belongs with whom, about who belongs where. Stepping outside the neighbourhood in which a young person has grown up can feel and be very threatening. There are many ways in which boundaries are staked and marked in neighbourhoods. Shared language can offer a way of marking insiders and outsiders, as can sporting (especially football) affiliations, music cultures and dress codes.

Informal learning strategies always need to 'start where young people are' and that includes particular places and neighbourhoods, but also to 'seek to move beyond where they are', and some youth work projects have been consciously designed to offer bridges across neighbourhoods in what has become segregated urban space. The Mahdlo project in Oldham offers a good example here. A decision was taken to build a new MyPlace Centre in the centre of the town as an area that was presently affiliated with no particular group. The size of the MyPlace centres also potentially creates the possibility of differently affiliated groups all using them, in contrast to small neighbourhood clubs which often have very local membership.

The creation of strong boundaries and places also creates 'safe enough' spaces for the risks of learning to be taken. It may be that young people need to develop the ability to counter the put-downs addressed to their own group from within their own space before being able to move on and connect with other groups. A common feature of accounts of working-class communities is that they 'lack aspiration'. Perhaps rather they need to be understood as sometimes showing strong attachments to particular places which have supported generations of young people in the face of poverty and hardship. The local youth club can sometimes remain popular despite its lack of refurbishment, precisely because of such attachments. The paradox here is that safe-enough spaces are essential and yet learning can sometimes happen fastest and most significantly when there is a 'shifting' and a riskiness that occurs when boundaries are challenged or breached. Boys are no longer allowed undisputed access to the pool table, for example ... or a street-based discussion leads to a meeting with the police where young people set the agenda.

The project of learning is one that unsettles, moves and crosses borders, and this is the case with informal learning too. In detached work, project teams often create temporary dwellings where the participants can be safe enough for a time, facilitating the regular appearance of support, encounter and relationship in the lives of project participants.

Processes of informal learning: thinking about people and relationships

Most youth and community projects are staffed by a combination of professionally trained workers and volunteers. The relationships offered to young people by youth workers, and the relationships enabled among young people, are the central vehicle for learning in youth and community work contexts. It should be understood as a relationship of professional friendship, as an educative and supportive relationship. It is important to find ways of supporting those relationships and enabling them to be properly professional. For this reason supervision has been a central theme for professional formation since the emergence of professional youth and community work in the 1960s, with 'conscious use of self in relation to others' being understood as a significant professional task. Youth workers need to be friendly but understand the distinctions between the friendship they offer in the context of their work and friendship in their personal lives. This is especially important because of the informality of the approach to practice, including the negotiation of relationship, and requires careful supervision and understanding of boundaries. The learning that occurs through relationship with a supervisor can mirror the learning relationships which youth workers facilitate with the young people with whom they work.

Such learning occurs through dialogue and through accompaniment, through conflict and through affirmation, both in staff teams and in the learning from the everyday which forms the substance of youth work practice. It involves checking out the position you are coming from and the position other people are coming from. It involves becoming aware of the strengths and limitations of our own 'situatedness'. Informal educators have to be alert to emerging new themes that enable people to make connections with one another and alert to their role as staff and the responsibilities this implies.

There are a number of strategies which youth workers can use to systematically free up space and time for reflection. Regular meetings with project reference groups and resource groups which have been deliberately brought together to enable reflection from a range of perspectives are immensely valuable. It is especially useful to explore the point of view of the most marginal or least visible participants in projects as this can lead to provocation and challenge: the challenge to see anew, to think differently or to change perspective.

Youth workers characteristically work with young people by engaging in everyday chat which then moves beyond that and beyond and through boredom to the opening up of possibilities for learning. The buzz or flatness of particular groups, the sense that 'it's boring' and what can open up from that point is the place from which youth workers engage. Relationship is built up in part through repetition and exploring the same topics over and over again, often at a light and superficial level: the soaps, football, music – all these are common starting points. Then the stories of everyday life – of school or college and sometimes of family life: the youth worker will become familiar with these and with the characters who regularly appear in them. Such low threshold intervention – by which is meant an approach in which young people do not have to overcome a high hurdle in order to maintain relationship and support – is fundamental to developing practice. Detached work in particular sees itself as 'low threshold' as the workers go to the young people and not the young people to the workers.

The practice of listening and attending to the young people and their adult associates and communities in this way can lead to a deepening of conversation. In this there are some invaluable clues: dissatisfaction; adult disrespect; and wind-ups are three very frequent starting points for a more developmental period in the work. There are some important questions to be asked and answers to be listened for at the beginning of the engagement process: What makes people round here happy? Or sad? Frightened or excited? Hopeful or despairing? These questions enable youth and community workers to both attend to the here and now of relationship and to imagine and design projects which move the work forward.

The sense of being disrespected by the adult world is a very powerful one for many young people and in some areas alternative codes of respect have been generated based in criminal hierarchies and control, where the payment of 'respect' may mean nothing more than the payment of money or participation in illegal actions on behalf of a gang leader. Informal educators develop ways of creating more open and mutual forms of respect and self-respect between and among young people. Often this is through partnership with others: such as creative practitioners, sports people or even people creating community businesses and co-operatives.

For many reasons, the lives of young people are a place in which these society-wide conflicts can be acted out. The skills of the youth and community worker in moving away from such entrenched conflict positions, in creating the pause before flight or fight, may be considered as one of the most skilful and powerful aspects of informal learning.

It includes, at least, the following:

- Delegitimising prejudice and put-downs by taking a questioning approach as distinct from laying down the law.
- Moving out of a regulatory approach to speech and comment to one which allows stories to be told which recognise the hurt, pressure and put-downs routinely experienced by people in deprived or marginalised communities, and looking for opportunities which affirm and create the chance for development and learning, internally to the community. Story projects and oral histories remain important and popular.
- Creating opportunities, where possible, for people from different communities to come together and learn about one another's histories, issues and needs.

- Noticing and addressing the ways in which 'folk devils and moral panics' are being created about particular figures or groups and considering how myth-busting can be done locally and nationally. Community meetings and in particular anti-poverty campaigning has been a valuable vehicle for this work in some places.
- Understanding the potential and limits of separate space based on the needs of a particular community, perhaps facing severe pressure at a particular time, and yet the need for reaching out connecting and welcoming newcomers.

Conclusion

The informality of youth work is the place from which learning can begin, rooted as it is in a sense of the whole person. But the learning which occurs is not necessarily different from the learning which occurs in any open educational process. It is often felt to include the learning of 'soft' skills – the development of competence in making informed choices, the development of confidence, the development of the ability to draw on support and build trusting relationships – but it also includes the ability to explore attitudes and values, moral and ethical dilemmas and to contribute to the development of democratic experimentation and the building of solidarities across communities and neighbourhoods. That on the way there may also be much growth of knowledge – whether of sport or arts or social and cultural history or languages or politics – is perhaps one of the least recognised benefits of youth work as informal learning.

References

Banks, S. (ed.) (2010) *Ethical Issues in Youth Work*. London: Routledge.

Batsleer, J. (2008) *Informal Learning in Youth Work*. London: Sage.

Batsleer, J. (2010) 'Youth Work Prospects: Back to the Future', in J. Batsleer and B. Davies (eds) *What is Youth Work? (Empowering Youth and Community Work Practice)*. Exeter: Learning Matters.

Bauman, Z. (2000) *Liquid Modernity*. Cambridge: Polity Press.

Bryson, V. (2007) 'The Politics of Time', *Soundings: A Journal of Politics and Culture*, 36: 100.

Coburn, A. (2010) 'Youth work as border pedagogy', in J. Batsleer and B. Davies (eds) *What is Youth Work? (Empowering Youth and Community Work Practice)*. Exeter: Learning Matters.

Green, M. and Christian, C. (1998) *Accompanying Young People on the Spiritual Path*. London: the National Society/Church House.

Sapin, K. (2009) *Essential Skills for Youth Work Practice*. London: Sage.

Sennett, R. (2003) *Respect in a World of Inequality*. London: Norton.

11

Thinking Ethically

Howard Sercombe

> This chapter lays out a core problem: the apparent lack of a consensus on what is right and wrong, and the lack of any kind of foundation on which a consensus might be based. However, that doesn't mean that ethical thinking can no longer be done, or that it is no longer possible to work together ethically.

The discipline of thinking ethically is no longer simple, if it ever was. The contemporary world is a pluralist world. Examples of different ways of living ethically confront us from other parts of the world, from other societies, and from different communities within our own society. In such an environment, it is hard to be clear about the boundaries of ethical action, about ways to be good to each other, about patterns of behaviour that can be relied on. We also live in a postmodern world, where, it is argued, the claims of external authorities of all kinds have collapsed (Bauman 1992), including not only organised religion and tradition, but also science and even rationality itself. This may not be true for individual people, but outside a single-ideology environment it is hard to find a common basis for ethical action. Paradoxically, this is precisely the kind of environment where it is ever more important to be clear about the principles under which we dare to intervene in the lives of young people and to act on their behalf.

Postmodernism and the ethics environment

There are lots of descriptions about what the postmodern condition is, and about how it might work out in different fields. As I see it, there are two central and related features of the postmodern condition. They are: (1) the rejection of essences and (2) the collapse of authorities.

This chapter is edited from Sercombe, Howard (2010) 'Thinking Ethically', Chapter 7, *Youth Work Ethics*, Sage.

First, the rejection of essences. Plato thought that somewhere, there must be a true and reliable and essential idea of what justice, or loyalty, or compassion, or virtue is, and it is the duty of the philosopher to find it and communicate it. Postmodernists suggest that such notions are not fixed, but that all meanings are negotiated, that all meanings flow out of social discourse and cannot be fixed or really even found. There is no 'essential' meaning of the term 'justice'. Indeed, there is no such thing as justice independent of the way that people generate the concept. 'Justice' is a symbol of a certain way of living together, or doing relationships, or of judging the fairness of events or situations, and it changes and fluctuates and is seen differently by different people in different places.

The collapse of authorities doesn't only mean that postmodernity rejects existing authorities. There is nothing new in that. In the West, up until the nineteenth century, ethics had usually been tied to the authority of God. For the moralists of the eighteenth-century Enlightenment, the authority of the idea of God had been cast off, and human beings were now free to seek a more rational basis for the ethical life. This established a new authority for ethics, different from the pronouncements of God as heard through the mouths of the priests: the rule of Reason and of the scientific method.

Commentators on postmodernity argue that in the postmodern world, even this authority has fragmented and broken down. Reason has lost its authority too.

In the postmodern world, we are frequently aware of how Reason can be a mask for particular interests. In the irrationality of food surpluses amid Third World famine, all impeccably justified on rational ethical grounds, children still starve. Because we are exposed to a huge diversity of human cultures through travel, the communications revolution and the media, we are familiar too with how relative authorities and customs and rules are, and how alien codes of behaviour have their own logic. In the face of this, it is not clear that the 'irrationality' of emotion or desire should not be just as good a basis for ethical action as Reason. Not that emotion or desire are now the new authorities. In the postmodern world there can be no authorities. The authorities have all collapsed (Baudrillard 1983).

I will argue, however, that living in the postmodern world doesn't mean that a decision to align oneself with a way of thinking about ethics is not possible (though some would dispute this). On the contrary, in order for us to live and work together, it becomes even more necessary. But there aren't any authorities that can command universal assent, that are able to style their pronouncements as absolute truth and expect everyone to comply – even the authority of Reason.

The basis of ethics

So what now is the basis for ethics? How is it that human beings act ethically at all?

And what is the basis for agreement about what is wrong and right, if there is any agreement worth speaking of? Is it that God has decreed how people should live, and will ultimately reward those who live well and punish those who live exploitatively or corruptly? More passively, is it in our nature, in the way God made us or in the way the evolutionary process has shaped us genetically? Or is it Reason, informed by careful observation and the collection of data, and informing appropriate action? Or simply the rules of our social and economic system, generated by the system and imparted through the processes of socialisation? Is it just by agreement, that human beings contract together to obey certain rules?

This is one of the questions that ethics as a discipline struggles with. Because it is about competing authorities, lots of argument goes on about it. For youth workers who are trying to work with people who have often been treated badly, and trying to get it right, it is not just an academic question, but a question also of where our own commitment lies (Bauman 1992).

Here are just a few questions that we need to consider:

- So where is all this leading? Do we no longer know what is right and wrong? Is it now impossible to make judgements about the actions of others, and for them to make judgements about our actions?
- Does ethics all depend on accidents of birth, what kind of family you were brought up in, what nation or cultural group, what economic situation, what period of history?
- The novelist Dostoyevsky said that if God is dead, everything is permitted. Is the idea of God now dead? Is, indeed, everything permitted?
- Is there nothing that we can say is absolutely wrong, no matter what the circumstances?

Absolutism and relativism

We can distinguish three positions regarding absolutism and relativism:

- The position that says no ethical meanings can be established is known as **nihilism**. This is not a commonly held view nowadays, and we will not discuss it here.
- The position that says there are no universal ethical norms but that there are still valid principles based on one's culture and circumstance is known as **relativism**.
- The position that says that, regardless of what a person or culture believes, there are universal ethical requirements, is known as ethical **absolutism**.

The standard position in most of the human services is relativism. As youth workers, we continually confront difference between our own ethics and those of the people we work with: about property, about sex, about drug use, about the care of children, about how outsiders should be treated. It makes sense to look at how different cultures have generated different ethical systems and how they work, and to refrain from imposing our own judgements on the situation. But there is an easy relativism, where we just tolerate everything and challenge nothing, and probably avoid potentially conflicting situations; and a more principled relativism which struggles with the facts of working with cultures (or the organisation that we work for!) where the ethics seem fundamentally askew. And they can be. To say that a belief or a practice is cultural doesn't mean that it isn't wrong. Cultures as well as individuals can become corrupt. Slavery was culturally acceptable in the eighteenth century.

Example 1

The philosopher Mary Midgley (1993a) discusses the samurai tradition, in which a new sword must be blooded by going to the nearest crossroads, and beheading the first person who comes along in a single blow. Her position is that while this is a very ancient tradition, it is just wrong. What do you think?

Example 2

There are youth workers who will be working in male subcultures (e.g. outlaw biker cultures or certain street gangs) where rape, under certain circumstances, is seen as perfectly legitimate behaviour. If a woman places herself in a position where she is accessible to the group, for example by going back to their space with them, and especially if she is drunk, then the question of whether she wants to have sex, or with whom, no longer arises. Whoever wants to have sex with her will. Can this be anything other than rape? And is rape anywhere, ever, morally justifiable behaviour? If it isn't, doesn't that mean that the ethic of sexual autonomy over one's own body, at least, is absolute? And if that ethic is absolute, is it the only one?

If relativism is sometimes seen as a cop-out, absolutism is often seen as arrogant. Like saying: 'I believe that I have the truth and, therefore, if you have a different stance, you are mistaken'. But there is also a more dialogic absolutism, which might believe that there are absolute values but that my understanding or appreciation of them is likely to be imperfect, especially given my inclination to self-interest and my potential for self-deception and rationalisation. And that anyway the standards are likely to play out differently in different circumstances. So while I might have an immediate reaction to behaviour that seems wrong to me, I am committed to dialogue, to talk about it, to try together to work out an understanding of where the truth lies.

These questions are especially relevant in youth work. Frequently, we are working across cultures. Different cultures frequently express different moral stances about things like sex and relationships, about attitudes to property (including not only theft but also ownership and sharing), about attitudes to authority, about loyalty and respect for tradition. How are we to deal ethically with this range of values?

Example 3

A key principle often promoted in basic youth work training is the principle of *non-judgemental practice*, influenced largely by the Carl Rogers' approach to counselling. Rogers (1961) advocated a stance of 'unconditional positive regard', so that no matter what kind of person you were working with, or what they had done, it was necessary to convey a warm positive regard for the person and not to stand in judgement of them or their actions. Non-judgementalism still stands as a core principle in most community work. Closely aligned with this is the principle that it is wrong for workers to impose their values on the young people with whom they work.

But consider a situation in which you are working with a young woman who is repeatedly beaten up by her boyfriend. You are also working with her boyfriend. Can you avoid judging him – and should you? Is it right to allow actions which are blatantly exploitative to pass without comment? Is it not only allowable, but obligatory, to name violence and injustice for what they are? Can tolerance go too far? By refusing to moralise, are we perpetuating wrongs?

Making moral judgements

We can now look briefly at a number of thinkers who argue, in different ways, that moral judgement is possible.

Mary Midgley (1993b) argues that the popular prohibition on moral judgement is inconsistent and not very helpful. Principles like respect for another's property, benevolence and so on are often shared. This is what makes it possible to understand the cultural practices of others, and to make intelligent cross-cultural comment about moral practices. The other point is that people often make statements which indicate a non-mainstream morality, but which are really justifications for unethical behaviour; for example, when a person justifies their sexual adventurism by criticising an out-moded morality, but gets very upset when someone else sleeps with their boyfriend or girlfriend, or when a thief is outraged at their goods being stolen.

Martin Buber (1965) argues that guilt is something real which needs to be addressed, and in order for it to be addressed, moral judgements must first be made. He describes an example of a young woman of his acquaintance who is helped by her therapist to deal with a guilty conscience so that it no longer gave her trouble. In the process, rather than healing her, capacities which she had previously were destroyed, and she was, according to Buber, permanently ethically damaged. Rather, Buber says, what is required is that I recognise my wrongdoing, recognise myself in my wrongdoing (and so the need for me to change), and undertake to make whatever compensations or reparations are possible or appropriate to the person I have injured.

Kerry Young (2006) suggests that the practice of youth work is precisely about producing a more moral situation, a situation in which violence is not done to young people, and in which young people do not do violence to others. This kind of practice necessitates making moral judgements, and assumes the right to inter-vene in situations in order to influence outcomes, and to intervene in relationships to reduce levels of exploitation and oppression. Anti-oppressive work, whether around sexism, heterosexism, racism or more micro situations such as bullying, all involve making ethical judgements and demonstrating a willingness to intervene.

At the same time, there *is* something objectionable in what is normally called moralising or judgementalism. Judgementalism generally refers not to the practice of making ethical judgements, but of making judgements in ignorance, in haste, in arrogance, and without due recognition of our own ethical blind spots, or of making judgements not in order to heal situations but to offer an opportunity for us to claim moral superiority and diminish or condemn the other.

On the other side, a refusal to judge or to intervene may deny young people the very thing that they need most from us at particular points. The young man who beats his girlfriend needs to know that it is not OK, and to look closely at the mechanisms through which he allows himself recourse to this kind of action. While he needs to be understood, and to understand the roots of his action, he does not need to be excused. This needs to be done sensitively and skilfully, and it may be wise to work slowly on things (depending on the issue) rather than jump in and reduce the chance of change. But that is a strategic matter, a matter of what mode of intervention will work best, rather than a denial of the principle.

Perhaps more importantly, we have an obligation to intervene when our colleagues are acting unethically, and they have the same obligation to us. Part of the point of this kind of ethical conversation is to come to some agreement about what the important ethical principles are in our engagement with young people. So while we have our own personal ethics in our practice (and there is no substitute for that), we are involved also in a community of practice that names itself 'youth work' and whose name we share. As we accept the identity and the benefits of youth work, we also accept its disciplines.

Conclusion

In the postmodern world, according to Zygmunt Bauman (1992), our personal ethics can no longer be compelled by external authorities. Nothing is compelling. The truth of our ethics is established by our own commitment.

As youth workers, we judge the exclusion of young people to be wrong by our shared commitment to what a society should be, and indeed our society's own claims to be a democracy. The same is true for other examples that we have talked about – the violence of young men, the tolerance of high levels of unemployment, the practices of racism. Even human rights can have no authority outside the commitment of persons, associations and states to the core values about human life and human society that are embodied in them. Is it possible to prove objectively that young people should not be excluded? Probably not. But that is our commitment, and youth workers work hard to address exclusion where they see it.

So when a difference of opinion about ethics arises (as it often does), there can no longer be an appeal to authority, unless we agree on the authority – as might be the case, for example, in faith-based work, or human-rights-based work, or when we have agreed to a code of ethics. In most cases, what is needed is a process of dialogue: a process where I deeply listen to you and your way of seeing the world, and try as openly and honestly as I can to communicate my own (Bauman 1992; Koehn 1994). If we can find common ground (and this is more often the case than not), then perhaps we can try to work towards a position that is consistent and reflects the values we share and to which we are committed. At their best, moral codes, including codes of ethics, are the product of a long process of that dialogue.

References

Baudrillard, J. (1983) *Simulations and in the Shadow of the Silent Majorities*, New York: Semiotext(e).

Bauman, Z. (1992) *Intimations of Post-modernity*, London: Routledge.

Buber, M. (1965) 'Guilt and Guilt Feelings', in M. Buber, *The Knowledge of Man*, New York: Harper and Row, pp. 121–148.

Koehn, D. (1994) *The Ground of Professional Ethics*, London: Routledge.

Midgley, M. (1993a) 'Trying Out One's New Sword', in C. Sommers and F. Sommers (eds), *Vice and Virtue in Everyday Life*, Forth Worth, TX: Harcourt Brace College Publishers, pp. 174–180.

Midgley, M. (1993b) *Can't We Make Moral Judgements?* New York: St Martin's Press.

Rogers, C. R. (1961) *On Becoming a Person: A Therapist's View of Psychotherapy*, Boston: Houghton Mifflin.

Young, K. (2006) *The Art of Youth Work*, 2nd edition, Lyme Regis: Russell House Publishing.

12

A Social Theory of Learning

Etienne Wenger

In arguing that learning is not a process of individual cognition directly related to teaching, but a social process related to our participation with others in everyday activities, this chapter questions the central assumptions of most institutions of learning. The author develops the idea of learning as participation in communities of practice, a radical perspective but one which allows us to adopt a broader and more inclusive way of looking at learning, and one which is particularly relevant to the kind of informal learning central to youth work.

Our institutions, to the extent that they address issues of learning explicitly, are largely based on the assumption that learning is an individual process, that it has a beginning and an end, that it is best separated from the rest of our activities, and that it is the result of teaching. Hence we arrange classrooms where students – free from the distractions of their participation in the outside world – can pay attention to a teacher or focus on exercises. We design computer-based training programs that walk students through individualized sessions covering reams of information and drill practice. To assess learning we use tests with which students struggle in one-on-one combat, where knowledge must be demonstrated out of context, and where collaborating is considered cheating. As a result, much of our institutionalized teaching and training is perceived by would-be learners as irrelevant, and most of us come out of this treatment feeling that learning is boring and arduous, and that we are not really cut out for it.

So, what if we adopted a different perspective, one that placed learning in the context of our lived experience of participation in the world? What if we assumed that learning is as much a part of our human nature as eating or sleeping, that it is both life-sustaining and inevitable, and that – given a chance – we are quite good at it? And what if, in addition, we assumed that learning is, in its essence, a fundamentally social

This is a revised version of the original text which appeared as pp. 3–17 in *Communities of Practice* by Etienne Wenger. First published in 1998 by Cambridge University Press.

phenomenon, reflecting our own deeply social nature as human beings capable of knowing? What kind of understanding would such a perspective yield on how learning takes place and on what is required to support it? In this chapter, I will try to develop such a perspective.

A conceptual perspective: theory and practice

There are many different kinds of learning theory. Each emphasizes different aspects of learning, and each is therefore useful for different purposes. To some extent these differences in emphasis reflect a deliberate focus on a slice of the multidimensional problem of learning, and to some extent they reflect more fundamental differences in assumptions about the nature of knowledge, knowing, and knowers, and consequently about what matters in learning.

The kind of social theory of learning I propose is not a replacement for other theories of learning that address different aspects of the problem. But it does have its own set of assumptions and its own focus. Within this context, it does constitute a coherent level of analysis; it does yield a conceptual framework from which to derive a consistent set of general principles and recommendations for understanding and enabling learning.

My assumptions as to what matters about learning and as to the nature of knowledge, knowing, and knowers can be succinctly summarized as follows. I start with four premises:

1 We are social beings. Far from being trivially true, this fact is a central aspect of learning.
2 Knowledge is a matter of competence with respect to valued enterprises – such as singing in tune, discovering scientific facts, fixing machines, writing poetry, being convivial, growing up as a boy or a girl, and so forth.
3 Knowing is a matter of participating in the pursuit of such enterprises, that is, of active engagement in the world.
4 Meaning – our ability to experience the world and our engagement with it as meaningful – is ultimately what learning is to produce.

As a reflection of these assumptions, the primary focus of this theory is on learning as social participation. Participation here refers not just to local events of engagement in certain activities with certain people, but to a more encompassing process of being active participants in the *practices* of social communities and constructing *identities* in relation to these communities. Participating in a playground clique or in a work team, for instance, is both a kind of action and a form of belonging. Such participation shapes not only what we do, but also who we are and how we interpret what we do.

A social theory of learning must therefore integrate the components necessary to characterize social participation as a process of learning and of knowing. These components, shown in Figure 12.1, include the following:

1 *Meaning:* a way of talking about our (changing) ability – individually and collectively – to experience our life and the world as meaningful.
2 *Practice:* a way of talking about the shared historical and social resources, frameworks, and perspectives that can sustain mutual engagement in action.
3 *Community:* a way of talking about the social configurations in which our enterprises are defined as worth pursuing and our participation is recognizable as competence.
4 *Identity:* a way of talking about how learning changes who we are and creates personal histories of becoming in the context of our communities.

Clearly, these elements are deeply interconnected and mutually defining. In fact, looking at Figure 12.1, you could switch any of the four peripheral components with learning, place it in the center as the primary focus, and the figure would still make sense.

Therefore, when I use the concept of 'community of practice', I really use it as a point of entry into a broader conceptual framework of which it is a constitutive element. The analytical power of the concept lies precisely in that it integrates the components of Figure 12.1 while referring to a familiar experience.

Communities of practice are everywhere

We all belong to communities of practice. At home, at work, at school, in our hobbies – we belong to several communities of practice at any given time. And the

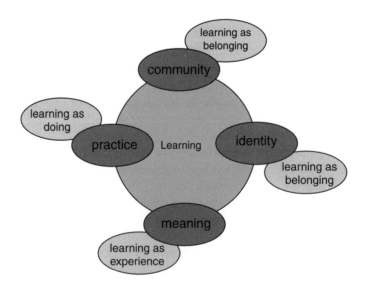

Figure 12.1   Components of a social theory of learning: an initial inventory

communities of practice to which we belong change over the course of our lives. In fact, communities of practice are everywhere.

Families struggle to establish an habitable way of life. They develop their own practices, routines, rituals, artifacts, symbols, conventions, stories, and histories. Family members hate each other and they love each other; they agree and they disagree. They do what it takes to keep going. Even when families fall apart, members create ways of dealing with each other. Surviving together is an important enterprise, whether surviving consists in the search for food and shelter or in the quest for a viable identity.

Workers organize their lives with their immediate colleagues and customers to get their jobs done. In doing so, they develop or preserve a sense of themselves they can live with, have some fun, and fulfill the requirements of their employers and clients. No matter what their official job description may be, they create a practice to do what needs to be done. Although workers may be contractually employed by a large institution, in day-to-day practice they work with – and, in a sense, for – a much smaller set of people and communities.

Students go to school and, as they come together to deal in their own fashion with the agenda of the imposing institution and the unsettling mysteries of youth, communities of practice sprout everywhere – in the classroom as well as on the playground, officially or in the cracks. And in spite of curriculum, discipline, and exhortation, the learning that is most personally transformative turns out to be the learning that involves membership in these communities of practice.

In garages, bands rehearse the same songs for yet another wedding gig. In attics, ham radio enthusiasts become part of worldwide clusters of communicators. In the back rooms of churches, recovering alcoholics go to their weekly meetings to find the courage to remain sober. In laboratories, scientists correspond with colleagues, near and far, in order to advance their inquiries. Across a worldwide web of computers, people congregate in virtual spaces and develop shared ways of pursuing their common interests. In offices, computer users count on each other to cope with the intricacies of obscure systems. In neighborhoods, youths gang together to configure their life on the street and their sense of themselves.

Communities of practice are an integral part of our daily lives. They are so informal and so pervasive that they rarely come into explicit focus, but for the same reasons they are also quite familiar. Although the term may be new, the experience is not. Most communities of practice do not have a name and do not issue membership cards. Yet, if we care to consider our own life from that perspective for a moment, we can all construct a fairly good picture of the communities of practice we belong to now, those we belonged to in the past, and those we would like to belong to in the future. We also have a fairly good idea of who belongs to our communities of practice and why, even though membership is rarely made explicit on a roster or a checklist of qualifying criteria. Furthermore, we can probably distinguish a few communities of practice in which we are core members from a larger number of communities in which we have a more peripheral kind of membership.

In all these ways, the concept of community of practice is not unfamiliar. By exploring it more systematically I mean only to sharpen it, to make it more useful as a thinking tool. Toward this end, its familiarity will serve me well. Articulating a familiar phenomenon is a chance to push our intuitions: to deepen and expand them, to examine and rethink them. The perspective that results is not foreign, yet it can shed new light on our world. In this sense, the concept of community of practice is neither new nor old. It has both the eye-opening character of novelty and the forgotten familiarity of obviousness – but perhaps that is the mark of our most useful insights.

Rethinking learning

As I will argue, placing the focus on participation has broad implications for what it takes to understand and support learning.

- For *individuals*, it means that learning is an issue of engaging in and contributing to the practices of their communities.
- For *communities*, it means that learning is an issue of refining their practice and ensuring new generations of members.
- For *organizations*, it means that learning is an issue of sustaining the interconnected communities of practice through which an organization knows what it knows and thus becomes effective and valuable as an organization.

Learning in this sense is not a separate activity. It is not something we do when we do nothing else or stop doing when we do something else. There are times in our lives when learning is intensified: when situations shake our sense of familiarity, when we are challenged beyond our ability to respond, when we wish to engage in new practices and seek to join new communities. There are also times when society explicitly places us in situations where the issue of learning becomes problematic and requires our focus: we attend classes, memorize, take exams, and receive a diploma. And there are times when learning gels: an infant utters a first word, we have a sudden insight when someone's remark provides a missing link, we are finally recognized as a full member of a community. But situations that bring learning into focus are not necessarily those in which we learn most, or most deeply. The events of learning we can point to are perhaps more like volcanic eruptions whose fiery bursts reveal for one dramatic moment the ongoing labor of the earth. Learning is something we can assume – whether we see it or not, whether we like the way it goes or not, whether what we are learning is to repeat the past or to shake it off. Even failing to learn what is expected in a given situation usually involves learning something else instead.

For many of us, the concept of learning immediately conjures up images of classrooms, training sessions, teachers, textbooks, homework, and exercises. Yet in our experience, learning is an integral part of our everyday lives. It is part of our participation in our communities and organizations. The problem is not that we do not know this, but rather that we do not have very systematic ways of talking about this familiar experience. An adequate vocabulary is important because the concepts we use to make sense of the world direct both our perception and our actions. We pay attention to what we expect to see, we hear what we can place in our understanding, and we act according to our world views.

Although learning can be assumed to take place, modern societies have come to see it as a topic of concern – in all sorts of ways and for a host of different reasons. We develop national curriculums, ambitious corporate training programs, complex schooling systems. We wish to cause learning, to take charge of it, direct it, accelerate it, demand it, or even simply stop getting in the way of it. In any case, we want to do something about it. Therefore, our perspectives on learning matter: what we think about learning influences where we recognize learning, as well as what we do when we decide that we must do something about it – as individuals, as communities, and as organizations.

If we proceed without reflecting on our fundamental assumptions about the nature of learning, we run an increasing risk that our conceptions will have misleading ramifications. In a world that is changing and becoming more complexly interconnected at an accelerating pace, concerns about learning are certainly justified. But perhaps more than learning itself, it is our *conception* of learning that needs urgent attention when we choose to meddle with it on the scale on which we do today. Indeed, the more we concern ourselves with any kind of design, the more profound are the effects of our discourses on the topic we want to address. The further you aim, the more an initial error matters. As we become more ambitious in attempts to organize our lives and our environment, the implications of our perspectives, theories, and beliefs extend further. As we take more responsibility for our future on larger and larger scales, it becomes more imperative that we reflect on the perspectives that inform our enterprises. A key implication of our attempts to organize learning is that we must become reflective with regard to our own discourses of learning and to their effects on the ways we design for learning. By proposing a framework that considers learning in social terms, I hope to contribute to this urgent need for reflection and rethinking.

The practicality of theory

A perspective is not a recipe; it does not tell you just what to do. Rather, it acts as a guide about what to pay attention to, what difficulties to expect, and how to approach problems.

- If we believe, for instance, that knowledge consists of pieces of information explicitly stored in the brain, then it makes sense to package this information in well-designed units, to assemble prospective recipients of this information in a classroom where they are perfectly still and isolated from any distraction, and to deliver this information to them as succinctly and articulately as possible. From that perspective, what has come to stand for the epitome of a learning event makes sense: a teacher lecturing a class, whether in a school, in a corporate training center, or in the back room of a library. But if we believe that information stored in explicit ways is only a small part of knowing, and that knowing involves primarily active participation in social communities, then the traditional format does not look so productive. What does look promising are inventive ways of engaging students in meaningful practices, of providing access to resources that enhance their participation, of opening their horizons so they can put themselves on learning trajectories they can identify with, and of involving them in actions, discussions, and reflections that make a difference to the communities that they value.

- Similarly, if we believe that productive people in organizations are the diligent implementors of organizational processes and that the key to organizational performance is therefore the definition of increasingly more efficient and detailed processes by which people's actions are prescribed, then it makes sense to engineer and re-engineer these processes in abstract ways and then roll them out for implementation.

- But if we believe that people in organizations contribute to organizational goals by participating inventively in practices that can never be fully captured by institutionalized processes, then we will minimize prescription, suspecting that too much of it discourages the very inventiveness that makes practices effective. We will have to make sure that our organizations are contexts within which the communities that develop these practices may prosper. We will have to value the work of community building and make sure that participants have access to the resources necessary to learn what they need to learn in order to take actions and make decisions that fully engage their own knowledgeability.

If all this seems like common sense, then we must ask ourselves why our institutions so often seem, not merely to fail to bring about these outcomes, but to work against them with a relentless zeal. Of course, some of the blame can justifiably be attributed to conflicts of interest, power struggles, and even human wickedness. But that is too simple an answer, and unnecessarily pessimistic. We must also remember that our institutions are designs and that our designs are hostage to our understanding, perspectives, and theories. In this sense, our theories are very practical because they frame not just the ways we act, but also – and perhaps most importantly when design involves social systems – the ways we justify our actions to ourselves and to each other. In an institutional context, it is difficult to act without justifying your actions in the discourse of the institution.

A social theory of learning is therefore not exclusively an academic enterprise. While its perspective can indeed inform our academic investigations, it is also relevant to our daily actions, our policies, and the technical, organizational, and educational systems we design. A new conceptual framework for thinking about learning is thus of value not only to theorists but to all of us – teachers, students, parents, youths, spouses, health practitioners, patients, managers, workers, policy makers, citizens – who in one way or another must take steps to foster learning (our own and that of others) in our relationships, our communities, and our organizations.

Part 3

The Practices of Work with Young People

13

Crossing the Boundaries? Working Informally in Formal Settings

Sheila Curran and Tyrrell Golding

Work with young people covers a broad range of practice and takes place in a wide range of settings. It includes work with young people in formal settings, such as schools and colleges, as well as in informal, community-based settings. Drawing on their own experiences of practice, which includes working as youth workers in schools, the authors explore ways in which practitioners can draw on ideas and approaches associated with informal education to support young people's learning and development, whatever setting or context they might be working in.

Introduction

Work with young people happens in a wide range of places and spaces, is conducted by a broad range of practitioners and encompasses a broad range of practices. In your own work, you might be working as a youth worker in a youth centre or on the streets; as a learning mentor or in a pastoral role in a school or college; as a leader with the Guides or Scouts; or you might have a role in a youth offending team or in a housing organisation. These are just some examples of the roles and settings in which practitioners work with young people.

What you set out to achieve in your work, your aims and purposes, will vary according to your role and the context in which you are working. Whatever your role, though, we would suggest that the ability to form relationships with young people, and to work in ways which support young people's learning and development, will be central to your practice. In this chapter we will be exploring ideas of informal education and informal learning, particularly in the context of work with young people. We will also be encouraging you to think about the implications that these issues and debates might have for your own practice, or practice that you might go on to develop in the future.

In writing this chapter we have drawn on our own professional experience, which includes working in a range of youth and community work settings, as well as our reading, debate and discussions. Our aim is to provide you with some ideas, or conceptual tools, which will help you to examine the practices of learning you are involved in, and perhaps to look at and understand them differently. Those of you who are working in more formal settings will, we hope, find this chapter useful in helping you to consider why and how you might incorporate informal strategies into your work. If your experience of practice has been mostly in more informal work, we hope that the chapter encourages you to think about ways in which you can also use and adapt your skills and experience to support young people in more formal settings.

Informal and formal education

One way in which learning and educational practice has been categorised and conceptualised is in terms of the degree to which it is 'formal' or 'informal'. The distinction between formal and informal education has been highly significant in debates about youth and community work in particular. This includes debate as to whether it is possible to work as a youth worker in formal institutional settings, for example in schools and colleges, in the youth justice system, including prisons and in more formal 'uniformed' youth organisations.

Within these debates, informal education is associated with learning that takes place outside formal educational settings, and with approaches to learning that are very different from those traditionally associated with schooling. Informal education is based on 'learning through conversation and dialogue' (Batsleer, 2008, p. 5), on listening and talking, and on the development of relationships. For Tony Jeffs and Mark Smith (2011):

> [I]nformal education [is] a spontaneous process of helping people to learn. It works through conversation, and the exploration and enlargement of experience. Its purpose, we suggest, is to cultivate communities, associations and relationships that make for human flourishing.

Informal learning takes learners' interests and concerns as a starting point, and recognises that learners as well as educators bring experiences, motivations and abilities to learning situations (Richardson and Wolfe, 2001). The experience or the process of learning is seen to be as significant, if not more significant, than the achievement of prescribed outcomes or qualifications. Informal educators see learning as a collaborative process, one in which learners participate in planning and managing their learning. There is an emphasis on association, on people coming together in groups and engaging in activity together, and on learning in an informal atmosphere.

Writing about informal education, particularly in the context of youth work, emphasises the importance of voluntary engagement as a core principle which informs this area of practice. Young people choose to be involved, often in their own time, and they are able to walk away if they decide what is on offer is not for them. They are also encouraged to be actively involved in their learning and to be creative and critical in their responses to what is on offer. As Janet Batsleer observes, rather than seeing young people as problems, or as people with problems: '... informal education starts from assumptions about the potential and the capacities of young people and their rights to develop these capacities' (2008, p. 21).

Informal learning draws on explanations of learning developed by, among others, David Kolb (1984) whose experiential learning cycle you can see in Figure 13.1. We learn from engaging in experiences and from interacting with other people, and from reflecting back over and analysing these experiences and interactions.

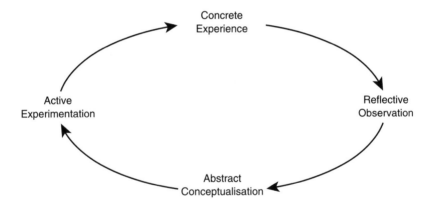

Figure 13.1   The experiential learning cycle

Source: Kolb, D.A. (1984) *Experiential Learning: Experience as a Source of Learning and Development*, 1st edn. © 1984, p.42. Reprinted by permission of Pearson Education, Inc., Upper Saddle River, NJ.

In contrast, 'formal' education is associated with the learning that takes place in formal educational settings, in schools and colleges, and in classrooms. It is based on a set and prescribed curriculum, which is carefully planned, monitored and assessed. The curriculum determines what is learnt and how learning takes place. The focus of much of the work is on gaining certificates and qualifications. Teachers are positioned as authority figures; they control what is happening and students have little power to influence the learning that takes place. Young people are required by law to attend, and their parents may be prosecuted if they don't.

Whilst these descriptions are a useful starting point, there is a need to be cautious about the apparently simple distinction between formal and informal learning. We believe that there are aspects of formality and informality in most learning situations. One of the difficulties that Tony Jeffs (2001) identifies is that discussions about informal learning often focus on how it differs from formal education, particularly schooling, rather than on ways in which we can foster learning in whatever situation we are working in. To a certain extent this is understandable; most of us will have had some experience of going to school and some understanding of the way that people learn and are taught in schools. The potential downside of this starting point, however, is that 'this encourages us to focus attention on what are often superficial differences, rather than on a shared responsibility to promote learning' (Jeffs, 2001, p. 35).

Mark Smith (2008) suggests that, rather than seeing informal and formal education as entirely separate processes, it may be useful to consider them as part of a continuum, with informal practice at one end and formal practice at the other, and an area in between where the curriculum is negotiated between practitioners and young people (Figure 13.2). This is a useful tool in helping us think through some of the debates about informal versus formal learning, including where different types of practice may be positioned.

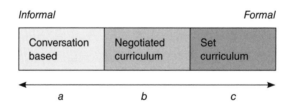

Figure 13.2   A continuum of informal and formal education (Smith, 2008)

Source: 'Informal learning', the encyclopaedia of informal education [online]. Available at: www.infed.org/biblio/inf-lrn.htm

Using the example of how a teacher in a school might work, much of their practice will be at the formal end of this continuum, focused on teaching or delivering a set curriculum, and on preparing students to be assessed and tested against prescribed learning outcomes. But there are also likely to be aspects of their practice that are more informal, such as the work they do building relationships and having conversations with young people in and out of classrooms, including through trips, visits and extra-curricular activities. While teachers may be expected to deliver a preset curriculum to students, in practice, any learning situation is likely to involve a process of negotiation, where teachers try to find out what interests and motivates students, and encourage them to take some responsibility for their learning. Lessons will not always work out to plan, and teachers need to be able to respond to the unexpected, to improvise and change what they are doing when necessary, just as a youth worker needs to be able to do, for example, when running a group work session in a community centre.

A changing practice and policy landscape

A difficulty in presenting informal education and formal education as either/or processes, and in terms of a binary divide, is that this tends to oversimplify learning in a way that is unhelpful to practitioners. It also fails to reflect ways in which educational practice may change over time, including in response to policy shifts. An example of this is the way in which youth workers, who would position themselves very much at the informal education end of Smith's spectrum, as informal educators, are increasingly being encouraged, or required, to adopt more formal approaches in their practice. This might include being required to plan and evaluate their work in terms of young people's achievement of accredited outcomes and qualifications.

Our own experiences also indicate that practitioners working with young people often move across and between different roles and work settings. This includes moving between more formal and less formal settings at different points of their lives and at different stages of their careers. This may be particularly the case in the early stages of their careers, when people often find themselves with a number of different contracts in different settings, or with a series of short-term contracts.

Pen picture

Teagan had just started working with young people after having a short career break to have her children. During the day she worked as a Learning Support Assistant in a secondary school, working with young people who needed extra support with their literacy and numeracy skills. One evening a week she volunteered at a youth club run by her local church. One of the biggest challenges she found when she first started was the two 'hats' she was working with. In the youth club the young people would call her by her first name and would chat to her about a range of topics, from issues with their family and friends to their best or worst teachers, as they played games and did arts and crafts activities. During the day the young people had to call Teagan 'Miss' and would be 'told off' if they strayed off the topic of conversation the teacher had set. Over time, Teagan used the space at youth club to discuss these different 'hats' with the young people so they could understand her different roles and the differences between the two settings in which she worked. Whilst she was always careful to be professional and not take sides if the topic of best and worst teachers came up again, she was able to support the young people to think about why different teachers had different styles and how the young people could get on better at school. She also found that her role in school helped her to understand the pressures facing young people who struggled with reading, as well as developing her understanding of some of the things she could do to help. She was interested to see how young people sometimes behaved very differently in the youth club, compared to how they behaved in the classroom.

At least some of this movement across different sectors of work with young people will be prompted by changes in funding and policy initiatives. As we write this chapter, we are very aware of the changes that are currently taking place both in the broad field of work with young people, and the specific practice that is described as youth work. New forms of practice are emerging with youth workers in particular working in roles and contexts where we might not have found them in the past. These include work with young people in hospitals, and the employment of youth workers in housing organisations, practice based on recognition of the importance of providing specialist services to meet the needs of young people.

Youth workers are also being employed in a range of roles in youth justice, particularly in youth offending teams, including supporting young people in and upon leaving prison. At first glance, these areas of practice may appear to have little in common with what we have identified as the characteristics of informal education. Our experience indicates that here as in other formal settings, youth workers are being employed precisely because the positive outcomes of adopting informal education approaches have been recognised and acknowledged.

In schools and other formal education institutions, we can also observe a growing recognition of the need to develop new approaches to working with young people, particularly young people who are most vulnerable, who are becoming disengaged from school, and who might be at risk of 'failing' or of being excluded from school. Recognition of the role that informal education and youth work in particular can play in supporting young people's achievement in formal education can also be seen at a policy level, particularly in educational policy being developed by governments in the Celtic nations.

For example, in Northern Ireland, the Department of Education has stated that within its vision for education: 'youth services play a key role in connecting formal and informal learning and contributing to the development of coherent pathways to learning for all young people' (Harland et al., 2005, p. 89). In Scotland, developments associated with the Curriculum for Excellence are setting out to transform education, including by creating a more flexible, coherent and enriched curriculum for all children and young people aged 3–18. The intention is to provide a more consistent package of learning and support that responds to young people's needs, and to prepare them with the knowledge and skills that that they will require for life and work, as well as helping them to achieve academic qualifications. Responsibility for implementing change and this new curriculum is seen to extend beyond schools and to include everyone working with children and young people in Scotland, including youth workers. The development of new school and youth work partnerships are identified as one way in which outcomes for young people can be improved (Learning and Teaching Scotland, 2009). There is recognition that youth workers have a broad range of skills. These include the ability to build relationships with young people and develop their confidence and interpersonal skills, including the ability to work in teams, and this can have a positive impact on young people's learning across the curriculum and in other areas of their lives.

Education policy coming from government in England at the time of writing may not be providing the same sort of vision or central steer as in other parts of the UK, but at a local level you may be aware of or indeed part of these sorts of changes in practice; for example, if you are working as a youth worker, learning mentor, student support worker, or pastoral support worker working alongside teachers to support young people's engagement in school.

Working across the boundaries of formal and informal education, and working across formal and informal settings, can present some challenges. In the next section of the chapter we will examine some of these challenges, and some of the strategies that you might adopt to help you deal with them in your own practice.

Challenges

One of the challenges for practitioners used to working in informal education settings, and moving to work in a formal environment, such as working in a school, will be learning to work in an organisation which may have a very different culture. This includes how the organisation views power and authority, and where adults are positioned in roles that give them authority over young people (Barnes, 2002). Schools tend to be hierarchical organisations, with adults largely making decisions and having responsibility for making sure that young people conform to the rules. One very obvious difference you may note is how adults in schools are usually addressed by young people. Teachers are called Miss or Sir, depending on their gender, and by their surnames rather than being on first-name terms with young people as they are likely to be in a more informal setting. This can be uncomfortable for practitioners whose practice is based on values that place an emphasis on equality and mutual respect between workers and young people (Richardson and Wolfe, 2001). Organisations such as Scouting also position adults in roles of authority, with titles that reflect this, for example, the use of the title 'Akela' in cubs. Alternatively, for some adults, young people calling them by their first name can be equally as uncomfortable.

Pen picture

When Mary first started to think about how she was working informally in her current work with young people, she just couldn't see it in her practice. She was a Sergeant in her local Cadets corps. Her sessions were always well planned and involved formal drills and training the cadets on key skills they needed. However, through discussions with her colleagues and spending time reading more about informal work with young people, she started to identify areas in her practice where she could adopt and adapt the way that she worked with the young people. In doing so, she identified two areas of her

(Continued)

(Continued)

practice that she could change. Firstly, she planned to ensure that she was always there when the young people were arriving. This gave her 15 minutes before the first drill of the evening began to chat to them. When she started this she decided not to have 'an agenda' for her discussions; rather she just tried to slowly develop a relationship with the young people, asking them open questions such as how their week had been to allow the young people to share and chat with her about anything they thought was important. Mary noticed that, because she had built stronger relationships with the young people, the drill and training sessions went better as she could now adapt them according to the young people's needs and moods. Secondly, Mary decided to work differently with older young people in the group. She discussed with them what they thought the cadets might benefit from doing, involving them in the planning and delivery of sessions, allowing them to take on more responsibility, and relieving Mary of some of the responsibility and time commitment of planning everything herself.

Another challenge for practitioners working within the values of informal education is working out how a commitment to young people's voluntary engagement can fit with practice that involves working with young people in settings where attendance is compulsory – work in schools or prisons, for example. Here it can be helpful to refer back to definitions of informal learning as being about a 'spontaneous process of helping people to learn' which works through conversation and through exploring experiences (Jeffs and Smith, 2011), which we believe can happen in many different settings. Secondly, we would argue that relationships are at the heart of informal education. If a practitioner is committed to the kinds of practice and professional relationships with young people which Sapin (2013) and others highlight, then they will be committed to developing relationships with young people that can only be developed if the young people enter into them voluntarily. After all, if you think back to your own time in school you might remember a particular teacher who you might go to if you needed help. They had the same statutory duty to teach you as every other member of staff but there was something about the way they spoke to you or treated you which meant you felt able to trust them.

Informal educators find themselves facing challenges from the opposite end of the spectrum. Changes in government policy, particularly over the last decade, have led to informal educators being required to adopt more formal approaches in their practice. Many youth workers, for example, will be working in situations where they are expected to plan and evaluate their work in terms of young people's achievement of qualifications and 'accredited outcomes'. Managing these different expectations can be challenging for practitioners. Some commentators take the view that where government sets 'outcomes' which prescribe how and what young people should learn, or where funders dictate the outcomes of the work they are commissioning, then it is no longer possible to work to the values of informal education (Nicholls, 2012). Others take the view that it is possible for informal educators to build meaningful relationships with young people and to work with them in creative ways, even in the most restrictive settings and contexts.

A final challenge we have identified can also be seen as an opportunity – working together. For many informal education practitioners, working collaboratively with 'formal' educators or in 'formal' settings can present challenges to their sense of professional identity and their sense of professional boundaries. We have already highlighted the issue of power; perceived differences in power will have an impact on relationships between different professionals, just as they will have an impact on relationships between practitioners and young people. If practitioners from different professional backgrounds are to work effectively together, including across formal and informal settings, then they need to understand each other's roles, priorities and perspectives, and to recognise the different ways in which they can contribute to young people's learning and development. It is also important to clarify different roles and responsibilities. Different organisations and professional cultures can each contribute to the successful 'flourishing' of young people. By working together organisations and individual practitioners can achieve what is known as 'collaborative advantage': the ability to achieve something together that they could not achieve alone.

Opportunities

Working in new ways, and adopting different approaches to the work you do with young people, brings opportunities as well as challenges. If we look at one form of formal learning, school, you might consider the classes which make up an average day as the building bricks of young people's learning. Through our experience of working with young people in schools, we have come to see the spaces and places between the classes, arriving at school, walking the corridors from one class to the next or waiting in the lunch queue as the mortar which holds these building blocks together. It is in these spaces that informal methods of learning can be applied to the benefit of all. Identifying the strengths and applications of informal education practices in formal settings comes from a position that informal learning is as valuable as formal learning. The authors of this chapter feel this strongly, however they also recognise the importance and remit of formal schooling in young people's lives. In their experience of working in a range of secondary schools in a number of different job roles, it is clear that adopting methods used in informal learning, such as conversation and dialogue, and developing relationships based on mutual respect and equality (Richardson and Wolfe, 2001) can play a big part in unblocking barriers to formal learning for all young people, but particularly those who have not traditionally found themselves successful in the schooling system.

Similarly, uniformed organisations such as The Cadets, Scouts and Girl Guides may work in quite a formal way from week to week but there may be aspects of their work with young people which is informal, such as free time at the end of a meeting or fireside time at camp. If you work in such an organisation we encourage you to take up and build on opportunities provided by everyday conversation and chat, just as 'Teagan' did.

Pen picture

Mark worked as a youth worker in a community college. His role was varied. During the school day he worked with young people at risk of exclusion, which included one-to-one support and small group work, with some young people working towards completing ASDAN qualifications. He also ran sessions with young people on drugs and alcohol education as part of the school's PSE curriculum, and contributed to training for teachers delivering these sessions. He co-ordinated a peer-mediation project, running lunchtime training and support sessions for young people who volunteered to be peer-mediators, as part of the school's anti-bullying work. During the evening, he ran youth club sessions in the youth centre on the school site, as well as a Duke of Edinburgh Award group. The dinner queue formed outside his office and at least twice a week he would plan to eat lunch whilst he chatted to the young people as they waited. This allowed him to slowly build relationships with a range of young people he might not meet normally, let the young people know about activities and projects he was developing as well as hearing from the young people themselves about what was going on in their lives.

The school also benefitted from the networks and relationships that Mark had developed in the surrounding community. For example, as a result of his contacts with health organisations, a specialist nurse now ran a smoking-cessation group for students who wanted to give up smoking. And as he developed good working relations with school staff, including teachers, they came to him if they had concerns about students he was working with, and began to understand more about youth work and what it had to offer for young people.

Research conducted in Northern Ireland suggests that 'For many years youth workers have been involved directly or indirectly with schools in terms of delivering programmes that complement and supplement the curriculum' (Morgan et al., 2008, p. 1). Informal educators aim to work with young people where they are, and many young people attend school at some point in their lives. Youth workers have traditionally worked in partnership with a range of other professionals and agencies in order to respond to young people's needs and concerns and schools are very significant in young people's lives. The values that underpin informal education focus on developing relationships and working with groups of young people, which has the potential to contribute expertise to particular areas of the school curriculum. Examples of this are sex and relationships education, personal and social education, and citizenship education, as well as work that supports young people's participation in decision making. In doing so there is the potential to share and develop practice with other professionals who are likely to have different skills and experiences.

Another opportunity for 'collaborative advantage' is the chance to develop new approaches to learning and teaching that support young people who are most disengaged or at risk of exclusion. Sapin suggests practitioners 'need to remember that whilst most young people attend school regularly, others only attend intermittently or not at all' (2013, p. 47). There is clearly, therefore, a need to support the engagement of the most vulnerable young people, who may have become 'switched-off' from learning; who may be at risk of leaving school with few if any qualifications; and who are likely to be particularly vulnerable to unemployment in a challenging employment market or to be in low-skilled and poorly paid work if they are lucky.

Conclusion

It is not the purpose of this chapter to suggest that all work with young people should be conducted informally or indeed that it can be conducted informally (though there are some interesting examples of ways of working informally in settings and practices that are always seen as traditionally formal, such as forest schools). Rather, we are highlighting the fact that there are ways in which most practitioners working in formal settings can consider, adopt and adapt informal working practices to add to and enhance their work.

Furthermore, settings which mostly adopt formal working practices can add to their work and enhance their students' experience and learning by working in collaboration and partnership with those who work informally. They should also consider the importance of what goes on during the 'mortar' times, the down times or non-timetabled parts of their day/sessions/projects, as clearly as they do the timetabled parts of the day, building in opportunities for reflection and for young people to have some say or influence in deciding how and what they want to learn.

Finally, we believe that informal practice can be woven into the most formal of timetables, if planned appropriately, and that it is the commitment to informal practice and the values which underpin it, which makes this possible.

We hope that reading this chapter has helped you to think about ways in which you can develop your practice with young people, including by drawing on ideas of informal learning. Above all, we hope that this chapter encourages you to use your understanding of informal education ideas and approaches to help you create spaces that enable you to foster the learning and development of the young people you are working with, whatever context and setting you are working in.

References

Barnes, P. (2002) *Leadership with Young People*, Lyme Regis, Russell House.
Batsleer, J. (2008) *Informal Learning in Youth Work*, London, Sage.

Harland, K., Morgan, T. and Muldoon, O. (2005) *The Nature of Youth Work in Northern Ireland*. Department of Education (N.I.).

Jeffs, T. (2001) 'First lessons: historical perspectives on informal education', in Richardson, L. and Wolfe, M. (eds) *Principles and Practice of Informal Education: Learning through Life*, Abingdon, Routledge.

Jeffs, T. and Smith, M.K. (2011) 'What is informal education?', *The Encyclopaedia of Informal Education* [online]. Available at: www.infed.org/i-intro.htm (accessed 7 January 2013).

Kolb, D.A. (1984) *Experiential Learning*, Englewood Cliffs, NJ, Prentice Hall.

Learning and Teaching Scotland (2009) *Bridging the Gap: Improving Outcomes for Scotland's Young People through School and Youth Work Partnerships* [online]. Available at: www.educationscotland.gov.uk/Images/Bridging_The_Gap_tcm4-552837.pdf (accessed 20 January 2013).

Morgan, T., Morgan, B. and O'Kelly, B. (2008) *Youth Work in Schools: An Investigation of Youth Work as a Process of Informal Learning in Formal Settings*, Bangor, Northern Ireland Statistics and Research Agency.

Nicholls, D. (2012) *For Youth Workers and Youth Work: Speaking Out for a Better Future*, Bristol, Policy Press.

Richardson, L. and Wolfe, M. (eds) (2001) *Principles and Practice of Informal Education: Learning through Life*, Abingdon, Routledge.

Sapin, K. (2013) *Essential Skills for Work with Young People*, 2nd edn, London, Sage.

Smith, M.K. (2008) 'Informal learning', *The Encyclopaedia of Informal Education* [online]. Available at: www.infed.org/biblio/inf-lrn.htm (accessed 6 February 2013).

14

Enhancing Young People's Participation

Kate Sapin

> Young people often have limited control over many of the decisions that affect their lives. This chapter looks at ways of facilitating young people's participation that provide opportunities for them to develop skills and confidence in making their own decisions and to participate in decision-making processes.

Focusing on participation

Youth work promotes young people's participation in decisions about issues that affect them, from relationships with their families and friends to environmental pollution, globalisation and world peace. Youth workers provide opportunities for young people to have a voice and a positive impact on the ways in which decisions are made. Young people's participation can improve existing services or make demands for new services to address community needs. Through youth work, young people express themselves socially, artistically and politically in ways that can make a difference. Young people who are brought together to learn from each other can find ways to improve their lives. Youth work practice aims to enable participation at different levels: with young people, with communities and with services and organisations. (Box 14.1 outlines some examples.)

According to Max-Neef's (1991) list of interdependent human needs (simplified here in Box 14.2), participation is fundamental. If young people's needs for participation are not satisfied, the effects can interfere with other aspects of their lives. For example, if young people are disempowered or alienated, the sense of belonging

This chapter is edited from Sapin, Kate (2013) 'Enhancing Young People's Participation', Chapter 9, *Essential Skills for Youth Work Practice*, 2nd edn, London: Sage.

Box 14.1   The aims of participation and related practice

Aims of participation	Work with young people	Work with communities	Work with services and organisations	Self-development
Young people have more control over the decisions they make about their lives	Providing opportunities to develop confidence and responsibility	Raising awareness of community issues with young people and enabling them to influence these issues	Enabling young people to feedback and contribute to the decision-making process and decisions that are made	Learning from young people and involving them in relevant research
Young people's services become more accessible and appropriate	Developing and promoting opportunities for young people to become involved in evaluation and development of services	Raising awareness of young people's needs for accessible services	Developing structures and opportunities for young people to affect service development and management	Networking to develop multi-agency links and services; developing an understanding of the barriers and shortcomings of services
Society develops positive attitudes towards young people	Developing their awareness of others' perspectives and any impact they may have on how they are perceived and treated	Raising awareness of young people's positive actions	Challenging negative and oppressive attitudes and practice, and enabling young people to do so	Researching to understand power, oppression and social structures
Young people are able to participate in decision-making processes	Involving young people in cross-generational work; enabling young people to develop the skills and knowledge required for participation	Providing opportunities for young people to be heard	Developing structures for participation and enabling young people to participate in existing decision-making structures	Researching to identify relevant issues, resources and opportunities for participation

and self-esteem that comes with identity can be adversely affected. On the other hand, if young people participate and have the opportunity to behave responsibly, they can be empowered in other ways. The skills and confidence developed through cooperative action or being able to dissent could have positive effects on their ability to understand others within their social groups, families, schools, communities and employment. Practice example 1 provides an example of how participation in planning projects and activities can enhance young people's confidence and address a range of other human needs.

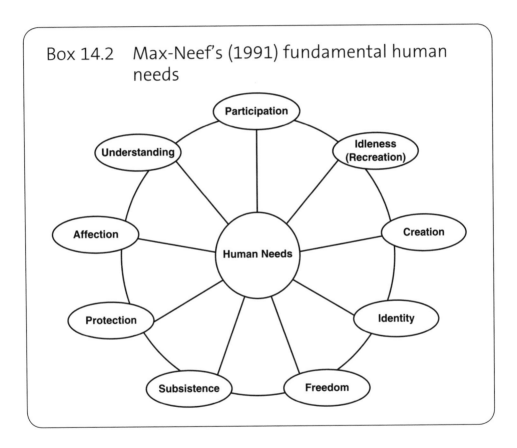

Box 14.2   Max-Neef's (1991) fundamental human needs

Addressing the barriers between young people and those in positions of power can involve youth workers in a variety of roles (see Box 14.3). Acting as an intermediary or advocate, youth workers can create links between young people and decision-makers. Youth workers need to be cautious about getting in the way of direct communication between young people and decision-makers and speaking on young people's behalf rather than enabling them to speak for themselves. Passing

Practice example 1   Developing skills through planning a camping trip

A youth worker's report identified that young people learned the following skills whilst planning and organising their camping trip:

- **Research:** identifying preferences in relation to destination, activities and food; finding out about accessible and available campsites and transport; learning about insurance, parental permission and risk assessment requirements.
- **Negotiation:** with local shopkeepers for donations of supplies, with campsite and transport for a good deal, with parents for permission, with each other to make decisions.
- **Fund raising:** organising sponsored activities, seeking out donations.
- **Budgeting:** planning and recording expenditure and resource requirements.
- **Cooking and healthy eating:** identifying ways to address individual diets and health requirements, preparing meals, clearing up.
- **Planning:** the registration process, the journey, the activities, the menus, the paperwork.
- **Teamwork:** sharing tasks, joint decision making, keeping each other informed, addressing responsibilities.
- **Critical reflection:** evaluation of the project, of their learning, of whether they want to be involved again!

on second-hand information, although clearly a second-best option, may be the only opportunity for young people's views to be heard. If called upon to be such a go-between, youth workers need to present young people's views as accurately and as fully as possible.

Successful campaigns for organisational or structural change to enable participation may require a youth worker to undertake a range of different roles. Some youth workers prefer to advise other organisations on ways to involve young people, whilst others focus on being advocates for young people. Youth workers engaged in networking and research seek out opportunities for young people's participation whilst an activist is involved in challenging those in power. Challenging organisational or societal ways of thinking or acting can provoke negative reactions. Pushing or overextending the boundaries of a remit or job description to increase young people's involvement needs to involve others within the organisation. Otherwise, should employers disapprove, this activist role can leave a youth worker unsupported. Some situations benefit from a strategy that builds good relations with those in power. Providing viable suggestions for change that can be clearly understood may address or pre-empt resistance or backlash.

Box 14.3   Examples of roles to develop participation

Role	Examples
Advisor	I enable young people to participate by making sure that organisations know about different ways that young people could contribute to their decision making. I have a number of proposals to address barriers to participation: structural changes, challenges to attitudes and examples of good practice.
Advocate	I enable young people to participate by making a point of acknowledging young people's contributions, ensuring that young people's views are taken into account and supporting young people in expressing their views. I always pass on young people's ideas to people who make the decisions and support or present proposals for structural changes that mean they have a greater say. For example, our organisation recently developed some procedural changes that delegated budgetary decisions 'downwards'. Enabling face-to-face youth workers to have greater control over their budgets means that young people have more direct access to decision making.
Networker	I enable young people to participate by building links between organisations and groups of young people or organisations. I seek out organisations who wish to take account of young people's opinions and match them with youth-led organisations who wish to have their voices heard. I make sure that young people know about meetings, conferences and training events.
Researcher	I enable young people to participate by consulting with them about their aspirations and interests, involving them in research to identify resources and funding, and making sure that they bring a global perspective to their planning, such as taking into account environmental issues and linking with young people from other countries.
Activist	I enable young people to participate by developing informal networks and forums that enable them to influence and share in decision-making processes. I support young people to challenge those in power, for example in their campaigns to influence decisions. I structure my own practice so that young people have a direct say in decisions such as staff selection, organisational priorities and resource allocation.

Recognising levels of participation

The level of power and control that young people experience ranges from passive recipients to active decision-makers. Various yardsticks to identify different levels of participation can be used (such as Arnstein, 1969; Hart, 1992) to identify young people's roles. (See Box 14.4 for a figure illustrating Hart's 'ladder'.) While accept-able levels of participation do not require young people to be managers in control all the time, young people need to know where they stand. Clear identification of roles and communication can protect against false expectations.

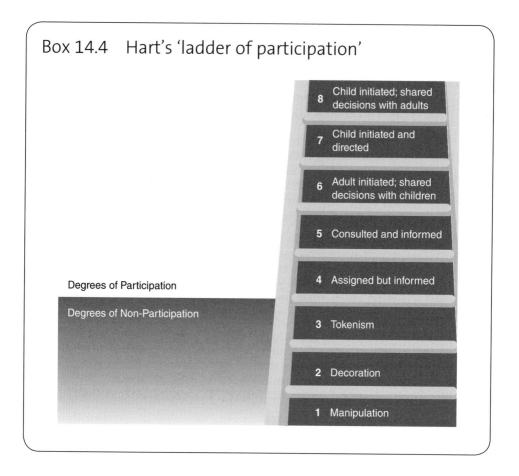

Box 14.4   Hart's 'ladder of participation'

8   Child initiated; shared decisions with adults

7   Child initiated and directed

6   Adult initiated; shared decisions with children

5   Consulted and informed

4   Assigned but informed

Degrees of Participation

Degrees of Non-Participation

3   Tokenism

2   Decoration

1   Manipulation

An important factor in young people taking control of a project or activity is the commitment of the young people, the youth workers and the organisation. Support for the development of participation may come from the organisational culture and individual staff members, as well as from positive policies and procedures. Provid-ing the right level of support at appropriate times without being overly directive is critical although not always easy to gauge. The degree of participation that young people are able to exercise may depend on the particular activity or organisation, or on what Shier (2001) defines as 'openings, opportunities and obligations':

At each level, an **opening** occurs as soon as a worker is ready to operate at that level; that is, when they make a personal commitment, or statement of intent to work in a certain way. It is only an opening, because at this stage, the opportunity to make it happen may not be available.

In the second stage, an **opportunity** occurs when the needs are met that will enable the work or organisation to operate at this level in practice. These needs may include resources (including staff time), skills and knowledge (maybe through training), development of new procedures or new approaches to established tasks.

Finally, an **obligation** is established when it becomes the agreed policy of the organisation or setting that staff should operate at this level. It becomes an obligation on the staff that they must do so. Working in a particular way, enabling a specific level of children's participation, thus becomes built in to the system. (Shier, 2001: 110)

Communication between youth workers and young people about the issues concerned in having a voice or making a difference needs to be regular and informative. Young people's understanding of the degree of influence or difference that their participation can make is often bluntly accurate. Experience of exclusion and being patronised, through ageism as well as other oppressive attitudes or practices mean that young people's cynicism about participation cannot be ignored. A 'map of participation' (such as in Practice example 2) or other means of communication can assist young people to identify and communicate information about their experience and the level of their participation, whether that is being excluded or having a leadership role.

Practice example 2   A map of participation

We use 'maps of participation' to let young people tell us and other members of the community where they feel that they can make a difference and where they feel excluded. We use a large map of the area that shows the community centre, school, shops and their homes. Sometimes it's just a rough drawing – at other times a printed one. For a group, we make one as big as the table. The young people decorate the map with symbols to highlight the places that are significant to them. Colours can show positive or negative feelings about certain areas. Sometimes we use stickers – a picture of a lion to be placed where they feel they can be leaders or a sheep where they feel like followers – although usually they decide on their own symbolism. Logos or graffiti 'tags' are put on areas that are 'theirs'. The map gives them a powerful way to compile information about experiences and a basis to work from to address the issues raised.

Promoting positive attitudes towards young people

Young people recognise that adults and their social structures tend to treat young people differently from mature adults. They experience the fact that adults generally have more political, social and economic power, which can be exerted over them to their benefit or detriment. Mutual mistrust between younger people and adults is often a result of reciprocal ageism, or generalised negative assumptions about different age groups. Ageism might be insignificant or oppressive, somewhat related to a truth or completely false. For example, assumptions are often made about the igno-rance of a particular age group in relation to what is going on around them despite evidence to the contrary. If these assumptions lead to unfair or unequal treatment, abuse, exclusion or ridicule, then the ageism is discriminatory or oppressive.

The involvement of young people in local organisations or community activities can effect change in relation to ageist attitudes and practice. In certain communities, young people may be seen as problems and youth work as the solution or at least a form of problem intervention. Meanwhile, the young people may feel misunderstood and unclear about how to address their negative image. Developing the participation of young people in partnership with com-munities can enhance the recognition of young people as individuals and build positive relationships.

A youth worker can work with communities and agencies to support the participation of young people as individuals with certain perspectives. At the same time, work with young people to build on their strengths and seek out their ideas, encourage their questions, respond to their energy and enthusiasm and support their creativity can build up their confidence. All parties can emerge from a project (see Practice example 3) with a very different and more positive image of the young people's capabilities.

Practice example 3   Promoting positive attitudes

A new community facility was being planned in an inner-city area. Initially, the planning committee was managed by local political leaders and representatives from certain services mostly related to primary healthcare. A group of young people came by the building site one day when one of the members of the planning committee happened to be visiting. Following an animated conversation about the plans, the young people were invited to come along to a meeting to present their views. The young people were able to present a few ideas and ask a few questions related to the plans. The enthusiasm, ideas and creativity displayed by the young people impressed the committee, who were able to see the benefits of involving the young people in planning the facility.

While it did not seem appropriate to invite a random group to participate fully in the planning meetings, the committee decided to ask the local youth services to find a way to involve young people. The youth service recommended that a subgroup of the planning committee be set up as a forum for young people to discuss their ideas for presentation at future planning meetings. This meant that the young people's views could be contributed – without having to sit through all of the 'boring parts'. The planning committee acknowledged the value of the young people's contribution to the planning process.

Developing young people's control

Different types of youth work provide different opportunities for young people to develop their capacity for taking responsibility and working with others (see Box 14.5). In a 'young people's project', young people are in control. 'Youth work activities and projects' have different degrees of control depending on the level of their involvement, whereas a 'youth service' may involve young people in participative youth work activities and projects or simply offer options from which young people select.

Through participation in youth work activities and projects, such as discussions and negotiations to make group decisions, young people develop clarity about the world and find ways to articulate and assert themselves. Being listened to and seeing the results of their contributions can be very positive learning experiences. For many young people, these opportunities to demonstrate capability provide useful and sometimes unique transitional experiences into adulthood and affect their confidence in other aspects of their lives.

Box 14.5   Working on participation

Participative roles

Organisation	Young people's role	Relevant youth work practice
Young people's projects	A group of young people decide on possible project options, select from them and carry out the work required.	A youth worker is in a supportive role, providing information, advice and access to resources, as well as encouraging the development of the project so that it is inclusive and accessible to others.
Youth work activities and projects	Representative young people are involved at various levels of organisation to inform planning and management.	A youth worker consults with young people and encourages their participation. Decisions are made in partnership to provide options based on young people's expressed needs and interests.
Youth services	Young people select from options designed by others and feed back their views.	A youth worker provides a programme of activities and information, listens to young people through monitoring and evaluation, and makes reasonable adjustments to the programme.

(Continued)

(Continued)

Non-participative roles

Setting	Young people's role	Worker's role and approach
'Care', entertainment, diversion	Young people are involved in activities that they do not understand.	The worker has control, designs a project and allocates the young people to certain activities.
Training	Young people are told what to do.	The worker instructs the young people without identifying their previous knowledge or interest.
Coercion (court order, compulsory education)	Young people have no say in the activities.	The worker requires compliance for the project, which may also have enforced attendance and record-keeping.

Youth workers encourage young people to pass ideas and information between themselves to develop and manage projects. Role conflict can arise when the drive for participation comes from external funding criteria or organisational aims rather than the young people concerned. Attention needs to be paid to the aim of youth work, that is, to address young people's needs and interests, and to the reasons for enabling their participation: to enable them to have more control over the decisions they make about their lives. Merton et al. (2004), for example, define some functions of work with young people which can conflict with youth work aims and values (see Box 14.6). 'Participatory' projects can be more about *socialisation* and control than young people's interests. Such projects may enable young people who enjoy taking on responsibilities to flourish whilst others feel excluded because managing a project 'is just like school'.

Box 14.6   Merton et al.'s (2004) functions of work with young people

Function	Application to work with young people
Integrative youth work	Is concerned with the socialisation of young people and introducing them into 'social norms, expectations, roles and institutions as preparation for the adult world. Seen in this way, social institutions remain broadly the same and it is the task of the young people and those working with them, to fit into what is expected of them' (Merton et al., 2004: 29).

Function	Application to work with young people
Reflexive youth work	Recognises that local, incremental and individual instances of social change are necessary as 'social structures and systems may serve to exclude and disadvantage certain groups and individuals, and that one of the purposes of youth work is to ensure that the perspectives of young people are better accommodated within these institutions' (Merton et al., 2004: 30).
Redistributive youth work	Is concerned with social justice and social capital (e.g. Putnam, 1995) and 'counters disadvantage, by raising the sights of young people and directing resources to those least likely to receive them' (Merton et al., 2004: 30).

Improving services for young people

Decisions taken within different structures, services and systems have widely varying expectations with regard to young people's participation, yet young people are affected by their decisions. Assisting young people to identify where the power lies, how procedures work and how to participate in their decisions can be part of a youth worker's role. In particular, youth workers support young people in dealing with the effects of inequalities. Youth workers who are able to identify how power operates within society and its institutions, employing organisations, families and social groups, can assist young people to find their way through these various arenas and enable them to participate more fully in decisions. Youth workers also need to be aware of their own power to identify whether their practice addresses or promotes oppression or liberation.

The ideas and perspectives of young people could usefully inform the design, development and implementation of services that they might use. When young people participate in management and evaluation, activity resources might be more sensibly allocated. Services might become more accessible and relevant. In addition, young people could develop more of a sense of ownership and responsibility for the services. Practice example 4 provides an illustration of the type of contribution that young people can make to a planning group, in that they could foresee a range of issues that may not have occurred to an adult planning group. In addition, they were able to make suggestions that were more feasible and interesting to the particular target group. Taking their ideas into account can give the young people a sense of pride that can precipitate their further involvement in maintaining a facility. If they had not been involved, the development may have been unused, dangerous and expensive. Their participation not only improved provision, but had the potential for benefits throughout the community. Through involvement in a socially responsible activity, young people can provide a positive image to their peers, families and community, which could have far-reaching effects.

This model of young people's participation can be seen as 'market research' and lead youth workers and others to lose sight of the purpose of participation. While improvement in services may be a worthwhile by-product, youth workers need to focus on enabling young people to have more control over the decisions that they make. Enabling participation is meant to be liberating for young people, not provide more restrictions.

Practice example 4   Young people's participation improves a park

A committee involved in re-designing a park involved some young people in discussing the plans. The young people pointed out that a skateboard facility under discussion would:

- be unlikely to interest the target age group unless certain design features were included
- only accommodate a limited number of young people at a time
- only accommodate one proficiency level at a time
- require access to expensive safety equipment, which was beyond their means
- need supervision to prevent younger children or alternative activities getting in the way.

The input of these young people meant that the plans were changed and the resulting facilities were well used and safe.

Involving young people in organisations

An understanding of organisational structures, roles, relationships, power and decision-making processes can assist a youth worker in identifying relevant practice to increase participation. Practice example 5 demonstrates how a project can fall through with a lack of clarity about relationships and who has the power to make decisions.

Practice example 5   Young people are duped

A Board of Directors for a youth organisation decided to set up a management group for a project made up solely of young people that would have responsibility for redecorating the youth centre, including the design and budget allocation. The project group put a lot of effort into considering different ways in which to involve other young people in the project. The final design included a mural with contributions from different groups using the centre. The centre was redecorated with a high level of participation by young people. A grand re-opening was planned by the project group and the organisation's Board of Directors was invited. Several key members of the Board, who were also funders of the organisation, were offended by the content of the mural. At the next Board meeting, it was agreed that the mural would be painted over.

A youth worker could have made a difference to Practice example 5 outlined above. Pointing out ways to enhance young people's participation at all levels of the project could have led to more positive outcomes. For example, an experienced youth worker could have ensured that the Board of Directors fully discussed the implications and consequences of the brief prior to establishing the group. The Board's discussion might also have been enhanced by the participation of young people as representatives or members on the Board of Directors, which could also have improved communication and relationships between the two groups. Continuous representation from the project group on the Board of Directors would have helped to keep them informed about the development of the project. A youth worker or young person may have sought clarification from the Board of Directors about whether the project group's designs would need approval. Although this would limit the young people's power, a revised brief would more accurately reflect the views of the Board. The project group would also have been clearer about the consequences of their decisions.

A youth worker may also have been able to suggest a different approach to the way in which the Board handled the disagreement. For example, the Board of Directors could have informed the project group about their concerns and asked them to come up with alternative proposals. A youth worker taking on an advocacy or networking role may have suggested that the Board of Directors keep in touch with the young people to be in tune with their interests, styles and attitudes. Relationships could have been based on two-way communication. Then the young people's views may have been valued and the Board may have been able to communicate their own values to the young people.

The example highlights a number of issues about enabling participation. For participation to be positive, young people need to be treated with respect. In this example, the young people may have known that the mural was offensive yet have gone ahead in order to antagonise the board or to highlight the bogus power on offer. Alternatively, they may not have known that the mural was offensive and have been denied the opportunity to put the situation right. Youth workers need to question who has the right, the power and the access to knowledge and who makes the decisions over who will have access. This analysis of groups, organisations and society will assist in the identification of meaningful participation.

While conflicts about power can be inevitable, a number of structural changes could enhance young people's participation. Identifying different structures and different ways in which young people can participate on committees can provide options for organisations looking to increase young people's participation. A youth worker may be able to advise young people about effective contributions in committees and provide an understanding of the implications as well as the limitations of various roles. Participation in committee discussions from the initial allocation of funds to a project may enhance all of the members' understanding of possibilities and limitations. Or young people's ongoing participation on an advisory committee could contribute a relevant perspective to policy development.

A youth worker can also set up structures to enable young people's participation. Relevant structures could be based on informal youth groups or more formally constituted groups and committees. The aim will usually determine the levels of formality and young people's influence – although sometimes the history of the group is also significant. The remit and procedures of a group established by young people are likely to be quite different from an adult group that young people join. For example, young people on a youth council would set the agenda themselves, whereas the contributions of young people invited to attend the board meetings of a housing trust may well be limited to certain agenda items. An understanding of the specific roles and responsibilities that members undertake when joining a committee can provide clarity for both young people and the committee. A youth worker can suggest different types of committee structures as options (see Box 14.7) to enhance the decision.

Box 14.7   Types of committees

Type of committee	Role of committee
Boards of directors Management committees	Provide direction Be responsible for projects or organisations Manage staff and budgets
Advisory boards Policy committees	Give feedback and advice Have no responsibility for management Discuss issues; develop proposals Present findings
Task forces Working groups Action forums Subgroups	Develop short projects with a specific purpose Report to another body Meet outside of the decision-making body
Youth councils Youth forums	Network to discuss issues Disseminate information Attend other bodies as representatives

Enabling young people to participate fully

Young people who feel involved in decisions and are able to contribute to the process and outcomes of decision making can be a great asset to any organisation that works with young people. Certain circumstances can encourage or enable individuals to participate fully, such as an understanding of the topic, the potential choices being made and the implications of the decision. Young people also need information about the decision-making process and how they fit in (see Box 14.8 for some examples). Simply adding young people as members to an existing adult committee without any thought to how they might be received or how either party might feel about the culture and procedures is not usually a very successful way to enable participation. Usually both the existing committee membership and the new younger members need some induction and training as to how to proceed.

Box 14.8   Young people's rights on committees

Rights	Potential roles
Voting and speaking rights	Chair, Secretary, Treasurer Full member Appointed member Worker or volunteer Representative of subgroup or other group
Speaking rights but no voting rights	Chair, Secretary, Treasurer Worker or volunteer Representative of subgroup or other group Contributing member
No voting rights and restricted speaking rights	Representative of subgroup or other group Invitee to discuss specific topics or make presentations Consultant Advisor
Right to attend only. No voting rights and no speaking rights	Observer Representative of network or forum Shadowing member or officer
Receive minutes and/or reports; no voting rights, no speaking rights and no right to attend	On mailing list

---

Honest and open discussion about participation and answers to questions (such as those outlined in Box 14.9) are important. If a youth worker is unsure about whether a young person will be listened to when attending an adult committee meeting, this needs to be honestly communicated. Encouraging a young person to go to a committee meeting without knowing what to expect could lead to disappointment and a lack of tangible outcomes. At the very least, a discussion of possible scenarios is advisable. Preferably, young people attending meetings should be prepared with clear explanations of their roles and the procedures of the meeting.

Box 14.9   Do I want to be involved in this decision?

Factor	Questions raised
Relevance	Do I understand the topic, the discussion, the decision and its impact? Am I interested in this topic or the decision? Do I care? Will the decision make any difference? Will my participation affect anything?
Purpose	What is the purpose of the decision? Is there another agenda? Is a decision being made? What is it? What are the choices? What are the implications of the different choices? What are the potential impacts of this decision? Will this decision have effects other than those intended? Do I want this responsibility? Do I have concerns about being involved in this decision (e.g. reputation, other repercussions, lack of confidence)?
Process	Do I have sufficient information on which to base a decision? Can I ask about this? Will my questions be answered? Will the options be discussed? Is there too much information? Are too many decisions being made? Do the others making the decision with me understand me or my perspective?
Power	Will my opinion or decision be listened to? Respected? Implemented? Do the mechanics of the process or culture of the organisation enable me to agree or disagree with what is being decided? How will my involvement be perceived by others?

Essential skills for developing participation

- Focusing on participation
- Recognising levels of participation
- Promoting positive attitudes towards young people
- Developing young people's control
- Improving services for young people
- Involving young people in organisations
- Enabling young people to participate fully

Further reading

Read about Arnstein's (1969) and Hart's (1992) ladders of participation. Driskell (2002) provides a wealth of ideas about ways to involve young people in community development. Wates (2000) outlines tools to use to develop participation. Ledwith and Springett (2010) examine a theoretical approach to participatory practice. Conger and Riggio (2007) discuss leadership and ways to develop young people as leaders. Hudson's (2009) book on managing third sector organisations has a wealth of examples about organisational structures that can be used to train young people and other managers about participation and responsibilities.

References

Arnstein, S. R. (1969) 'A ladder of citizen participation', *Journal of the American Institute of Planners*, 35(4): 216–24.

Conger, J. A. and Riggio, R. E. (2007) *The Practice of Leadership: Developing the Next Generation of Leaders*. San Francisco, CA: Jossey-Bass.

Driskell, D. (2002) *Creating Better Cities with Children and Youth: A Manual for Participation*. London: Earthscan.

Hart, R. (1992) *Children's Participation: The Theory and Practice of Involving Young Citizens in Community Development and Environmental Care*. London: Earthscan.

Hudson, M. (2009) *Managing Without Profit: Leadership, Management and Governance of Third Sector Organisations* (3rd edn). Directory of Social Change.

Ledwith, M. and Springett, J. (2010) *Participatory Practice: Community-based Action for Transformative Change*. Bristol: Policy Press.

Max-Neef, M. A. (1991) *Human Scale Development: Conception, Application and Further Reflections*. New York: Apex Press.

Merton, B. et al. in the Youth Affairs Unit, De Montfort University (2004) *An Evaluation of the Impact of Youth Work in England*. Research Report RR606. Nottingham: Department for Education and Skills.

Shier, H. (2001) 'Pathways to participation: openings, opportunities and obligations, in line with article 12.1 of the United Nations Convention on the Rights of the Child', *Children & Society*, 15(2): 107–17.

Wates, N. (2000) *The Community Planning Handbook: How People can Shape their Cities, Towns and Villages in Any Part of the World*. London: Earthscan.

15

Developing Generative Themes for Community Action

Dave Beck and Rod Purcell

Young people often have limited control over many of the decisions that affect their lives. This chapter takes a learner-centred approach, arguing that young people themselves are best placed to identify their own needs and interests. Adopting this approach requires practitioners to dismantle hierarchical barriers and be prepared to share power with the young people they are working alongside. The authors outline the philosophy which lies behind this approach and the practical strategies for delivering it. Their aim is to enable young people to develop skills and confidence in making their own decisions and to participate in decision making processes.

The main rationale for participative methods is based on the belief that people themselves are best placed to know what their problems are and, with the right support, can develop the most appropriate solutions to those problems. It is therefore incumbent on workers to develop approaches which tap into that local knowledge and capacity for change. To do anything else is to impose external culture and values and, even for the best of reasons, further disempower the communities we work with. As Paulo Freire puts it: 'One cannot expect positive results from an educational or political action program which fails to respect the particular view of the world held by the people. Such a program constitutes cultural invasion, good intentions notwithstanding' (Freire, 1972, p. 93).

There is no such thing as a neutral position, and it has to be recognised that youth and community work is about taking sides. The National Occupational Standards for Community Development Work recognise this and identify promoting social justice as a core value underpinning practice. As the great American community organiser Saul Alinsky commented, this means taking the side of the have-nots, those who are

---

This chapter is edited from Beck, Dave and Purcell, Rod (2010) 'Developing Generative Themes for Community Action', *Popular Education Practice for Youth and Community Development Work*, Exeter: Learning Matters.

left out and overlooked (1989). Workers therefore have to be on their guard for policies and initiatives which, although purporting to be for community empowerment, actually impose the vision, values and agenda of outside bodies.

The current social policy context in the UK has much to say about participation, but not everything which claims to be participative gives local people a genuine say in the issues that affect their lives. Often what is described by professionals as participation is simply information giving, or a consultation exercise where the community is presented with a limited range of pre-determined options. Even where partnership structures are established there are usually significant power and resource imbalances between the community and agencies. Genuine examples of participation where the community has equality with agencies are rare.

It would be fair to say that youth and community workers often find themselves in the situation where they are trying to develop local participation in issues, services and events which have been decided outside the community. This could range from trying to get people to use the new 'one-stop shop', to getting participants for pre-decided training courses, to persuading people to engage in local authority-led community planning processes.

There are several implications which flow from this model of practice. Firstly, the fundamental power relationships within the community have not changed; external bodies are still making decisions on behalf of local people, albeit with some marginal choices being left to them. Secondly, the worker has to put large amounts of time and emotional energy into trying to persuade people that these are issues and services which are important to them. This can lead to workers burning out and communities feeling as if they are being battered by regular waves of new policies and initiatives and becoming even more 'apathetic' and 'hard to reach'. This calls into question the sustainability of this model, both for workers and communities. Finally, if all of this energy and effort is going into working with issues that are not necessarily the community's main concern, it means that our practice masks these real concerns and further silences and disempowers the community.

An alternative form of practice must therefore be employed. In the rest of this chapter we suggest that workers need, as their first point of departure, to help communities focus on the issues which are of concern to them and, importantly, which they are prepared and able to do something about. Let us then consider the role of the worker in this alternative model of practice.

What is the worker's role?

Since the 1960s most youth and community workers have come to believe that their role is not that of the expert who decides what is best, but to help people themselves decide what their needs are and how best to meet them (Batten, 1967). However the role is multi-faceted, complex and contested by different theorists and stakeholders in the field of community development.

In the current social policy context in the UK, workers find themselves caught between conflicting role demands. Indeed, this has always been so. On one hand, the principles and values of community development cast workers in the role of developing people's ability to think critically and act to effect authentic, sustainable social change.

On the other, there are expectations for them to be deliverers of services with prescribed targets and outputs to be met. Workers will have to negotiate and sometimes fight to have a space to practise under the first set of expectations in order to make a difference in the communities which they serve. As Peter McLaren puts it: 'We require a revolutionary movement of educators informed by a principled ethics of compassion and social justice, a social ethos based on solidarity and social interdependence' (1998, p. 451).

Theorists such as Freire, McLaren and Ledwith suggest an approach to practice which is underpinned by particular concerns and commitments. Ledwith (2005) identifies five vital areas: a commitment to collective action for social and environmental justice; a process of empowerment through critical consciousness and participation; an analysis of power and discrimination; an understanding of the dominant ideas and the wider political context; and collective action based on this analysis which deals with root causes and not just symptoms. It is clear from this that the worker is not a blank canvas who, with no previous experience or values, seeks only to work with the community's agenda. Rather they are intentionally agents of change seeking to encourage sustainable social change through critical reflection and collective action.

This is particularly important here at the early part of the twenty-first century, because the current dominant ideology that shapes social policy and practice is that of the individual. Explanations of social problems centre increasingly around individual pathology or family inadequacies. Therefore, issues of youth unemployment might be understood in terms of lack of appropriate parenting and not in the context of wider societal and structural issues.

It becomes clear then that approaches to empowerment of communities in which workers simply go and ask people what they want are surely doomed to failure since, without a process of critical reflection, people will inevitably respond to symptoms rather than root causes and even the symptoms will be understood and responded to in the light of the dominant discourse of individual pathology.

And so the role of the worker in a model of practice which leads to genuine empowerment is this. Firstly, to have a thorough understanding of the issues which are important to the local community. Secondly, to understand the wider social and political context that gives rise to those local conditions. Thirdly, to develop processes whereby local people can critically reflect on their experiences in the context of the wider world. And finally, to support a process of collective action that aims to achieve personal and social transformation.

Problem-posing methods

As we have established, the first step in the process of a transformational practice is helping people to question the social reality in which they live, with all its injustices and contradictions, but which they experience as normality. Ira Shor (1993, p. 26) describes this as a process of questioning answers rather than merely answering questions. Through this process people cease to be objects and become writers of their own story (Jesson and Newman, 2004).

Within this model of practice workers develop materials and processes which enable people to critically reflect on their social conditions and analyse them in the context of the wider world. This suggests a democratisation of learning since the knowledge which is created and the conclusion which is drawn are not within the gift of the worker but are created by the group. It also indicates a shifting of power from the individual expert to the group. Not that this is an easy or automatic process – far from it. Because of the unequal social relations we all live in, we automatically default to our socially conditioned roles. It is very common for workers to feel that they must have all the answers and for the groups they are working with to defer to their expertise and look for direction and answers. These ingrained social roles must be struggled against if real empowerment is to be achieved.

Problem-posing methods use codifications of generative themes as their starting point. Essentially, these are concrete representations of an aspect of people's lived reality. For example, a group could be presented with photographs of housing conditions on their estate. This has the effect of enabling them to see again images that have become invisible to them. It is at this stage that the problem-posing method starts.

A typical range of questions that the group might explore are:

Think of a group situation that you have been involved with recently.

- Who officially had power in this setting?
- Who else might have executed power through personality, relationships, etc.?
- How did that affect the functioning of the group?
- What messages were implicit in this about gender, class, ethnicity, etc.?

Assume that you are working with this group.

- How might you promote personal and social transformation?
- What power does the worker bring to this situation?
- What are the range of effects this could have on the group?
- How do you ethically justify intervening in this way?
- What do you see happening?
- Why is it happening this way?
- How do people feel in this situation?
- Whose interest does it serve?
- Who holds power in this situation?
- Is your experience the same or different to this?
- Are there any things happening economically or politically which are having an impact on this situation?
- Is there anything being done to improve this situation?
- Is there anything we could do to improve it?
- How might we do this?
- Who else could be involved?

The result of these discussions will be a critical understanding of the issue, personal awareness of the individual's relationship to the issue, understanding that the issue is experienced collectively, and an outline for a programme of action. The role of the worker is to facilitate this process, to learn from it, but not to direct it. Inevitably this often raises issues for the worker when the programme of action may conflict with agency agendas.

Dialogue

Inherent in the worker's role to facilitate discussion is an understanding of the idea of dialogue. Freire describes dialogue as a form of revolutionary communication (Freire, 1972). From this we can see that he is describing not a mere conversation but communication set in a context of two transformed relationships; this is an intentional process. Although it is not prescriptive in its outcomes it is trying to achieve something in particular and that is *conscientisation*. This is a state which Freire describes as:

> [a] particular quality of critical awareness which enables people to consider a range of options in the ways they act, and enables them to choose a course of action deliberately and with the intention to change some aspect of their reality. (1972, p. 101)

It is built on two sets of transformed relationships: the relationship between teachers and learners, and the relationship between learners and knowledge.

> Educator and learners all become learners assuming the same attitude as cognitive subjects discovering knowledge through one another and through the objects they try to know. It is not a situation where one knows and the others do not; it is rather a search, by all, at the same time to discover something by the act of knowing which cannot exhaust all the possibilities in the relation between object and subject. (Freire, 1976, p. 115)

In order to achieve this transformation, the worker must understand the culture and community which is the social location of the learner and then cross the border. In that way they act in solidarity with the learners; no longer seeing them as *the other* (Mayo, 1999). The starting point for this learning process is that no one knows the full picture, neither the teacher nor the learner, but that together we can discover new knowledge. This does not mean that the worker has the same role as the learner but that they have complementary roles in the group as the whole group both teaches and learns.

As an example, a youth worker might want to discuss sexual health with a group of young people. In a traditional form of practice what was to be learned would be decided by the worker; this could be the use of condoms, the nature of sexual diseases, and/or available health resources. The worker might then set up group discussions, screen videos, distribute leaflets and arrange visits to other projects in order to enable the group to learn what the worker had decided were the important lessons for the group. We can see that in this model, the worker does not learn but only teaches, and the group learns. No matter how well meaning, this is external knowledge imposed on the group from outside. For people to act on knowledge they must believe in it, and this is unlikely to happen when it is simply the case of adults once again telling them what is right and wrong.

By contrast, a transformational approach to the subject of sexual health would be qualitatively different. The worker, realising she does not know all there is to know about the sexual health issues that are important to the group, would seek to know what young people understand, experience and feel about sexual health issues, as well as understanding the received wisdom about safe sex practices. These elements would then be explored by the group through dialogue. Within this, understandings and assumptions would be challenged in order to develop an authentic understanding of how people are positioned within the issue. The outcome of the dialogue would not be known since it is developed by the group and not the worker. They might think that issues of identity and power are more central to them in making positive decisions about their sexual behaviour. This might also include much of the information contained in the traditional approach but the young people themselves would decide what was useful and how it fitted into their own understanding of the world. In this way an internal impetus for change is developed rather than the external imposition of the traditional approach.

From this we can see that within traditional forms of practice, knowledge is seen as a commodity which must be successfully transmitted from teachers to learners. To paraphrase Foucault, *knowledge is power*, and youth and community workers need to recognise this fundamental point. Within transformative education, existing knowledge is the starting point and is to be critically examined through co-investigation of the learning group. Through this process of co-investigation new understandings are developed and new knowledge is created. Because this knowledge is created and owned by the group it has power.

Part of the effectiveness of this social approach to learning is its ability to enable us to analyse our assumptions – why we think the things we think. This can reveal the boundaries which block us from developing new ideas and new action.

What is a generative theme?

In order to galvanise community action, the worker must first identify issues about which people have a passion and a willingness to take some action. Freire calls these issues generative themes. He identifies domination and liberation as the overarching or global generative themes. These global themes are expressed at every level within society. People experience them as boundary situations. An example of a boundary situation from community-based education is the very common experience of working with a group of community activists who, although intelligent and able, feel stupid and non-educable. This understanding of themselves could have been produced by things teachers have said to them, failing in formal education and believing when they are told by other members of the community that education is not for them. However it is produced, it feels like a real and insurmountable barrier which will effectively keep them from risking education, which further strengthens the barrier. Only when they begin to see an alternative future for themselves and are able to see the injustice of the education system that failed them and a society which is prepared to put them on the scrapheap – and get angry about it – do they have the ability to challenge that barrier.

A generative theme is an issue about which people feel strongly and willing to take some action. Much of the government-sponsored youth and community work we see today flows out of centrally determined strategies by which local issues and projects are identified. This results in workers spending much of their time recruiting local people into programmes that they did not choose. This is not only inefficient but it casts workers as subjects and the community as objects to be worked on, thereby strengthening feelings of alienation and disempowerment.

However, a generative theme is not something that comes automatically; it has to be worked for. This is in part because our education system does not invite us to be critical thinkers, leading us to passively accept the situations we find ourselves in. On one occasion I was talking to a young man who lived in a run-down area of Glasgow. When I asked him if he had ever experienced any discrimination in his life he said no. This was despite the fact that he had been unemployed for several years, had addiction problems and was living in poor-standard housing in a state of long-term poverty. It was several days into the programme we were going through that he came back to me in amazement. 'I've been discriminated against all my life!' he said, but up to that point he hadn't been able to see it and could not therefore take any steps to change.

It is also difficult because encounters between workers and the people they work with are encounters of power. The workers, whether they want it or not, have status, experience, and access to resources. The community have learned to be dependent, reliant on authority figures and passive. An essential element in the process of individual and social transformation is the struggle to transform this worker/client – teacher/learner relationship. Through dialogue, which we discuss in detail below, people find voice and value which can enable, even briefly, these contradictions to be transcended. It is this experience that begins to build a vision of a more human, more democratic, more nurturing and creative world.

Often communities are described as apathetic but their education and experience have taught and conditioned them to be passive and silent. The worker must therefore find creative ways to enable people to re-see their lives and to examine their assumptions and what they have taken for granted. This examination is often a disturbing and emotional process, leaving people feeling angry that they have endured the situation for so long. This emotional energy is an indispensable aspect of a transformational process; it is the fuel that initiates and sustains action. If the issue you are working on does not engender emotion and passion, it is not a generative theme; any action that flows from it is likely to fizzle out or require the worker to cajole people along.

Listening surveys

Traditional forms of practice usually rely on qualitative and quantitative research methods to provide an evidence base for practice. The inherent danger in these approaches is that inevitably the worker's own experience and value-base will shape the issues focused on, and the questions asked will in turn shape the answers obtained and the action that results. For example, an organisation which has been set up to deliver skills training to get people back into work may well carry out some initial research to identify what the community wants. It will of course ask training-related questions and get training-related answers. This will then justify the action they take within the community as being 'community-led'. It is obvious that if you asked the same group of people different questions, you would get a very different picture of what the community needed.

Often these studies treat local communities and the people within them as data sets to be analysed. Needs are usually ascribed according to agency priorities rather than the openly expressed views of local people. The overall effect is to treat people as objects for analysis rather than subjects who have the right to self-determination. The Freirean approach seeks to reverse these power relationships and support local people to define both the needs of the area in which they live and the solution to their problems. Key to this process is the creation of generative themes. An example of a generative theme is shown in Table 15.1.

One practical way of identifying a generative theme within a community is by carrying out a listening survey. Listening in this context denotes a permanent attitude on the part of the subject who is listening, of being open to the word of the other, to the gesture of the other, to the differences of the other (Freire, 1998, p. 107). The key skill in a listening survey is having an open mind. As Purcell commented:

> For this (listening survey) to work it is important to adopt the Zen approach of expecting nothing. That is to be open to anything and any interpretation and not to approach with a mind fixed on particular sets of issues or an attachment to a specific course of action. (Purcell, 2006, p. 239)

A listening survey can be a challenging task as people's feelings may be contradictory and are seldom clearly expressed. Often a 'presenting issue' such as young people on the streets may be a symptom which hides the underlying issues (for example, the lack of youth provision and difficult home environments).

Hope and Timmel (1999) outline the nature of a listening survey. Teams of workers, often made up of a mixture of development workers and local people, seek to identify the issues within the community that people have the strongest feelings

Table 15.1 Generative themes

Theme	Economic causes of the problem	Who controls the decision-making on the problem?	What are the culture, values and beliefs held about the problem?	What is the present national, provincial, and/ or local policy on the problem?
Young people drinking on street corners	Limited disposable income; access to cheap drink; lack of job prospects; few youth venues	Parents; shop owners; police; local authority	Drinking is a sign of being grown up; need to drink to be accepted by peer group	WHO Declaration on Young People and Alcohol, 2001; Crime & Disorder Act 1998; Parenting Orders; Confiscation of Alcohol (Young Persons) Act 1997

about. The process is to find situations where people are involved in informal conversations – shops, bars, outside schools, waiting rooms, etc. – and listen for the issues about which people are worried, happy, sad, angry or fearful. In particular, the team is listening for issues which relate to six themes which are common to groups of people living together:

1 meeting basic physical needs;
2 relationships between people;
3 community decision-making processes and structures;
4 education and socialisation;
5 recreation and beliefs;
6 values.

The key issues are then presented back to the community by the use of codes, which leads to critical reflection and collective action.

Conclusion

Workers must seek out generative themes within communities in order to harness the energy and passion to achieve social change. Genuine participation will come about through engaging people in the critical examination of their lives and providing structures to support action on the themes that emerge. This approach to working with people seeks to support empowerment that leads to genuine change. As such it acts as an antidote and stands as a critique of top-down approaches which seek only to ameliorate symptoms and pacify people.

References

Alinsky, S.D. (1989) *Rules for Radicals: A Practical Primer for Realistic Radicals*. New York: Vintage Books.

Batten, T.R. (1967) *The Non-Directive Approach in Group and Community Work*. Oxford: Oxford University Press.

Freire, P. (1972) *Pedagogy of the Oppressed*. Harmondsworth: Penguin.

Freire, P. (1976) *Education: the Practice of Freedom*. London: Writers and Readers Publishing Cooperative.

Freire, P. (1998) *Pedagogy of Hope: Reliving Pedagogy of the Oppressed*, Freire, AMA (notes), Barr, R.R. (tr.). New York: Continuum.

Hope, A. and Timmel, S. (1999) *Training for Transformation, Vol 4*. London: ITDG Publishing.

Jesson, J. and Newman, M. (2004) 'Radical adult education and learning', in Foley, G. (ed.) *Understanding Adult Education and Training*. Crows Nest, NSW: Allen & Unwin.

Ledwith, M. (2005) *Community Development: A Critical Approach*. Bristol: Policy Press.

Mayo, P. (1999) *Gramsci, Freire and Adult Education*. Basingstoke: Palgrave Macmillan.

McLaren, P. (1998) *Life in Schools: An Introduction to Critical Pedagogy in the Foundations of Education*. New York: Longman.

Purcell, R. (2006) 'Lifelong learning and community: social action', in Sutherland, P. and Crowther, J. (eds) *Lifelong Learning: Contexts and Concepts*. Abingdon: Routledge.

Shor, I. (1993) *Education is Politics: Paulo Freire's Critical Pedagogy*. New York: Routledge.

16

Working with Groups of Young People

Jane Westergaard

Changes in education have led to the creation of new roles intended to provide 'support' for young people. Much of the work that 'youth support workers' do is focused on working with individuals, but it also requires them to develop skills in working with groups. This chapter looks at the benefits of working with young people in groups, the different forms that group work can take, and the roles that different practitioners can play in supporting young people's learning and development in groups.

Introduction

The changing education landscape in recent years has placed an emphasis on employing a range of individuals whose role is to provide 'support' to students. The focus in teaching and learning has been informed by an argument for greater emphasis on the *individual* and supporting them in meeting their needs. What this support consists of and who delivers it is not always easy to unravel. There is an ever-increasing list of job titles that describe specific functions for those who work closely with young people in schools and colleges, but who are not them-selves teachers. These 'para-professionals' make up a significant proportion of the work force in secondary schools and further education colleges, and in the UK these roles include teaching assistants, classroom assistants and learning mentors.

This chapter is edited from Westergaard, Jane (2009) 'The Role of Youth Support Workers with Groups of Young People', Chapter 1 in *Effective Group Work with Young People*. Open University Press. Reproduced with the kind permission of Open University Press. All rights reserved.

In the USA, Europe and Scandinavia, alternative job titles describe similar roles: tutors, learning support staff or student advisers, for example. There will be others for whom the support of young people in education is central to their work; however, they are not based permanently in educational institutions, but are regular visitors to them. These 'visiting' youth support professionals are likely to include careers' advisers, personal advisers, school counsellors, and youth, community and health workers. It would be foolish to argue that this wealth of support for young people is not welcome – it is. But it would also be true to say that for many working in education, including teachers and managers, the plethora of roles can lead to confusion.

Much of the support provided by those in the roles outlined above is likely to be one to one, whereby helping relationships are established between a young person and an identified worker. Through these relationships, the individual needs of the young person are recognized and strategies for development and change are discussed and implemented. However, increasingly youth support workers are finding themselves in situations where they are working with groups of young people, not just individuals, in order to offer support. Initially, providing support in a group context may feel daunting, as many youth support workers will not have had extensive training in how to prepare, plan and deliver group learning. However, it is important to recognize the benefits of offering support to young people through group work as well as in one-to-one relationships. Group work provides youth support workers with the opportunity to access and utilize possibly the greatest 'support' resource they will have at their disposal – the young people themselves.

This chapter begins by focusing on the range of youth support roles currently in evidence in schools and colleges and it 'unpicks' the key tasks undertaken by these youth support workers. Once the range of youth support work roles has been examined, the chapter establishes the *key features* of group work that takes place in educational environments (e.g. school, college), but is *not* delivered by teachers or those with extensive training in learning and teaching methods. The distinction between 'supporting' group work, which focuses on the group members' 'personal learning and development', and other activities, which involve young people working together in a group in educational settings, will be made clear. The chapter compares personal learning and development (PLD) group work delivered by youth support workers with three other forms of group activity:

- teaching;
- informal education;
- therapeutic group work.

By undertaking a comparison of teaching, informal education and therapeutic group work, the distinctive features of PLD group work will be made clear. But first, who are these youth support workers and what do they do?

The youth support worker role

A visit to any secondary school or further education college in the UK (and in many other countries in Europe and throughout the world) will introduce the visitor to a range of professionals who are working together to support students and to ensure that young people are encouraged and enabled to achieve their full potential. The case studies that follow will help to provide some clarity about the range of youth support roles in education (note: all case study examples included in the chapter are drawn from experience, but do not represent real people or institutions).

Kelly – the teaching assistant in Manor Way School

Kelly works with designated students who have been identified as needing additional support in the classroom. Kelly's role is to accompany these students to lessons and to plan with each individual subject teacher how she can support these young people in the classroom. This support may involve assisting with literacy and numeracy, or it may require Kelly to offer help in dealing with emotional or behavioural problems. Sometimes, the students who Kelly supports are disruptive in class. On a number of occasions Kelly has been asked to work with small groups of young people away from the classroom to assist them to develop their personal skills.

Lloyd – the learning mentor in Manor Way School

Lloyd, like Kelly, works with pupils who have been assigned to him for additional support. The young people Lloyd works with have poor attendance records and are at risk of exclusion. Lloyd supports these young people on a one-to-one basis, inside the classroom and outside it. He also works with groups of young people who have been identified as needing help with particular issues such as anger management or family breakdown.

Ashraf – the Manor Way School personal adviser

Ashraf is based in the school and he works with young people who have been referred to him because they are experiencing barriers to progression. These barriers might include disruptive behaviour, lack of confidence or other issues including poor housing, risk of exclusion or social problems like bullying. Ashraf works on a one-to-one basis with young people, but he also runs group sessions when shared issues or problems emerge with students in the school.

Sam – the youth worker employed by the local youth service

Sam is not based permanently in the school. But he visits every evening to work as part of an extended schools project where students (and their families) are invited to use the facilities of the school to encourage their development outside school hours. Sam works with groups of young people who have been identified as needing support with personal and social issues. He runs group sessions on confidence building, assertiveness, drug and alcohol awareness and team building.

Crystal – the careers adviser based in the local careers centre

Like Sam, Crystal is not based in the school, but visits regularly to talk to individual students about their options and progression during and after school. Crystal mainly works on a one-to-one basis with young people, but she also delivers group sessions on topics like job applications, CV writing and interview skills.

Joe – the sexual health personal adviser, Julie – the looked after children personal adviser, Jatinder – the teenage pregnancy personal adviser, Karin – the youth offending personal adviser and Carl – the intensive needs personal adviser based in the local youth support service

Joe, Julie, Jatinder, Karin and Carl are not based in the school, but are frequent visitors to it. Young people are referred to them as needs are identified by teachers in the school. They work with 'targeted' young people on a one-to-one basis, but they also work with groups when appropriate. Jatinder, for example, is delivering a 'cyber baby' course (where young people prepare to look after a 'baby', programmed to cry and demand attention) to a group of 16-year-old girls.

> ## Pat – the pupil referral unit worker
>
> Pat works in the Pupil Referral Unit that is attached to Manor Way School with young people who have been excluded. These young people have not responded positively to the school environment or are school-phobic. Like many of the other youth support roles, Pat offers one-to-one help and he also undertakes group work that focuses on the personal learning and development needs of pupils in the unit.

This is a brief and by no means comprehensive glimpse of the range of para-professionals working in one school and its associated services. All the roles identified involve building one-to-one relationships with young people, and this element of youth support work is dealt with extensively on training courses and through the literature (Egan, 2002; Nelson-Jones, 2005; Reid and Fielding, 2007). However, what has become clear is that youth support work is not focused solely on one-to-one work with young people. In all the case studies outlined above, group sessions form an aspect of the work. So, what kind of group work do youth support workers deliver and how is it different from other forms of group activity?

What is a group?

The concept of 'a group' is familiar to us all. We are each likely to be involved in groups as part of our everyday lives. For example, we are almost certainly members of a family group, a friendship group, a group of colleagues and other social groups. In addition, we are likely to have played an active part in an educational group (i.e. school) from the age of 5 to 16 and we may, at points in our lives, have accessed other groups: support groups, protest groups, political groups, religious groups, sport groups and special interest groups. Each group would have performed a specific function at a particular time, fulfilling a range of requirements from our very basic human needs (food, warmth, shelter) to more complex emotional and psychological needs (belonging, being loved, being understood, developing knowledge, learning a skill). 'Group work' therefore can mean different things at different times.

However, the purpose of this chapter is to consider ways in which practitioners can work with a specific kind of group. The definition of this group is: *a group made up of individuals with shared needs who will benefit from the opportunity to work with, and learn from others in order to develop skills, knowledge and attitudes.*

What kind of group work takes place in education?

In addition to PLD sessions, there are three recognized forms of structured group work in education in which young people may be engaged. These three group activities are different from the PLD sessions facilitated by youth support workers in significant ways. As stated earlier, the three activities are:

- teaching;
- informal education;
- therapeutic group work.

By examining each of these in some detail and comparing them with PLD sessions, it is possible to distinguish what makes PLD group work delivered by youth support workers different.

Teaching

Teaching has seen a significant shift both in terms of philosophy and delivery in the last 50 years. Gone is the focus on 'chalk and talk', underpinned by an emphasis on the transfer of knowledge from 'expert' to beginner. This has been replaced by the concept of the student as 'learner' (Brandes and Ginnis, 1996), taking an active part in students' learning and gaining knowledge, skills and attitudes by engaging with a range of activities in the classroom. However, in spite of this philosophical shift towards students as engaged participants in their own learning, the focus of teaching tends to remain curriculum-driven and therefore largely abstract. Simply put, this means that the subject matter being taught will, generally, be focused on a preset curriculum. This curriculum is likely to be driven by the need to develop understanding and skills in relation to a specific subject. The level of this understanding will be 'tested' at regular intervals, culminating in a nationally recognized qualification that demonstrates the acquisition of knowledge and competence in a particular field of study.

As part of a nationally set curriculum, most students are required to study specific subjects in school. These are likely to include English, maths and science – all subjects which, it could be argued, will be of value in later life, but none of these sets out specifically to address the personal and developmental needs of the individual learner. For example, learning about the 'theory of relativity' does not necessarily meet the individual personal development needs of a 15-year-old, whereas learning about how to 'manage my time effectively' does.

It is the role of teachers to ensure that they plan their lessons based on the requirements of the curriculum, and for many there may be little flexibility in the way in which this is delivered in the classroom. Teachers will be experts in their own academic, creative or technical subject matter and they will strive to make their teaching interesting; to engage and inspire the learner and to encourage success in the subject.

Although teachers will have an understanding of the ways in which young people learn, their primary concern is to deliver knowledge about *something* (i.e. their chosen subject). Those involved in delivering PLD group sessions are more interested in helping young people to acquire knowledge about *someone* (i.e. themselves) rather than a 'subject'. The case study below provides an example of what teaching involves.

Bob – the history teacher in Manor Way School

As a subject teacher, Bob is responsible for ensuring that his teaching adheres to a nationally established curriculum, where he has little choice in selecting the subject matter or topic, but some flexibility in choosing appropriate learning methods. To a large extent, the purpose of Bob's role is to ensure that pupils have knowledge of a specific subject area and will gain a qualification in it. This may encourage pupils to develop an interest in the subject; it may inform future choices they make concerning career, but it is unlikely to have a direct impact on their lives in terms of addressing their personal needs.

There have been recent developments in the UK in relation to the introduction of a social curriculum that includes personal, health and social education (PHSE) and citizenship lessons (Department for Education and Skills, 2003). This goes some way to raising awareness of issues that may impact on young people as they make transitions into adulthood. This aspect of the curriculum bears close resemblance to PLD group work in that it aims to assist young people to understand their world and to consider how they can play an active and useful part in society. It is likely that students will be involved in discussions and will undertake activities to broaden their knowledge and understanding, just as they will in PLD group sessions. Although for the most part, the PHSE curriculum is delivered by teachers, youth support workers are often involved, as their expertise in areas related to personal learning and development is recognized and welcomed.

Informal education

The subject of informal education has been written about extensively in recent years (Jeffs, 2004; Davies, 2005) and many youth workers will have undertaken training in informal education. It is not possible, within the remit of this chapter, to explore in depth the theory and concepts underpinning informal education. However, it is important that the distinction between informal education and PLD group work in education settings is made clear.

Adams provides a useful definition of informal education:

> Groups are made up of individuals who are defined a 'group' because of a common task. The aim of the group is to achieve the chosen task, such as build a carnival float, organise a party, canoe a river or just have fun together. Facilitating achieving the task is not the only area on which the worker needs to focus, equally important is the individual in the group and the group itself. All three aspects need maintaining by the worker, rather like juggling three balls in the air. If too much attention is paid to one, another may fail. (Adams, 1993: 311)

What is evident here is that learning takes place by engaging with, and setting out to achieve, a specific task. It is, for example, by building a carnival float or organizing a party that participants begin to work together, to learn more about themselves and to understand how they work with, and fit into, the structure of the group. Similarly, in PLD group sessions, participants are encouraged to address their issues and needs by developing greater self-awareness through working alongside others. However, in PLD sessions this 'learning about self' is achieved in a variety of ways by undertaking a range of activities. These activities would not necessarily focus on one overarching project as described by Adams. In fact, the focus of PLD group work is on the needs of each individual in the group, and activities are planned to enable group members to achieve their own personal outcomes. Thus, the individual group members themselves and not the 'project' or 'task' form the focus of the sessions.

Clearly then there are similarities between informal education and PLD group work. For example, the methods of educating are likely to draw on experiential learning techniques (Kolb, 1984), and the success of the sessions will depend on the relationship between the facilitator/educator and the group. But there are differences too. The PLD session, unlike informal education, is likely to take place in a formal setting and will have preset, specific aims and objectives. These aims and objectives are unlikely to link to a piece of project work (i.e. building a carnival float) but will focus on the individual needs of the group members (i.e. developing anger management techniques). Furthermore, PLD sessions are likely to be bound by time (within a school day) and are less likely to be attended on a voluntary basis.

The case study outlined below provides an example of a piece of informal education group work.

Ade – a youth worker in Manor Way Youth Club

Ade is a youth worker based in a youth club near Manor Way School. Ade does not have any direct involvement with the school, but does work with groups of young people who attend the school. In particular, Ade works with young men who come to the club. He takes groups of young people on residential trips and involves them in project work. The group he is working with currently are helping to develop a plot of scrubland at the back of the youth club into an area where they can play ball games.

Therapeutic group work

Teaching and informal education are examples of two types of group activity that are likely to take place in educational settings. The third, therapeutic group work, delivered by a counsellor, has a different emphasis again. Geldard and Geldard explain:

> Generally, the purpose of therapy groups is to attempt to alleviate specific symptoms or problems (e.g. depression or anxiety). Their focus is either on identifying and treating emotional and/or psychological difficulties seriously interfering with the child's functioning and/or addressing developmental and social problems. Therapy groups are remedial, help to promote personal adjustment and are reconstructive. (Geldard and Geldard, 2001: 17)

At certain times in the lives of many young people, emotional, psychological and behavioural issues can become hard to manage and seemingly impossible to resolve, resulting in detrimental and sometimes harmful effects. It is during puberty and adolescence that significant physiological and emotional changes are taking place. Many young people are able to 'manage' these changes in a positive way, with the support of family, carers, friends, teachers and others, but some young people struggle to make sense of, and deal with, the new pressures that becoming an adult brings.

It is when barriers to the emotional and psychological development of the young person are identified, and their behaviour is a cause for concern, that it may be helpful to consider counselling or therapy as a means of enabling young people to understand and manage their life better. So, how is counselling or therapy in a group context similar to PLD group sessions, and, importantly, what are the distinctions between the two?

First, both counselling and PLD group work focus on the needs of young people. Both counsellor and facilitator will have an understanding of the issues affecting the group with whom they are working. However, in a counselling setting, it is likely that the issues or 'topic' that form the focus of the session will require in-depth emotional and psychological exploration, and the counsellor will be skilled in enabling this to happen. In PLD sessions, a specific topic or focus for discussion is also identified that meets the individual development needs of the group. However, the PLD topic is less likely to require group members to explore their emotions and psyche in such depth. For example, a school counsellor may work with a group of students who have eating disorders. The counsellor will help the group to explore their feelings, consider causes and work with the emotional trauma present. By contrast, a youth support worker may undertake a PLD session on 'keeping healthy' for a group who have been identified as being 'at risk' of not eating healthily. This session will encourage group members to reflect on their eating habits, to understand more about what healthy eating is and to consider what they need to do in order to eat healthily.

Second, both therapeutic group work and PLD sessions are planned. Group members in both cases will know where the session is being held, how long it will last, why they are there and who will be leading it. However, in the case of counselling sessions, although a broad topic is identified, the agenda for the session is set by the group themselves, and the content of the discussion and the issues that are raised are not usually directed by the counsellor. Generally, there are few planned activities within these sessions. Group members are talking about feelings and the counsellor will use therapeutic techniques to encourage positive change. By contrast, PLD sessions will have been prepared in detail by the facilitator prior to the group meeting. This means that the facilitator will have a session plan that will identify aims and objectives, they will have considered activities to use and they will have identified timings for these activities. Although this plan is negotiated and agreed with the group at the outset, and can be amended if necessary, the PLD session will follow a clear structure.

The third similarity between the two activities is that the aim of each is to work towards positive outcomes. The purpose of both the therapeutic groups and PLD sessions is, in part, to enable participants to make some kind of change or development in their lives. In the case of therapeutic groups, these changes may be needed in order to ensure group members' physical and psychological well-being, or even survival (e.g. changes in relation to self-harming, eating disorders and drug/alcohol abuse). This may involve attending a number of sessions and ultimately may require referral to medical professionals. PLD group work, by contrast, focuses on the positive changes that young people can make in order to help them to achieve specific life goals and transitions (e.g. changes concerning decision making, assertiveness, job seeking). However, unlike therapeutic group work, PLD sessions do not set out to provide in-depth emotional or psychological support in a therapeutic context.

Finally, and probably most importantly, therapeutic groups and PLD sessions are likely to share a philosophy based on humanistic (or person-centred) principles (Rogers, 1965) that can be applied in both a therapeutic and an educational context. Both counsellors and facilitators, for the most part, believe that young people are best placed to make their own decisions. They also believe that young people have the resources at their disposal to make informed decisions and to plan and take action in relation to these, leading to positive change in their lives. However, where the work of a counsellor in a therapeutic context will be informed mainly by established counselling perspectives (e.g. cognitive behavioural therapy or solution-focused approaches), the PLD facilitator will be drawing on a range of theoretical approaches (including learning theory, group dynamics and counselling concepts) to underpin their work with groups.

The case study detailed below provides an example of a therapeutic group session facilitated by a school counsellor.

Jaya – the school counsellor at Manor Way School

Normally, Jaya's work is with individuals who have been referred by staff in the school (or by pupils themselves) when issues or concerns have arisen. However, recently a group of young people in the school has been identified as self-harming. Jaya has agreed to work with this group, providing them with a safe place in which to discuss their thoughts and feelings about what they are doing and why. At times these sessions can become very emotional as the young people share difficult and painful experiences with their peers.

Having examined teaching, informal education and therapeutic group work, a sense of the key features of personal learning and development group sessions delivered by youth support workers is beginning to emerge. Let us explore this further.

Personal learning and development: group work delivered by youth support workers in educational settings

The case study set out below provides an example of a PLD session delivered by a youth support worker in school.

Lloyd – the learning mentor (a youth support worker) in Manor Way School

Six 15-year-olds have been referred to Lloyd for support. They are at risk of exclusion because their attendance is poor. What has become clear, through an assessment of needs, is that each of the young people concerned finds it difficult to concentrate in class, becoming easily bored and distracted. Lloyd has put together a programme of eight sessions for this group that focus on developing each member's concentration skills. The sessions are also aimed at raising self-esteem and confidence. Lloyd has structured the sessions with activities and input that will draw on the experience and expertise of group members. At the end of each session, every group member will develop an action plan to work towards before they next meet.

It is clear that the personal and social issues facing many young people in education (which may include having a lack of confidence, experiencing low self-esteem, encountering barriers to opportunities, making decisions about their lives and experiencing difficulty in managing their behaviour) can be addressed to great effect in a group context. The purpose of PLD 'group work' is to attend to these personal issues, focusing on each *individual's personal and developmental needs*, but in a group setting. To state this in simple terms, the *young person* rather than a specific curriculum area or subject provides the focus for the PLD group. Gerrity and DeLucia-Waak describe PLD group work as 'psycho-educational/guidance groups', whereby young people work together in a group involving:

> Role-playing, problem-solving, decision-making, and communication skills training to teach specific skills and coping strategies in an effort to prevent problems (i.e. anger

management, social skills, self-esteem, assertiveness, making friends). (Gerrity and DeLucia-Waak, 2007: 98)

Higgins and Westergaard (2001) define PLD sessions as 'guidance' group work, citing the activity of group work within the broader curriculum area of careers education and guidance. They acknowledge that delivering group work forms part of the role of the careers adviser, with topics such as 'decision making', 'choosing options', 'team building', 'preparing for transitions' and 'exploring occupations' being addressed in 'one-off' group sessions as part of a careers education and guidance programme. However, PLD sessions are increasingly being delivered outside the education curriculum as part of a larger, integrated personal, social and health education strategy within schools. It is true to say, however, that Higgins and Westergaard describe with accuracy the key characteristics of guidance group work and these features can equally be applied to PLD sessions. They identify three underpinning principles:

1 The topic to be addressed in the session should focus on the *personal needs of the individuals* in the group. It is the responsibility of the facilitator to identify a topic for the session and they will set out to ensure that it will be relevant and useful to the group members at that time. Consideration should be given to a number of points: Where are the participants 'at' in terms of their personal and educational development? What are the key issues that may be around for them at this point in their lives? Is there a specific need (developmental, educational, emotional or behavioural) for this group of young people that could be addressed through group work? What might be the underpinning issues related to the topic? *In the previous case study, Lloyd is working with a small group of 15-year-old pupils to address their lack of concentration in the classroom. He has prepared a series of sessions that focus on the needs of this group. One of the sessions is entitled 'Developing Concentration Skills'.*

2 The session should include an opportunity for group members to focus and reflect on *their own position* in relation to the topic, otherwise known as 'What's in it for me?' Although the topic has been identified as being 'of use' and relevant to a number of young people, each individual's response to it may be quite different. *For example, every young person in Lloyd's 'Developing Concentration Skills' session will have the opportunity to consider 'Why do I find concentrating hard?' and 'What gets in the way of me being able to concentrate?' and 'What might I do about it?'*

3 The session should consider the specific *action that each individual needs to take* in relation to the topic. It is not enough that the topic is discussed; underlying issues are explored and the session ends with a greater understanding for individuals within the group. Positive though this is, PLD group work goes further. Individuals within the session are helped to think about how they would

like 'things to be different' and to identify specific actions that they can take as a result of the session to effect some change. *For example, the young people in the 'Developing Concentration Skills' session will have the opportunity not only to consider what the issues are for them in relation to the difficulties they experience in concentrating, but they will also make specific plans in relation to developing their own concentration skills: 'How am I going to change?' and 'What do I need to do now?'*

The theory that supports PLD group work draws from a range of disciplines. Practitioners undertaking PLD sessions may be familiar with approaches and concepts underpinning education and learning, but they should also acknowledge skills and models that derive from other disciplines, such as counselling and guidance. PLD facilitators are not teachers, although they may use knowledge of learning theory (Kolb, 1984; Gardner, 1993; Brandes and Ginnis, 1996) and group management techniques (Young, 2005) in their work. Neither are they counsellors, although they may use counselling skills and methods in order to build a rapport with the group (Westergaard, 2005). PLD facilitators perform a unique function with an emphasis that is different to teachers, informal educators and counsellors. However, PLD facilitators are skilled professionals who are clear about what they are setting out to achieve. Institutions in which youth support workers are employed should recognize and celebrate the fact that these practitioners are able to offer something unique and valuable to their pupils.

Table 16.1   A comparison of different group work sessions

	Personal learning and development	Teaching	Informal education (youth work)	Therapeutic groups
Purpose	To develop self-awareness and make positive change	To gain knowledge, understanding and skills relating to an academic, creative or technical subject	To develop personal skills and abilities through interaction with others	To gain greater self-understanding, receive support and work towards change
Content	Based on an assessment of individual needs Interactive and experiential	Based on a curriculum/syllabus Range of teaching methods used	Based on developing skills in working together Project-driven	Determined by participants Sharing thoughts and feelings
Style of leadership	Facilitating	Managing the class	Leading by example Role-modelling	Counselling

Conclusion

In this chapter, two key points have emerged. First, the job titles associated with youth support work are many and varied. However, there is a common link between the roles in that all youth support workers aim to assist young people to engage with their learning, manage their lives and achieve their aspirations. This is done using a range of techniques and interventions, one of which involves working with groups. Providing support to young people in a group context can have advantages over one-to-one interactions. The single most significant advantage is that there is an additional resource to be had in the shape of the group itself. By sharing feelings, thoughts, ideas and experiences with each other, young people can often be helped to find solutions to the problems they face and the decisions they need to make. By so doing, they can be enabled to manage their lives more effectively.

Second, what has become evident is that the types of group session delivered by youth support workers are different to other, established forms of group activity. For example, where teachers focus on delivering a preset curriculum, youth support workers engage with the needs of the individual. Where informal educators develop the skills and qualities of group members by undertaking project work or informal learning opportunities, youth support workers deliver structured, time-bound sessions. Where counsellors focus on the in-depth emotional needs of their clients, youth support workers attend to social, behavioural and personal issues. Of course, youth support workers will draw on theoretical concepts from the other disciplines to inform their work with groups, but they will also be clear that what they are offering young people is something quite different and of value in its own right.

References

Adams, J. (1993) 'Group work in the youth service', in K. Dwivedi (ed.) *Group Work with Children and Adolescents*. London: Jessica Kingsley.

Brandes, D. and Ginnis, P. (1996) *A Guide to Student-centred Learning*, Cheltenham, Nelson Thornes.

Davies, B. (2005) 'Youth work: a manifesto for our time', *Youth and Policy*, 88: 527, Leicester, The National Youth Agency.

Department for Education and Skills (DFES) (2003) *Citizenship: The National Curriculum for England*, London, DfES.

Egan, G. (2002) *The Skilled Helper: A Problem-management and Opportunity–development Approach to Helping*, 7th edn, Pacific Grove, CA, Brooks/Cole.

Gardner, H. (1993) *Frames of Mind*, 2nd edn, New York, Basic Books.

Geldard, K. and Geldard, D. (2001) *Working with Children in Groups*, Basingstoke, Palgrave.

Gerrity, D.A. and DeLucia-Waak, J.L. (2007) 'Effectiveness of groups in the schools', *The Journal for Specialists in Group Work*, 32 (1): 97–106.

Higgins, R. and Westergaard, J. (2001) 'The role of group work in careers education and guidance programmes', *Career Research and Development,* 2: 4–17, Cambridge, CRAC.

Jeffs, T. (2004) 'Curriculum debate: a letter to Jon Ord', *Youth and Policy,* 84: 55–61, Leicester, The National Youth Agency.

Kolb, D. (1984) *Experiential Learning: Experience as the Source of Learning and Development,* Englewood Cliffs, NJ, Prentice Hall.

Nelson-Jones, R. (2005) *Theory and Practice of Counselling and Therapy,* 4th edn, London, Sage.

Reid, H.L. and Fielding, A.J. (2007) *Providing Support to Young People: A Guide to Interviewing in Helping Relationships,* London, Sage.

Rogers, C. (1965) *Client-centred Therapy,* Boston, MA, Houghton Mifflin.

Westergaard, J. (2005) 'Counselling and the youth support worker role: are these connected?' In Harrison, R. and Wise, C. (eds) *Working with Young People,* London, Sage.

Young, J. (2005) *100 Ideas for Managing Behaviour,* London, Continuum.

17

Youth Work in a Digital Age

Jane Melvin

Young people are living in a world where technology is rapidly changing and where digital literacy is increasingly important. New technologies provide opportunities for youth workers to engage with young people and support their learning in different ways. They also present a number of challenges for youth workers and for organisations working with young people. This chapter looks at a range of research into young people's use of technologies, and considers some of the practical ways in which youth workers can make use of digital technologies in their day-to-day practice with young people.

The case for promoting digital youth work

Social network sites, online games, video-sharing sites, and gadgets such as iPods and mobile phones are now fixtures of youth culture. They have so permeated young lives that it is hard to believe that less than a decade ago these technologies barely existed. Today's youth may be coming of age and struggling for autonomy and identity as did their predecessors, but they are doing so amid new worlds for communication, friendship, play, and self-expression. (Ito, 2009: 1)

Youth work is a practice that is 'young people-oriented and young people-centred' (Davies, 2005: 12), which might lead us to assume that the use of new technologies in youth work is commonplace. Youth workers take young people's concerns and interests as a starting point, and aim to create 'safe spaces' to support young people in their learning and development (NYA, 2001–2011). The concept of 'digital safe spaces', therefore, has a relevance to the youth worker of today. A key challenge for practitioners and for organisations working with young people is how to keep up with the pace of technological innovation and 'the rapidity with which children and young people are gaining access to online, convergent, mobile and networked media' (Livingstone et al., 2011: 4) in order to respond to young people's needs in a way that is both current and relevant.

A recent report by EU Kids Online found that 60 per cent of European 9–16-year-olds go online daily, with a further 33 per cent reporting that they go online at last weekly. Eighty-seven per cent of young people are able to access the internet at home, with 33 per cent also accessing the internet through a mobile device or smartphone (Livingstone et al., 2011: 12). In its claim to be a truly young person-centred discipline, these statistics are not something that youth work can afford to overlook: the opportunities for creativity, collaboration and education are perhaps too great to pass up, and the risks too great to ignore.

Learning in the twenty-first century involves much more than just accessing content. It requires us to be able to 'think critically and solve complex problems, work collaboratively, communicate effectively, and pursue self-directed learning' (Oblinger, 2010 [online resource]). Youth work, which is underpinned by concepts of experiential learning and informal learning, aims to provide opportunities that support young people's learning, whether this is through them successfully achieving an outdoor problem-solving task involving planks and oil drums, or through using Facebook to campaign against cuts to services.

The case for promoting digital literacy

Digital literacy has been defined as 'those capabilities which fit an individual for living, learning and working in a digital society' (Charlton, 2012). Youth work, which aims to support young people's learning and development, has an important role to play in developing young people's digital literacy. This includes helping young people to develop the skills and understanding they need in order to communicate effectively online, and develop their competencies in 'participation, collaboration, network awareness, and critical consumption' (Rheingold, 2010: 16), as users of social media and members of online communities.

James Gee (2009) identifies three key ways in which new technologies are changing the way we communicate, collaborate and learn which are also relevant to a discussion about the relationship between new technologies, learning and youth work. Firstly, technologies are changing how we interact with the media, information and society. They provide people with new opportunities to share ideas and information and to be creative. In a youth work context, developments in social media mean that it has never been easier for young people to search for information, to communicate with people with similar interests or ideas, and to contribute to debates about issues that they feel strongly about.

Secondly, Gee also highlights the potential for digital technologies to change the balance of 'participation and spectatorship' (2009: 20). Participation, as a cornerstone of the youth work curriculum, is about enabling young people to understand and contribute to democratic processes and to make their voice heard. Digital media provides new opportunities for doing this. There are some excellent examples of work being done by the British Youth Council (BYC) and the UK Youth Parliament (UKYP) where they are using social media not only to communicate, but also to promote their work and the profile of young people.

Gee's third point is that 'digital tools are changing the nature of groups, social formations, and power' (2009: 20). A key challenge for formal and informal educators alike is how to develop the skills of being 'tech-savvy' (Gee, 2008: 23). This requires practitioners as well as young people to have the confidence to use digital sources in a discerning, enquiring and safe way. Youth workers need to develop their skills and confidence in the use of digital tools and technologies, including through training and staff development, in the same way that they might develop their skills in offering advice on substance misuse or the issuing of condoms.

A quick search of Facebook using the words 'save+youth+club' shows what young people are able to do for themselves when their services are threatened. This perhaps represents a power shift which could result in feelings of professional disempowerment for youth workers who are less familiar with or less confident in using new technologies. Given the principles that underpin youth work, I would suggest that working in the digital world is no different to working with young people in other unfamiliar surroundings, such as outdoor education activity or on a trip abroad. Here, most youth workers would think nothing about exploring the context and environment alongside the young people, facilitating the discovery process and being honest about the things that they are not skilled at or don't know.

In a context where online social networks are increasingly being used to connect people, and to support communication and collaboration, new technologies can help youth workers to extend their practice, building on what they are already doing face-to-face with young people. For youth workers, new technologies present 'a huge opportunity to engage with young people and have real dialogue, especially those who have previously been off our radar' (Davies and Ali, 2009: 1).

Natives, immigrants, residents, visitors or outsiders?

Young people are a common target for stereotyping, and today's generation are no different. Labels such as 'Millenials' (Howe and Strauss, 2000), 'Digital Natives' (Prensky, 2001) and the 'Net Generation' (Tapscott, 2009) have been used to describe the current generation of young people who are seen as being competent and confident users of new technologies. They are presented as being very different to previous generations of 'digital immigrants' (Prensky, 2001), who are less confident and skilled, and who have had to learn the new language and culture of the digital age.

It has been claimed that 'digital natives' are people who have been born and brought up in a digital age, and have specific learning styles and preferences that are different from those of their educators, the 'digital immigrants'. Small and Vorgon (2008) even propose that the brains of children and young people today are neurologically wired in a different way to the pre-digital generation, in that they process information simultaneously rather than sequentially. Other commentators are more sceptical about claims they see as 'an academic form of a "moral panic"' (Bennett et al., 2008: 775), rather than being based on solid empirical evidence. In a youth work context, a potential danger of these sorts of labels is that they might prevent youth workers from looking at the wider issues surrounding young people's use of new technologies, including issues of digital exclusion. Davies (2011) identifies that many young people might be more confident in picking up new digital tools and exploring them. But that does not mean all young people have that confidence, nor does it mean that those who are using digital tools really understand them.

White and Le Cornu (2011) are critical of the 'digital native' typology, and have proposed a continuum model as a way of looking at how individuals of any age might approach and use new technologies (Figure 17.1).

Visitor  Resident

Figure 17.1 Digital visitors and residents' continuum (White and Le Cornu, 2011)

Source: 'Visitors and residents: a new typology for online engagement', *First Monday* [online], 16.

They suggest that individuals could be placed in a number of positions along this continuum and that their position will be related to their motivation for engaging digitally. If someone is largely positioned as a Visitor, for example, this does not mean that they have less skills and knowledge than someone who might be classified as a Resident, just that their motivation or perception is different. Visitors need to see some concrete benefit from their use of particular tools; they will only use tools if they think they will help them to achieve a defined goal or task.

Thinking about this in relation to youth work, it might be that some youth workers would position themselves as Visitors because they do not see a need to work with young people in their digital spaces. They may competently use the new technologies that they need such as email, search engines and websites, but 'won't get' other technologies, or 'don't want' to embed themselves further. Here, the question about the digital spaces that young people inhabit and whether youth workers should have a presence in those spaces is relevant. Is digital youth work about the youth worker's needs and preferences, or is it about working from the starting point of the young person?

In contrast, Digital Residents are seen as people who see digital media as a resource that they frequently engage with, including for sharing information about their life and work:

> A proportion of their life is actually lived out online where the distinction between online and off-line is increasingly blurred ... When Residents log off, an aspect of their

persona remains. This could be in many forms ranging from status updates to social networking platforms, to artefacts in media sharing sites or opinions expressed in blog posts or blog comments. (White and Le Cornu, 2011)

Here the challenges are different. The 'Resident' youth worker may use all the new technologies at their disposal to engage, communicate and build relationships with young people. But they also need to be mindful of overlaps between their personal and professional identities and the traces that they may leave behind online. For example, if you use Facebook to engage with young people, do you have a professional profile that separates your professional identity from your personal identity? If not, how do you avoid young people seeing your 'off-duty' self, or avoid being included 24/7 in the world of the young people who are your 'friends'? Some youth workers just use organisational or youth centre pages simply as a communication tool, circumventing the issue of live messaging or having young people as 'friends' (Melvin, 2012). Different youth organisations also have different policies about the use of social networking sites, which can work to support, restrict or frustrate the youth workers who have to comply with them.

Using digital technologies

Recent research involving 33 youth workers working in a variety of UK youth work settings (Melvin, 2012) shows the typical digital tools that are being used (Figure 17.2):

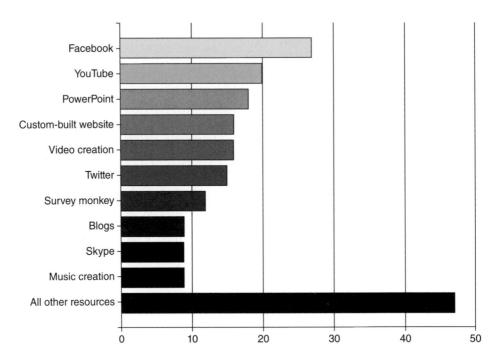

Figure 17.2   The digital tools being used in youth work contexts with young people (Melvin, 2012)

Tools covered by the 'other' category in the chart are mainly those of specific web-sites such as careers-based sites, music-based sites such as iTunes or www.spotify. com, photo-sharing sites such as www.flickr.com or www.picassa.google.com or animation/presentation sites such as www.xtranormal.com or www.animoto.com.

Youth workers were using a wide variety of tools in their practice, including for publicity, communication, animation and film-making, interviewing, photo manipu-lation and sharing. They were also using search engines and custom-made websites to seek information, advice and guidance. The outcomes they identified as achiev-ing through their use of digital tools were often achieved despite restrictive policies and out-dated equipment. This throws up potential ethical dilemmas for youth workers who might be using their own laptops or smartphones, or those of young people, to support their work.

Youth workers identified additional outcomes that had resulted from their use of digital technologies. Figure 17.3 relates to outcomes that youth workers iden-tified from their use of the top five digital tools identified, which were Facebook, Twitter, YouTube, custom-built or organisational websites and video creation:

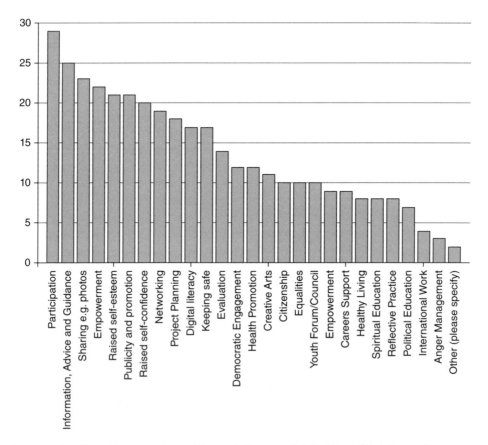

Figure 17.3   The outcomes achieved through the use of digital tools (Melvin, 2012)

Given this evidence, it might seem strange that youth workers would choose to with-draw from, or separate themselves from, tools that would enable young people to be more 'literate' in today's world. The question of whether new technologies should be incorporated into youth work practice in the same way as other youth work tools – sport, creative arts, conversation – is one that is proving challenging to promote, mainly due to the decisions made by policy makers and managers that err on the side of safety rather than learning and development. Green and Hannon identify that:

> The current generation of decision-makers – from politicians to teachers – see the world from a very different perspective to the generation of young people who do not remember life without the instant answers of the internet or the immediate communica-tion of mobile phones. It is these decision-makers who shape the way that digital technologies are used in the system and who set them up to limit their use and role in everyday life. (2007: 15)

Recent research involving English youth workers has identified a number of barriers, including organisational policy and outdated hardware and software, that prevent them from working effectively in a digital context:

> ... then the policy was clarified to me by a senior youth worker and it said that part-time youth workers could no longer have a profile. ('Lucy' as cited in Melvin, 2012)

> ... they had a very restrictive IT policy and in fact, I've just tried to open up a file earlier, and I've been told 'oh no that's social networking, you can't get on it' so I then have to go to the IT department to get them to lift the restrictions in order to allow us to do things. ('Robbie' as cited in Melvin, 2012)

Livingstone identifies educators as being divided into two camps: optimists and pessimists (2002, 2005: 2). Optimists see the opportunities that new technologies offer for promoting participation, creativity and debate. Pessimists, on the other hand, see these technologies as posing a threat to authority, traditional values and childhood innocence.

For youth workers trying to promote the use of digital technologies within their work, there are often organisational barriers in the way and complicated processes to go through:

> I spent about a year just setting up the protocols and procedures for being allowed to use Facebook and working with [the] policy makers ... to try and overcome some of the barriers. For example, I wanted to be able to send Bluetooth messages out on behalf of the detached workers if they were out in the park, just a mass Bluetooth say-ing 'We're in the park. Come along' but we couldn't do that because the policy says that it's dangerous for young people to have their Bluetooth turned on all the time and that we should be encouraging them to turn it off when they're not using it. ('Sharon' cited in Melvin, 2012)

Whilst the safeguarding of young people using digital media is undoubtedly impor-tant, discussion about young people's use of these tools is often dominated by fears which are often based on lack of knowledge and lack of practical experience.

Some youth organisations have even taken the step of banning the use of sites such as Facebook altogether. Even where social networking is permissible, youth workers identified restrictive policies that prevented them from working effectively with young people (Melvin, 2012):

> The youth service would say 'you're not allowed to have Facebook' and [even if you get permission] … you're meant to have the privacy settings on so you can't see what any of them are doing … As a youth worker it's quite important to see what's going on in the community, to know what they're all talking about … I might know that someone's been done for drugs or … that there's been a fight at school … I actually believe that I'm a part of [an online] community [Facebook]. ('Georgia' cited in Melvin, 2012)

Whilst some might say that it is not morally justifiable for youth workers to seek to be included in the online spaces that young people use, there are perhaps two important elements to consider. Firstly, there is the issue of young people's awareness of their online identity and the information that they share about themselves. If a youth worker is presenting a professional profile that young people can 'friend', it is also an opportunity for awareness-raising in relation to privacy settings and what is appropriate to share publicly.

Secondly, the issue of what youth workers do with information that they overhear or become aware of, particularly in relation to illegal or risky activities, is one to which there are often no set answers. The context of young people's online discussions can be likened to that of a camping trip where young people are in their tents, chatting about all manner of things as they prepare to go to sleep. The youth worker who is wandering around outside, trying to encourage them to quieten down, might be party to a number of different conversations, and has to make decisions about whether they comment or challenge at the time, bring up the issue the next day, keep a watching eye or simply ignore it. The same can be said of posted comments, or inappropriate images that are shared: the youth worker has the opportunity to then be proactive in raising issues of concern.

Where organisations allow the use of social networking sites, youth workers need to be particularly aware of their own online identity and what they allow to be public or private. Many youth workers now adopt a professional profile for social networking sites such as Facebook or Twitter, which clearly identifies them as a youth worker, states the purpose of their presence and sets the boundaries for contact, for example not using the live or direct messaging function, which can be difficult to record. The creation of centre or organisation pages rather than individual profiles, enables the tasks of updating and moderation to be shared, and many youth workers have worked with a group of young people to become 'admins', thus increasing their ownership and input into the project (Melvin, 2012).

Other issues that need to be considered when using social networking sites for youth work include how to respond to the posting of inappropriate comments and/ or images, whether posts should be moderated prior to going public, and how pages reflect the image of the youth worker and/or organisation.

The digital divide

So-called techno-evangelists often assume that the digital world applies to all users equally. Whilst researchers have found that the digital world is accessed by many young people for a variety of activities, they have also found that a significant percentage may not have the access and/or the skills that 'digital natives' are credited with having (Bennett et al., 2008). This could result in the 'neglect' of those young people who are less able to access or who are less interested in using digital media, particularly those whose 'socio-economic and cultural' status means that their choices are limited. The existence of a 'digital divide' is an issue that has been identified by youth workers:

> I would say 60/70% have it at home but there are those who don't and I would say it was the ones who were maybe a bit more neglected or who didn't have as much money and so often bullied, and wanted to be on Facebook so that they could then become part of the Facebook thing. It's kind of like 'of course they want to be on Facebook' so that they can make comments to their friends and talk about things. ('Debbie' cited in Melvin, 2012)

The Understanding Digital Exclusion Research Report identified users of digital media as being in one of a number of categories:

- **Digitally included:** have easy access to the internet at home, work or place of education, and make use of it.
- **Digitally determined:** use the internet, but do not have access at a convenient location (home, work or college).
- **Connected non-users:** are those who live in a household which has internet access but do not use it.
- **Disconnected non-users:** are those who don't have access at home and do not use the internet (Freshminds, 2008: 24).

These definitions can be helpful for youth workers when they are determining the needs of a young person in relation to digital media and learning, rather than just assuming that all young people will be the same.

The report also identified that many young people who are not in education, employment or training (NEET) often do not have access to new technologies at home, and rely on 'pay-as-you-go' mobile phones, which they use for texting rather than calls because of the cost. A 'significant minority' of young people did not have good digital literacy skills but would use digital media of all types more if they had better access or could afford it.

These findings throw up challenges for youth workers responding to the needs of young people who will have varying levels of digital literacy, and who might have very different levels of digital access. It also indicates an issue of equality that youth workers need to respond to:

> ... being in a really deprived area, I know I get young people that are coming here simply to go on Facebook because they haven't got a computer at home and they can't

access it on their phones. A lot of their homes don't have Wi-Fi. I have so many coming in and asking for the Wi-Fi code and it's purely because they don't have that facility at home, so I feel that to be fair and equal in society we have to offer that because not everyone has it at home. ('Georgia' cited in Melvin, 2012)

Safeguarding young people in a digital age

There is a role for youth workers to play in relation to digital safeguarding and this is no different to any other safeguarding or harm minimisation work that might be carried out, for example, in relation to safer sex or smoking cessation.

The Child Exploitation and Online Protection Centre (CEOP) strongly promotes the message that digital technologies are a powerful resource that should be used by young people. The role of educators is to work with young people to 'communicate and exchange information (including digital communication) effectively, safely and responsibly' (CEOP, 2010: 3)

The CEOP websites (www.ceop.police.uk/ and www.thinkuknow.co.uk/) both contain useful information and resources for youth workers, as well as details of training in relation to working with young people around online protection issues.

Research conducted by EU Kids Online in 2011 found that 40 per cent of children and young people had experienced one or more form of online risk including:

- 14% of European 9–16-year-olds have seen sexual images online.

- 6% of 9–16-year-olds have been sent nasty or hurtful messages/been bullied online.

- 30% of 9–16-year-olds have had contact online with someone they have not met face to face.

- 15% of 11–16-year-olds have seen or received sexual messages online. (Livingstone et al., 2011: 30)

It also found that 9 per cent of 9–16-year-olds had met someone off-line that they had initially met online (Livingstone et al., 2011). Research conducted by the National Centre for Missing and Exploited Children in the USA suggests that, when young people had met someone offline after meeting them initially online, 25 per cent of these meetings involved the young person going alone, or taking a friend rather than trusted adult. Young gay men or those who are questioning their sexuality were seen to be particularly at risk. Four per cent of young people had received an online sexual solicitation where the perpetrator had also tried to make offline contact (National Center for Missing & Exploited Children, 2001–2011).

The CEOP Report Abuse button is an easy way for young people to report someone who behaves inappropriately online (Figure 17.4). This is now to be found on many popular sites and can also be downloaded as an 'app' to customise websites and browsers. Many sites also have their own reporting processes which can usually be found under 'account settings'.

Figure 17.4 The Click CEOP Report Abuse button

Issues that young people need to be aware of in terms of their online (as well as off-line) safety include 'sexting', where young people send pictures of themselves in provocative poses or states of undress. In the age of the smart phone with built-in camera and video functions, it has become increasingly easy for young people to put themselves into vulnerable positions simply by sending a photo to a friend. CEOP advises young people as follows:

> Before you post a photo of yourself, think whether you would be happy to pass it around the dinner table to your parents, your grandparents, your teacher or even your future employer or university. If you wouldn't, it's probably not a good idea to pass it on to anyone. (CEOP, 2010)

Cyberbullying is just as distressing for the victim as other forms of bullying. It commonly involves the use of tools such as Internet Messenger (IM) or Blackberry Messenger (BBM), social networking sites, or texts. It is more common on sites where people can comment anonymously, create a false profile or where contact details or phone numbers can be withheld, meaning that the victim won't necessarily know who the bully is. It also has the potential to involve many more people, as others are able to read posts and comments. If the 'friends' of someone being cyber-bullied decide to join in by 'liking' comments, this will just compound what is happening. Keeping privacy settings locked down, only accepting friend invitations from people that they know, 'unfriending' people who do not behave appropriately, and reporting cyber-bullying, are key areas for youth workers to promote as ways of keeping safe online:

> We have young people coming in here to the youth club who are upset and we say 'what's happened?' and they say 'somebody's said this about me on Facebook' or 'I've received this text on my mobile' ... Young people are friends with everybody in an internet sense, so then everybody has access to their information, and if they post information on their Facebook account which for them seems quite innocent, there are young people that will say 'you know what, we're going to do something with that information to make that young person's life miserable.' Our workers have to spend time supporting that young person in understanding that this is going on and trying to help them understand how they can stop it – without stopping using Facebook, so it is difficult. ('Martin' cited in Melvin, 2012)

Support for those experiencing cyber-bullying can be sought from a number of sources, including Cyber Mentors (www.cybermentors.org.uk/), Childline (www.childline.org.uk/Explore/Bullying/Pages/CyberBullying.aspx) and Cybersmile (www.cybersmile.org/).

Creating critical consumers

As well as working with young people so that they keep themselves safe online, youth workers also have an important role to play in helping young people to become 'critical consumers' of digital media, people who can make judgements about the quality and validity of the websites and platforms that they use. Dan Gillmor (2008) suggests five 'Principles of Media Consumption' that can usefully be adopted by youth workers when they are working with young people to promote awareness of issues about their use of the internet: 'the principles come mostly from common sense. They include scepticism, judgment, reporting, expanding one's own vision and understanding how it all works' (Gillmor, 2008: 7).

Young people need to be aware of how their internet usage can be tracked, as well as what they are showing or sharing publicly. Social networking sites will often use default privacy settings when an account is set up, and the user has to know this and then be proactive in relation to changing them.

How familiar are you with issues like privacy settings on social media sites or determining what counts as a reliable source of information? How would you support a young person to check out whether the information given in a YouTube video is correct? Many people claim to have learnt new skills from watching YouTube: check out the 'How To Peel a Head of Garlic in Less Than 10 Seconds' video (www.youtube.com/watch?v=0d3oc24fD-c) – is it as easy as they claim?

> I struggle to work with the under 13's who legally shouldn't have a Facebook account, but who lie about their age in order to get one to be like their mates. It's slightly better if the date of birth that they give means that they are technically under 18, but if they sign up to an adult profile because they've given themselves that birth date, they don't get any of the 'protection' that they'd get from setting up an initial child's account. There's also the issue that they've lied to get the account and that parents don't seem to care. ('Bill' cited in Melvin, 2012)

This comment throws up some interesting thoughts about how young people 'consume' new technologies, as well as what youth workers can do to help young people develop critical thinking. Young people are often described as hedonistic or seeking immediate gratification, which can mean that they can act impulsively without thinking through the implications, especially if there is peer pressure to follow what their friends are doing. What is the role of the youth worker who works with under 13s who have Facebook accounts? A young person is unlikely to cancel their Facebook account just because a youth worker tells them that they are underage, so how could you support them to become critical consumers?

Conclusion

The use of digital tools contributes to improved outcomes for young people such as increased communication skills, information-sharing, conversation and discussion, creativity, campaigning, networking, participation and agency, as well as promoting digital literacy at a number of levels. However, the promotion of new technologies within youth work contexts often relies on the passion and interest of individual youth workers rather than being linked strategically to the twenty-first century learning needs of young people.

Organisational restraints and policies that are frequently determined from a safe-guarding or managerial perspective may not take into account the educative aims of youth work, meaning that youth workers are sometimes frustrated in their efforts to work with young people effectively using digital tools. As a profession, there are still many other challenges to overcome in relation to professional values, training, inter-net access and safety, and access to equipment that is fit-for-purpose.

Youth workers who are engaging young people digitally promote the use of social media sites such as Facebook, Twitter and YouTube, as effective communica-tion and engagement tools, and as a way of positively promoting the image of young people. New technologies also offer opportunities for creativity, collaboration and agency that have the potential to enhance not only digital literacies, but also social and emotional literacies.

As youth workers, we are working with young people in an extraordinary world, where technological and digital advances are moving faster than anyone could have predicted even 20 years ago. This is the challenge for youth work: keeping pace with young people to ensure that they become safe and critical users of the digital world, and facilitating improved access for those young people on the other side of the digital divide.

References

Bennett, S., Maton, K. and Kervin, L. (2008) 'The "digital natives" debate: A critical review of the evidence'. *British Journal of Educational Technology*, 39(5), 775–786.

CEOP (2010) 'Lesson plan: Positive use of technology'. Child Exploitation and Online Protec-tion Centre. Available at: https://www.thinkuknow.co.uk/teachers/resources/

Charlton, J. (2012) *Developing Digital Literacies* [online]. Joint Information Systems Committee (JISC). Available at: www.jisc.ac.uk/developingdigitalliteracies (accessed 28 October 2012).

Davies, B. (2005) 'Youth work: A manifesto for our times'. *Youth and Policy*, 88 (Summer), 1–26.

Davies, T. (2011) 'Skills for the job: Digital literacy'. *Children and Young People Now*. Haymarket Media.

Davies, T. and Ali, J. (2009) *Social Media Youth Participation in Local Democracy*. London, The Children's Services Network.

Freshminds (2008) *Digital Exclusion Profiling of Vulnerable Groups – Young People not in Education, Employment or Training (NEET): A Profile – Communities and Neighbourhoods*, Department for Communities and Local Government. Wetherby, West Yorkshire, Communities and Local Government Publishers.

Gee, J. (2008) *Getting over the Slump: Innovation Strategies to Promote Children's Learning*. New York, The Joan Gantz Clooney Center at Sesame Workshop.

Gee, J. (2009) 'Digital media and learning as an emerging field: Part 1 – How we got here'. *International Journal of Learning and Media*, 1(2), 20.

Gillmor, D. (2008) *Principles of a New Media Literacy*, New Republic/Berkman Center for Internet and Society at Harvard University. Available at: http://cyber.law.harvard.edu/sites/cyber.law.harvard.edu/files/Principles%20for%20a%20New%20Media%20Literacy_MR.pdf (accessed 16 April 2013).

Green, H. and Hannon, C. (2007) *Their Space: Education for a Digital Generation*. London: Demos. Available at: www.demos.co.uk/publications/theirspace (accessed 4 July 2013).

Howe, N. and Strauss, W. (2000) *Millennials Rising: The Next Great Generation*. New York, Vintage Books.

Ito, M. (2009) *Living and Learning with New Media: Summary of Findings from the Digital Youth Project*. Cambridge, MA, MIT Press.

Livingstone, S. (2002, 2005) *Young People and New Media*, London, Sage Publications Ltd.

Livingstone, S., Haddon, L., Gorzig, A. and Olafsson, K. (2011) *EU Kids Online Final Report*. London, London School of Economics/EC Safer Internet Programme.

Melvin, J. (2012) Using activity theory to explain how youth workers use digital media to meet curriculum outcomes', unpublished work, University of Brighton.

National Center for Missing & Exploited Children (2001–2011) *Internet Safety Statistics* [online]. National Center for Missing & Exploited Children. Available at: www.netsmartz.org/safety/statistics (accessed 22 July 2012).

NYA (2001–2011) *What is Youth Work?* [online]. Leicester, National Youth Agency. Available at: www.nya.org.uk/about-nya/what-is-youth-work (accessed 13 September 2011).

Oblinger, D. (2010) *A Commitment to Learning: Attention, Engagement, and the Next Generation (EDUCAUSE Review)* [online]. Educause Review Online. Available at: www.educause.edu/ero/article/commitment-learning-attention-engagement-and-next-generation (accessed 3 August 2012).

Prensky, M. (2001) 'Digital natives, digital immigrants'. *On the Horizon,* 9(5), 1–6.

Rheingold, H. (2010) 'Attention and other 21st century literacies'. *EDUCAUSE Review*, 45, 14–24.

Small, G. and Vorgon, G. (2008) *BRAIN: Surviving the Technological Alteration of the Modern Mind*, London, Collins.

Tapscott, D. (2009) *Grown Up Digital: How the Net Generation is Changing Your World*, New York, McGraw-Hill.

White, D. and Le Cornu, A. (2011) 'Visitors and residents: A new typology for online engagement'. *First Monday* [online], 16. Available at: www.uic.edu/htbin/cgiwrap/bin/ojs/index.php/fm/article/viewArticle/3171/3049

18

Faith-based Youth Work – Lessons from the Christian Sector

Naomi Stanton

Faith-based youth work is becoming increasingly important in Britain today, but its relationship to wider youth work values is complex. Research into Christian youth work in Birmingham reveals a fundamental division between an approach based on traditional youth work values such as informal education, voluntary participation and young people's choice, and an approach whose purpose is to transmit the Christian faith. On the basis of these and other findings, a model of how Christian youth work operates is developed in which three 'domains' are identified – social provision, small study groups and wider integration – each with a different focus and purpose. Other researchers have found that similar themes are also important in youth work based on other faiths.

The fastest growing part of the youth work field over recent years has been the faith-based sector. The number of full-time youth workers employed by the Church of England has outnumbered those employed by the state since the early twenty-first century (Brierley, 2003; Green, 2006), and this does not take into account the growth in numbers of youth workers employed by other Christian denominations or the effect of the most recent statutory funding cuts to young people's services during the recession. There are also well established Jewish and Muslim youth work movements (Khan, 2006; Marsh, forthcoming). In addition to this there are smaller pockets of youth work provision in other faiths.

This chapter is based on research undertaken with young people and their youth workers across the Christian denominations in Birmingham.[1] After providing some information on the research study, the rest of the chapter is presented in three main sections. The first section outlines the main themes from my interviews. The second section presents an illustrative model of Christian youth work that has emerged from my research and explores how it might apply to wider faith-based youth work. The third section explores the themes presented in section one in relation to other research that has been undertaken with young people from a range of faith groups.

The chapter explores the relevance of faith-based youth work to wider youth work values. In particular it explores the tensions between understandings of youth work as a process of informal education (Jeffs and Smith, 2005), with an emphasis on choice, conversation, relationships and voluntary participation, and understandings of Christian faith-based youth work (Collins-Mayo et al., 2010) which look for a greater emphasis on faith transmission. My research found that the emphases on choice, dialogue, relationships and participation in Christian youth work settings were crucial to young people's engagement. I also found that there were tensions in Christian youth work between meeting social, spiritual and institutional agendas and explored the ways in which youth workers manage these tensions. The conflict between starting with the needs of young people and meeting institutional demands strikes a parallel with the wider youth work field where current debates are centred on the tensions between outcome-driven, targeted provision, and the soft outcomes that are often associated with universal, open access youth work. Churches often want to impose what they perceive as young people's 'spiritual needs' on all those who engage with Christian youth work, whereas youth workers recognise that young people want to choose and negotiate these needs for themselves. Similarly, in the wider youth work field, funders often define young people's specific 'social needs' whilst youth workers look for young people's participation in defining these needs.

Research sample and method

Young people who are engaging with Christianity (and their youth workers) were identified via their youth groups and churches. Interviews took place with 42 people. Thirty-four young people were interviewed and eight youth workers. The denominations of Christianity represented within the sample were Anglican, Methodist, Baptist, United Reformed, Catholic, Pentecostal, and a black majority church of no specified denomination. The interviewees were based in eight different church-based groups. The young people interviewed were aged between 13 and 21 years. Twenty-one of the young people were male and 13 were female (the gender balance was affected by the fact that two of the groups were Boy's Brigades). Three of the groups accessed had significant numbers of young people from minority ethnic backgrounds. Of the eight youth workers, two were female and six were male. Five of the youth workers were volunteers and three were paid employees of their churches.

Narrative-inquiry technique was employed: open-ended interviews in which interviewees structure and control the conversation and the researcher then uses follow-up questions for clarification (Bell, 2005: 21). In this way, my sub-questions were defined by the young person's narrative rather than their narrative being defined by my questions.

Youth workers were asked about their backgrounds, motivations, awareness of and involvement in the institutional agendas, and their understanding of the relationship between youth groups and the wider church. All the names used within the research discussion are pseudonyms.

Section one: research themes

The origins of youth work in this country are rooted in the practice of faith-based volunteers and movements, namely Christian and Jewish organisations (Clayton and Stanton, 2008; Pimlott, forthcoming). It should be of little surprise then that the characteristics of faith-based youth work might bear similarities to the values of the wider youth work field. In this section the main themes that have emerged from my research in Christian youth work settings are explored. These are 'choice and voice', 'relationships and belonging', and 'consumerism and participation'. These themes correlate with the principle elements of youth work that this chapter defends.

The themes are not distinct from each other but overlap and link together. Allowing young people to have a choice and a say in how their provision is defined is a process based on relationships and helps establish a sense of belonging. Choice and voice are linked together as one theme because together they allow for the process of negotiation that facilitates young people's participation and sense of belonging. In Christian youth work settings there is a distinction between choice and voice being offered in regards to doctrine and activities. Young people may be offered choice and voice in relation to issues of faith but not in terms of defining church provision and vice versa. In my research, young people often had more experience of choice and voice in regards to both faith and activities in their youth groups than they did in the wider church. Moreover, their sense of belonging and opportunity to participate was more developed in their youth groups than in wider church structures.

A distinction should be made between faith-based youth work in social and spiritual settings. Christian youth workers operate in both. The social settings are to provide open access youth provision for any young people who wish to attend. Spiritual settings are for smaller study groups to explore the Christian faith. Collins-Mayo et al. distinguish between youth work and youth ministry and see the open access youth provision as the former and more specific teaching groups as the latter (2010: 24). They acknowledge Brierley's (2003) assertion that youth ministry is a specialist branch of youth work. The youth workers in my research were aware of the distinction in focus between their social and spiritual settings.

Choice and voice

My research found that youth workers recognise that young people have a choice to engage with their provision as well as whether to accept the values and beliefs of the organisation. Whilst Collins-Mayo et al. (2010: 97) criticise liberal youth work for its emphasis on choice over 'truth', Nick Shepherd (2010: 152) argues that belonging to a Christian youth group nurtures faith choices. Shepherd emphasises that successful youth ministry groups are social, participatory, relational, experiential and a place where faith is connected to real life (2009: 230–231).

This was evident in the narratives of the young people I interviewed who did engage with the Christian teaching element of their youth work programmes where they praised the opportunities they were given to discuss the issues together.

> We'll have a session where we discuss something from the Bible or discuss a topic about Jesus' life, or something going on in the world and we all offer opinions, and it's good to hear different opinions. (Pete)

In addition to promoting choice, the youth workers appeared to value young people's 'voice' in defining provision. Barry explained how he develops opportunities for youth leadership:

> I believe in young leaders … We've got this thing, for the want of a better title, we call it the youth council … and they all got nominated by the young people … They're aware of budgets, they're aware of how much a youth weekend is to put on … We need to make sure, you know, they're in on those decisions … they're involved with services, they have a say. (Barry)

In this setting, the young people do influence not just their youth activities but also wider church decisions. In other settings, however, there appeared to be a distinction between the capacity for young people to exercise their choice and voice in their youth activities and the wider church.

Relationships and community

All of the young people interviewed valued the social element of their youth work provision, with relationships and social belonging being the most widely quoted reason for engagement. Connor explains it as follows:

> I've got a lot of friends here and I enjoy what we do and, you know, every day is different, like every time we meet is different … it's just a different experience and most of my friends are here. (Connor)

Danni (aged 14) explained her attendance at her youth group in similar terms: 'I like it because I meet all my friends and stuff'. The establishment of social and faith communities was significant in young people's engagement with the social provision offered by youth workers and in the smaller Christian teaching groups they provided. Matthew, aged 18 and from a non-church background, discussed his experience of moving from just the social 'youth club' type provision into these Christian teaching groups:

> As soon as I walked through those doors it was like a sense of being welcomed. A sense of love that I felt was just 'Okay, I belong here' and it was that, that initially made me keep on coming every week. (Matthew)

This illustrates how the facilitating of a social community may be significant in young people's choice to engage with a faith community. Young people expressed frustration where this sense of community was not on offer.

However, this setting was not without its tensions. Matthew went on to explain how, having felt a sense of belonging in the youth activities, he did not feel so accepted in the wider church:

> It does seem as if it's like you've got the young people and then you've got the adults
> ... There's always a divide ... And it's like the adults think they know more than the
> young people when, if they'd go to talk to some of the young people then they'd
> understand that they do know quite a lot. (Matthew)

This sense of frustration with the wider church was present in several of the young
people's narratives. However, there were those who had a positive experience
within their churches. Nancy explained how she is accepted in her church community despite facing problems in other social arenas:

> Autism is very, very isolating. I've also had eating disorders as well and that's been
> isolating ... If I've had a difficult day at college or I get bullied or something, then
> I can just come in here and know that no one's going to treat me differently because
> there are people who have been in prison and they admit that, and they know they
> won't get judged here and it's just the faith and just the Christian family, in general,
> here is just so strong. (Nancy)

The more positive experiences of church tended to occur in the less traditional
denominations and the more evangelical churches. This qualitative finding links
with the quantitative findings from the 2005 Church Census which found that
these newer churches have, on average, both younger and larger congregations
(Brierley, 2006).

The disconnection between youth work and the wider church in several of the
settings had implications for young people's transition into adult church, as seen in
the example below from an interview with a youth worker:

Naomi: ... how easy is it for the young people to make the transition to adult church
as they outgrow the youth activities?

Theresa: It isn't.

Naomi: Does it happen?

Theresa: No. And this is the big issue. I have held on to the young people, and you've
met one or two of them, some of them are 18, 19, 20.

Naomi: So you just have to keep them in the youth work, do you?

Theresa: Because it's too dull out there and I struggle. And, yes, if I'm accused of
diversifying the church because of it then I put my hands up and say, 'yes I am,
probably' but that's partly because I don't think they're taking responsibility for
the fact that they need to meet the needs of the young people.

Even in the settings where young people were well connected with their wider church,
the transition to adult church was an issue because of the numbers of young people
leaving for university. Two young people from fairly traditional denominations had
already left for university. They found it difficult to integrate into the local churches of
their home denomination in their university towns as no other young people attended
and they did not feel welcomed by the wider church. The lack of a sense of belonging
has affected their motivation to attend on a regular basis. Both these young people
have, however, retained a connection with their home youth group.

Consumerism and participation

Whilst the role of 'choice and voice' in Christian youth work settings emphasises a desire for participation, sociologists of religion suggest that there has been a move from obligation to consumption in people's engagement with religion (Collins-Mayo et al., 2010; Davie, 2007). Kendra Creasy Dean criticises the 'consumer-driven thera-peutic individualism' that she observes in American youth groups which she suggests does not inspire any real commitment to Christian beliefs and practices (2010: 5). Others have taken issue with this, pointing out that social action plays a large part in Christian youth work programmes (Clayton and Stanton, 2008; Pimlott and Pimlott, 2008). A global research project into young people's spiritual development (by the Search Institute in Minneapolis, USA)[2] found that three of the six most significant methods young people identified when asked how they nurtured their spiritual development 'involved acts of compassion, service or generosity' (Roehlkepartain et al., 2008). All of the young people I interviewed were involved in some form of volunteering, fundraising or social action through their youth programmes – both those who were just involved with social activities and those engaged with faith-specific groups. Maria explained her involvement in a number of voluntary activities within her church:

> On Sundays I steward, I'm a steward at church … On Sunday afternoons I do a dance class for the younger children … And then on the weekdays I work for a magazine and a website … I work for them as a journalist. … We put on events … so I'm part of the concert and the street team as well … I've tried to make sure that me being a Christian is not just for myself. (Maria)

The youth workers recognised young people's desire to participate, creating space for this in their youth programmes and expressing frustration where it was difficult to implement in their wider churches. Bill suggested that young people were unlikely to attend church without some element of participation in services. Many of the young people who attend his open access youth club provision are not involved with the church in any other way but the majority of them got involved with a youth-led service he coordinated that took place on Valentine's day.

> Well a church like [this one] … unless they look at their youth, you're not going to get the normal Joe from round the corner to come to church. You're going to have to give them something, and by giving young people time in the services, by allowing them to do their own services; that's how we're going to get people back through the door. (Bill)

Rather than young people acting as consumers, they were seeking youth programmes that gave them opportunities to serve, whether through fundraising for their own activities, social action in their own or other communities, participation in services (through readings or music, for example) or volunteering as leaders for younger groups. Many young people felt their contributions were not recognised. Theresa expressed her frustration with this lack of recognition and with her church's expectation that young people should fit with an institutional agenda:

> I don't think they're taking responsibility for the fact that they need to meet the needs of the young people. They don't think twice about the young people meeting their needs. (Theresa)

There are some links between the tensions outlined above and those within youth work more generally. Within the church settings I observed, youth workers attempted to start with the needs of young people, but at the same time were required to meet a church agenda; usually that of 'bums on seats' on a Sunday morning. Similarly, statutory and even voluntary sector youth workers are required to meet certain targets and outcomes, whether those of engaging particular 'at risk' groups, accrediting young people for their participation, or moving young people from NEET to EET.

Section two: towards a model for faith-based youth work

In order to manage the tensions between young people's needs and their church agenda, the youth workers I interviewed and observed appeared to separate their work into different domains. The three main domains I observed were: firstly, that of open access youth club-type provision (Domain 1); secondly, small Bible study groups for young people who were exploring Christianity (Domain 2); and thirdly, integration with Sunday services (Domain 3). The domains emphasise three categories of focus for Christian youth work: the social, the spiritual and the institutional. There is some overlap between these domains; small Bible study groups are social as well as spiritual spaces and the wider church spans all three categories. Therefore, it may be appropriate to view the domains as moving from a singular focus on the social in Domain 1 to a dual focus on the social and the spiritual in Domain 2 and a multiple focus on the social, the spiritual and the institutional in Domain 3. However, the distinction between them serves to highlight what, from my research, appeared to be the youth workers' main focus in each domain.

There are three key purposes of Christian youth work that stem from the three domains. These purposes may also be applicable more widely to other forms of faith-based community work. They are as follows:

- meeting community needs;
- allowing people to engage with faith on their terms;
- integration with the rituals and practices of a specific church/organisation.

The first of these purposes is based on the identification of and response to the social needs of the community being served and acts as the starting point for engagement with those outside of the faith community. In some settings, this might be more focused on the meeting of needs within the faith community by providing a social space for those young people from religious families. However, in most of the Christian settings I visited it was an access point for young people from non-church families into youth provision that was inclusive and non-threatening. Many young people accessed only the social domain and did so long-term. The second purpose is the space for people to reflect on and discuss faith in small groups, should they choose to. These small groups are usually informal and combine time for socialising as well as religious discussions. The final purpose of youth work I identified in my research, but by no means the most significant, was to support young people's integration into the religious organisation. Significantly, each of these purposes is based on the formation of relationships between the practitioner and the community being served, and movement between domains especially so. In the churches where this model was most developed and each of the purposes valued and supported, there appeared to be greater levels of engagement with and movement through the domains. The three domains come together to form a model of faith-based youth work that illustrates their relationship, as shown in Figure 18.1.

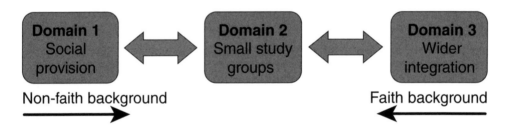

Figure 18.1 The three-domain model of faith-based youth work

The model has been developed from what was originally published as 'the three-domain model for Christian youth work' (Stanton, 2012).[3] In the Christian settings observed, young people from church families usually accessed Christian youth work initially via Domain 3 and young people from outside of the church accessed via Domain 1. Some young people moved through the domains and others remained in one domain. As explored in the previous section, the research themes of 'choice and voice', 'relationships and belonging' and the opportunities for 'participation' are often key aspects of young people's engagement with the different groups facilitated by the youth workers.

There was clear evidence in the young people's narratives of the value of the social domain, as illustrated by the examples below:

> It's really fun and you can learn a lot. And I've got a very good friend here. It's really good here. And it just gives you something to do, like on a Friday … Instead of going

out and getting drunk you can come here instead and have a laugh without alcohol involved and stuff. (Annette)

The activities that are run, as well as the people, are just nice. So it's a very nice atmosphere here and … you feel very comfortable, like there's nothing to be afraid of. You can just be yourself. (William)

The youth workers also saw the value of responding to community needs but some of them found that their wider churches did not value the social provision they offered. One youth worker was told that if the young people were not in church on a Sunday then the work 'didn't count'. Whilst this represents a rather extreme example of the issue, it was not uncommon for the success of the youth work to be measured by the number of young people in Sunday services.

There was evidence for the value that youth workers placed on the spiritual domain, as a space for young people to explore Christianity without their conception of faith being tied to a particular church. The example below illustrates this:

What [the lead youth worker] and I are doing is teaching them Christian values … so really it doesn't matter about this building. They can take what they've learned into later life … it's about each individual and what they take away from this. (Liam)

However, this enhanced tensions in settings where 'filling the church' was seen as the key purpose of having a youth worker. Yet, even in settings where young people's integration into adult church was viewed as the ultimate outcome of having a youth worker, it was often not something the wider church helped to facilitate, as exemplified earlier under the themes of 'relationships and belonging' and 'consumerism and participation'.

There is no specific domain or purpose relating to proselytising or evangelism within the model. This is due to the relational aspect of faith-based youth provision and that movement through the domains appeared to occur as a result of relationships, dialogue and social belonging rather than through preaching. Pete Ward (1997) distinguishes between 'inside-out' and 'outside-in' youth ministry. The former involves churches working primarily with the young people from within the church and the latter involves starting with young people outside of the church and engaging them in some form. The model of faith-based youth work in this chapter illustrates how youth workers are engaging a range of young people as part of their interconnected provision. Where they are engaging young people from outside of the church in the social domain, the focus is on young people's self-identified need for open access youth club provision. Only where young people choose to engage with the spiritual domain does the focus shift to what might be perceived as their spiritual, as opposed to social, needs. There was overlap in some settings, for example through a 10-minute 'God slot' at the end of a youth club session, but there were youth workers who actively avoided this overlap. In all settings, there was a clear distinction between provision that was primarily social and that which was primarily spiritual in focus.

As the model was developed in Christian settings, it does need testing as to its applicability to other faith groups. The purpose in widening it to encompass faith-based youth work generally is to begin to explore this relevance.

Section three: some defining characteristics of faith-based youth work

Because the research themes presented in this chapter stem from Christian settings, this section explores how they apply in other faith settings. Topics around young people and faith have received some recent research and theoretical focus. Some of this literature is explored below and links to the themes of my own research are identified.

Jasjit Singh (2011) found that young British Sikh adults organise their own informal faith spaces outside of institutional settings. Through organising Sikh camps, which appear to resemble some of the equivalent Christian youth festivals, young Sikhs are exercising their 'choice and voice' in developing their faith identities. The organisation of such events for other Sikh young people to share in is also evidence of their active participation and voluntary effort through their religious engagement.

Based on research with young British Muslims, Sughra Ahmed (forthcoming) suggests that Muslim youth work needs to allow space for young people to engage in open discussion and peer-facilitated learning, thus emphasising the importance of 'choice and voice'. She also emphasises the need for young Muslims to feel a sense of 'belonging' in the communities they access and for marginalisation to be broken down. Sadek Hamid (2006) distinguishes between Muslim youth work and Islamic youth work; the former represents social provision with the latter spanning the spiritual and institutional agendas. Hamid outlines tensions similar to those in my research over whether youth work focuses on young people's individual needs or the institutional agenda. He emphasises that best practice Muslim youth work supports young people's identity formation and belonging. He gives examples of young people in Muslim youth programmes being encouraged to take on leadership roles. His analysis shows that 'choice and voice', belonging and participation are key concerns in Muslim youth work despite the institutional barriers.

Shelley Marsh (forthcoming) acknowledges that early Jewish youth work was founded not just on activities but also activism. She notes the development of volunteering opportunities and, more recently, peer leadership within Jewish youth work. She gives the example of older young people organising and leading trips to Israel for other Jewish young people. The emphasis on informal education within contemporary Jewish youth work allows for young people's 'choice and voice', the development of relationships, and an emphasis on active participation, reflecting again the themes of this chapter.

In research around the issues of sex and sexuality for young religious adults, Sarah-Jane Page (forthcoming) found that overall there was a lack of space for discussion within institutional religious structures. Her research involved young people aged 18–25 from across the Buddhist, Christian, Hindu, Islamic, Jewish and Sikh traditions. Young people emphasised their desire for discussion around sexuality and often facilitated such among their peers. In some religious settings, there was simply silence on issues of sex and sexuality. In others, a non-compromising mode of teaching had implications for young people's sense of belonging and inclusion, particularly around homosexuality. The research emphasises the importance of young people's 'choice and voice' and their participation in religious discussions around controversial issues, and for faith-based youth work to facilitate this.

It appears then that the defining characteristics of faith-based youth work are the emphasis on 'choice and voice', the development of relationships and the provision of opportunities for active 'participation'. These are not dissimilar to the wider field of youth work. The barriers to facilitating these elements in faith-based youth work settings also appear to be similar to those in the wider field – caused by an institutional agenda taking precedence over the self-identified needs of young people.

Conclusion

Nigel Pimlott (forthcoming) outlines how faith-based youth workers have, both historically and in the present, encouraged civic participation. However, he suggests that tensions exist in determining how the markers of participation and citizenship are defined – by the by institution, by the Government, or from the concerns of young people. There are clear links between the tensions that exist in faith-based and statutory youth work, as outlined throughout the chapter. From an informal education perspective, youth workers start with young people's needs in whatever setting they are operating in. Skilled youth workers advocate for young people and their concerns to the employing organisation and manage the tensions between institutional demands and young people's self-identifiable needs.

My research in Christian settings raises the question of whether faith-based youth work exists to serve church or community. Youth workers across all sectors of the field face conflicting demands between providing qualitative experiences for young people and number-crunching for their agencies. Practitioners are well aware of their institutional demands, whether they be government-imposed targets, such as that for accreditation or reducing the numbers of NEETs, or a church's desire to increase the number of 'bums on seats'. In the Christian youth work settings that featured in my research, citizenship and social participation were more effectively facilitated when negotiated with young people rather than imposed from an institutional level, as shown by the numbers of young people not in church services but engaging in social action and volunteering. Whilst the tensions between social concerns and institutional agendas continue to exist in Christian youth work settings and similarly in the wider faith-based sector, youth workers are seeking to start with the concerns and interests of the young people they serve. Perhaps most significantly, in an era of shrinking statutory provision, many faith-based youth workers are meeting a need for open access, inclusive youth work in their communities.

Notes

The research informing this chapter was undertaken as part of the author's doctoral studies with the Open University.

1 The research was undertaken as part of a collaborative doctoral award funded by the AHRC/ESRC Religion and Society programme and co-supported by Christian Education.
2 The research was undertaken as part of a collaborative doctoral award funded by the AHRC/ESRC Religion and Society programme and co-supported by Christian Education.
3 The model of Christian youth work was part of my PhD thesis (Stanton, forthcoming) and is also published in the *Journal of Beliefs and Values* (December 2012). The original domain names were: Domain 1 'social club'; Domain 2 'cell group'; Domain 3 'Sunday service'.

References

Ahmed, S. (forthcoming) 'The voices of young British Muslims: Identity, belonging and citizenship'. In Smith, M., Stanton, N. and Wylie, T. (eds) *Youth Work and Faith: Debates, Delights and Dilemmas*. Lyme Regis: Russell House.

Bell, J. (2005) *Doing Your Research Project* (4th edition). Maidenhead: Open University Press.

Brierley, D. (2003) *Joined Up: An Introduction to Youthwork and Ministry*. Carlisle, Cumbria: Spring Harvest Publishing/Authentic Lifestyle.

Brierley, P. (2006) *Pulling out of the Nosedive: A Contemporary Picture of Churchgoing*. London: Christian Research.

Clayton, M-A. and Stanton, N. (2008) 'The changing world's view of Christian youthwork'. *Youth & Policy* 100, 109–128.

Collins-Mayo, S., Mayo, B., Nash, S. and Cocksworth, C. (2010) *The Faith of Generation Y*. London: Church House Publishing.

Davie, G. (2007) 'Vicarious religion: A methodological challenge'. In Ammerman, N.T. (ed.) *Everyday Religion: Observing Modern Religious Lives*. New York: Oxford University Press. pp. 21–36.

Dean, K.C. (2010) *Almost Christian*. New York: Oxford University Press.

Green, M. (2006) *A Journey of Discovery: Spirituality and Spiritual Development in Youth Work*. Leicester: The National Youth Agency.

Hamid, S. (2006) 'Models of Muslim youthwork: Between reform and empowerment'. *Youth & Policy* 92, 81–89.

Jeffs, T. and Smith, M.K. (2005) *Informal Education: Conversation, Democracy and Learning* (revised edition). Nottingham: Educational Heretics Press.

Khan, M.G. (2006) 'Towards a national strategy for Muslim youth work', *Youth & Policy* 92, 7–18.

Marsh, S. (forthcoming) 'On renewing and soaring: Transformation and actualisation in contemporary Jewish youth provision'. In Smith, M., Stanton, N. and Wylie, T. (eds) *Youth Work and Faith: Debates, Delights and Dilemmas*. Lyme Regis: Russell House.

Page, S. (forthcoming) 'Sex talk: Discussion and meaning-making among religious young adults'. In Smith, M., Stanton, N. and Wylie, T. (eds) *Youth Work and Faith: Debates, Delights and Dilemmas*. Lyme Regis: Russell House.

Pimlott, N. (forthcoming) 'Faith-based youth work and civil society'. In Smith, M., Stanton, N. and Wylie, T. (eds) *Youth Work and Faith: Debates, Delights and Dilemmas*. Lyme Regis: Russell House.

Pimlott, J. and Pimlott, N. (2008) *Youthwork after Christendom*. Milton Keynes: Paternoster.

Roehlkepartain, E.C., Benson, P.L., Scales, P.C., Kimball, L. and King, P.E. (2008) *With Their Own Voices: A Global Exploration of How Today's Young People Experience and Think about Spiritual Development*. Minnesota, MN: Search Institute.

Shepherd, N. (2009) *Trying to be Christian: A qualitative study of young people's participation in two youth ministry projects*, Unpublished PhD thesis: King's College, University of London.

Shepherd, N. (2010) 'Religious socialisation and a reflexive habitus: Christian youth groups as sites for identity work'. In Collins-Mayo, S. and Dandelion, P. (eds) *Religion and Youth*. Farnham, Surrey: Ashgate. pp. 149–156.

Singh, J. (2011) 'Sikh-ing beliefs: British Sikh camps in the UK'. In Jacobsen, K.A. and Myrvold, K. (eds) *Sikhs in Europe: Migration, Identities and Representations*. Farnham, Surrey: Ashgate.

Stanton, N. (2012) 'Christian youthwork: Teaching faith, filling churches or response to social need?' *Journal of Beliefs and Values* 33(3), 385–403.

Stanton, N. (forthcoming) 'From Sunday schools to Christian youth work: Young people's engagement with organised Christianity in twentieth century England and the present day'. PhD thesis, The Open University.

Ward, P. (1997) *Youthwork and the Mission of God*. London: SPCK.

19

Supervision as a Youth Work Tool

Liesl Conradie

Supervision is a valuable tool that youth workers can use to support their reflection and to help them develop their practice. This chapter explores some of the functions of supervision and the different forms it can take. It also examines what youth workers can do to establish effective supervisory relationships, whether they are engaging with supervision as a student, or as a qualified and experienced practitioner.

Introduction

Working with young people can be fun, energising and exciting, but also tough, demanding and frustrating. Opportunities to receive support and guidance and to discuss your practice can help you to learn and develop, whatever your level of experience. Supervision is one of the tools that we as youth workers should have in our metaphorical bag of professional resources.

The aim of this chapter is to introduce you to supervision as a process, and to help you explore the different functions it can fulfil. It focuses particularly on supervision in the context of youth work, though many of the ideas and issues explored will be relevant to other areas of professional practice that involve working with people.

What is supervision?

Supervision is a process used in youth work and in work with young people more broadly, as well as in other areas of the human services, including in counselling, health and social work. However, the form supervision takes and how it is used in practice, varies across these different professional contexts (Davys and Beddoe, 2010).

The word 'supervision' comes from the Latin 'super' meaning 'over' and 'videre' meaning 'to see', hence 'to watch over' or 'to oversee'. So one interpretation of supervision at a very basic level is that it involves one person watching over the work of another and simply checking on the quality and quantity of their work (Kadushin, 1992). In the context of work with young people, supervision is seen to be much more than this. Kate Sapin, for example, describes supervision as: 'a process of critical reflection in which youth workers discuss ongoing work and professional development issues with another practitioner, such as a manager, a practice tutor or a peer in order to identify clarity about roles, and the relationship between values, practice and development' (Sapin, 2013: 220).

Supervision is based on a relationship, involving a minimum of two people: the supervisee, who is the person being supervised, and the supervisor. The supervisor is tasked with their role because of their experience, professional qualifications and knowledge of the professional field and because of their ability and commitment to support learning. The emphasis of the relationship, however, should be on sharing and learning, not just for the supervisee but also for the supervisor. As Sapin goes on to observe: 'Supervision, like youth work, can be a process of dialogue and problem-posing with both parties working together and learning from each other's understanding. ... [It] can enable both supervisor and supervisees to learn from each other's perspectives in a relationship that is both supportive and challenging' (Sapin, 2013: 220).

All practitioners, whatever position they are in, and however much experience they have, will always have something to learn.

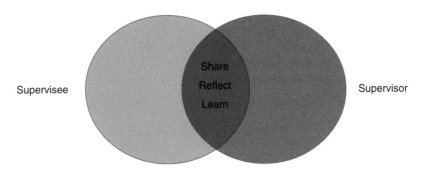

Figure 19.1   Bringing supervisee and supervisor together

Why is supervision important?

Youth work as a profession places a huge emphasis on reflection and reflective practice. Supervision is intended to support this reflection, providing a space where practitioners can discuss their work and develop a better understanding of their practice (Woods, 2001). It is based on the assumption that we learn from having opportunities to collaborate and to explore ideas with other people. As Carroll has observed, 'my own work and experience have taught me that I cannot learn some things on my own. I need others' (Carroll, 2009: 213). It also requires us as practitioners to be prepared to discuss what has gone well and what has not gone so well in our work, as a basis for learning and development.

An important part of the role of the supervisor is to ensure that this process of reflection incorporates the different perspectives of the main parties involved in the professional relationship – the youth worker, the young person and the organisation – as opposed to just focusing on the needs of the individual practitioner. The supervisor can then provide input, support and guidance that reflects these different perspectives and interests.

Supervision will be influenced by the wider context in which practice is taking place, including the policies and priorities of the organisation, the expectations of funding bodies, the requirements of professional bodies, and relevant legislation. Other influences on practice, and on supervision which explores this, may be events in the wider community and innovations and developments in the professional field. Figure 19.2 illustrates the range of factors that may influence supervision.

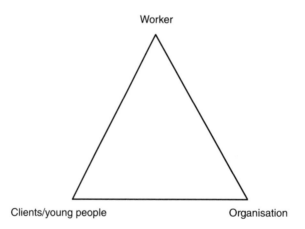

Figure 19.2   The range of factors that influence supervision

In a youth work context, the ultimate aim of supervision should be to benefit young people by providing them with the best possible service (Tash, 1967). Writing in the context of social care and children's services, Rowe and Haywood (2007) also emphasise the importance of supervision in providing good professional practice:

> If we are to deliver the best services across adults' and children's services we need to have the very best workforce who are well trained, highly skilled and passionate about their role. We know from our research that the key to building this workforce is the support, guidance and opportunities we provide to our colleagues. High quality supervision

is one of the most important drivers in ensuring positive outcomes for people who use social care and children's services. It also has a crucial role to play in the development, retention and motivation of the workforce. (Rowe and Haywood, 2007: 2)

Rather than just being something that needs to be done 'because your line manager says so' or because it is a requirement of study leading to a professional qualification, supervision should be seen as integral to the development of good practice and to our learning as practitioners.

The functions of supervision

A number of authors have written about supervision and the different functions and purposes that it fulfils. Alfred Kadushin (1992), a key author in this field, identifies what he sees as three key functions:

- **An administrative function** – concerned with promoting and maintaining good standards of work, and ensuring that practice fits within the policies and procedures of the agency.
- **An educational function** – focused on ensuring that workers have the knowledge, attitudes and skills necessary to practise effectively.
- **A supportive function** – focused on providing workers with support in order to keep their morale positive and to ensure that they are content and satisfied within their jobs.

The emphasis placed on each of these functions will vary according to the context in which supervision is taking place. For example, the *educational function* of supervision will be particularly important for a student being supervised as part of the requirements of a professionally qualifying course. But it is also likely to be important for a qualified and experienced worker, providing them with an opportunity to look at their professional development and to discuss ways in which they can develop the knowledge and skills they need to work effectively in a changing policy and practice environment.

The case study below illustrates how one student reflected on her experience of supervision.

Case study: Elizabeth

Professional supervision helped me to reflect on my practice and helped me to keep going. My supervisor has treated me with respect, made me feel welcome and offered support when I needed it. At university I sometimes struggle with putting my thoughts and ideas into a clear order. Talking through real situations with my supervisor has

(Continued)

(Continued)

helped me to see things more clearly. It's also helped me to see how the things that are happening in my practice link with the theory that I've been learning and reading about on my course. My supervisor has given me some good feedback when observing my practice which has helped me to reflect on what has gone well, and ways in which I might approach things differently in my future practice. My supervisor has also suggested when I'm being overcritical of myself. She reminds me that in work with young people, there are not always 'right' or 'wrong' approaches.

You will also see, though, that the student's account also touches on other functions of supervision. She identifies that supervision has 'helped me to keep going', indicating that it has had a *supportive function*. This function will not only be important for students, who may be practising in a new and perhaps challenging environment; supervision also has a supportive function for workers at any stage of their career. It can provide a valuable space where they have the chance to express and to begin to process their feelings about their work, rather than being consumed by them (Inskipp and Proctor, 1993).

Figure 19.3 aims to illustrate how each of these three functions is present in the supervisory relationship. Each is important, though depending on the situation and the context, some functions of supervision might take priority over others.

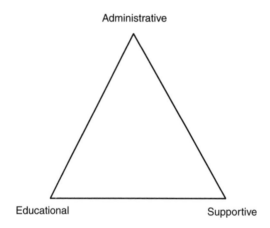

Figure 19.3   A triangle of supervision functions (adapted from Turnbull, 2005)

For example, in a situation where the supervisor is also the supervisee's line manager, the *administrative function* of supervision is likely to be particularly important; part of the role of the supervisor as line manager will be to ensure that the work of the supervisor fits with the policies and priorities of the organisation. I would suggest though that, even in this context, supervision also needs to focus on other areas of the triangle: to include time for discussion about the supervisee's learning and professional development, as well as to provide them with support. And where the supervisor is not the line manager, the supervisee will also benefit from having opportunities to discuss issues of good practice, including how the organisation's policies and procedures might be impacting on the work they are doing with young people, and ways in which they might set priorities and evaluate their practice.

In looking at the different function of supervision, it is also important to differentiate between support and counselling. The role of the supervisor is not to act as a counsellor, and the focus of supervision should not be on the supervisee's personal problems or issues. A difficulty might arise if, for example, a situation at work triggers memories of a negative experience in the supervisee's past. In this sort of situation, the supervisor can support the worker as far as the practice experience is concerned but is not there to provide counselling to overcome the past (Kadushin, 1992). They can, however, suggest that the worker seeks additional counselling support outside the supervisory relationship.

Table 19.1, devised by Hawkins and Shohet (1989) and adapted by Mark Smith (1996, 2005), identifies 10 key purposes or areas of focus for supervision, and categorises them in terms of the different functions of supervision. You will notice that they use the word 'managerial' to describe the 'administrative' function of supervision.

One difficulty with the table is that it may give an impression that different functions and purposes can be clearly identified and easily separated out from each other. In reality, there may be a great deal of overlap between different aspects of supervision. Practice with young people is complex. The issues that youth workers are dealing with, and the responses we have to them, are also complex and interlinked.

For example, a discussion about an incident which involved the youth worker needing to deal with intoxicated young men in a rural youth club, will probably touch on the organisation's health and safety policy (the administrative function), as

Table 19.1   Focus areas for supervision

To provide a regular space for the supervisee to reflect upon the content and process of their work	Educational
To develop understanding and skills within the work	Educational
To receive information and another perspective concerning one's work	Educational/supportive
To receive both content and process feedback	Educational/supportive
To be validated and supported both as a person and as a worker	Supportive
To ensure that as a person and as a worker one is not left to carry, unnecessarily, difficulties, problems and projections alone	Supportive
To have space to explore and express personal distress, restimulation, transference or counter-transference that may be brought up by the work	Managerial/supportive
To plan and utilize their personal and professional resources better	Managerial/supportive
To be pro-active rather than reactive	Managerial/supportive
To ensure quality of work	Managerial

Sources: Hawkins and Shohet (1989) and Smith (1996, 2005).

well as the worker's feelings (the supportive function). As a result of the conversation, the worker might identify a need to learn more about dealing with young people's drinking (the educational function) and the supervisor might suggest some reading or some training that might be useful.

There can sometimes be tensions between the different functions of supervision, and these can be difficult to manage. The focus can easily become skewed in favour of one function at the expense of the other, an issue that we will consider in more detail when we look at different forms of supervision.

Different forms of supervision

Supervision can take a number of different forms, including group supervision, where an individual supervisor supervises more than one supervisee at the same time; and peer or co-supervision, which, as the title suggests, involves practitioners working together to explore each other's practice. Peer supervision can be particularly useful if you are working in a situation where you are not receiving supervision, or if you are interested in learning more about supervision and want to develop your skills as a supervisor before taking on a more formal role as a supervisor yourself.

For the purposes of this chapter, however, we will focus on two forms of supervision that you are more likely to come across in your own experience of practice, including if you are studying on a course leading to a professional qualification: line management supervision and professional supervision.

Line management supervision

In line management supervision, the supervisor is also the supervisee's line manager and has responsibility for the quality of their work (Gopee, 2011). Its primary purpose is to manage the work and to ensure it fits with the organisation's goals. Line management supervision is also intended to provide support for staff working in situations that can be difficult and demanding. It provides them with time and space in which they can talk, and also receive feedback on their work.

A difficulty that can arise in line management supervision is that it has a tendency to overly focus on the administrative function of supervision, at the expense of the educational and supportive functions. When the supervisor has line management responsibility, there is a danger that the supervision sessions might be dominated by discussion about whether the worker is, or maybe isn't, meeting the needs of the organisation and its priorities, including any targets that they might be expected to meet.

It is important for both the supervisee and supervisor to have a discussion about the role of line management supervision, how it will be utilised and what both parties expect from each other. The tension between the different functions of supervision needs to be acknowledged within this relationship and efforts made to meet the needs of all three parties within the supervision triad: the worker, organisation and the client or young person. Only then can line management supervision truly be effective.

In line management supervision, it can also be difficult for the supervisee to open up and to be honest about any challenges or problems they are experiencing in their work because of fears about the implications this might have for their job.

Professional supervision

Professional supervision is also sometimes referred to as educational, non-managerial or consultant supervision (The Open University, 2011). Professional supervision has an educational function and is a requirement for students studying on courses leading to professional qualification in youth and community work. Professional supervision is also a key part of social work professional education.

Professional supervision in the context of study for a professional qualification focuses primarily on the student's learning and on the development of their practice. It provides a space and time where they can set the agenda for what they want to discuss, and where they will be encouraged to analyse their work and make links between their experience of practice and their study of theory. It also provides students with an opportunity to reflect on their personal values and how they interact with professional values and ethics. While the main focus should be on learning, discussions are also likely to touch on the feelings and emotions that will be entangled in the process, linking to the supportive function of supervision (Lomax et al., 2010).

The supervisor's task in this context includes taking responsibility for 'imparting expert knowledge, making judgements of the trainee's performance, and acting as a gatekeeper to the profession' (Holloway, 1997: 251). In order to be able to impart this 'expert knowledge', and to competently and confidently make judgements on the student's practice in the placement or work setting, the supervisor needs to be professionally qualified and also experienced in a similar or related field of practice.

Depending on the requirements of individual courses, the student's supervisor may or may not be part of the student's immediate placement or work environment. There are a number of advantages to the student being supported by someone outside their day-to-day practice setting. A key advantage is that it creates a distance which allows the student to talk more candidly about what they are experiencing and feeling, including any difficulties they might be having in their practice setting. In my experience as a supervisor, a key part of the role is encouraging students to think about and unpack their role within different settings, even if it is uncomfortable and unsettling. Where the supervisor is involved in the student's day-to-day practice, particularly if they are also in the position of being the line manager, it may be more difficult for them to open up and discuss more difficult issues, especially if one of the issues they are struggling with is a difficulty in the relationship between them and their line manager.

Even if the supervisor is positioned outside the student's practice environment, however, the reality is that they will have some level of responsibility and accountability for the student's practice, including in the role they play in determining whether the student has successfully completed the work-based aspects of their professional qualification.

In reality, professional supervision is frequently provided by a qualified practitioner who works in the organisation where the student is working or on placement, and they may also be their line manager. There are some advantages to the supervisor being someone who is close to the student's day-to-day work. They are more likely to be on hand and available for the student to 'pick their brains' and they will be familiar with the organisation and how it works.

Where the professional supervisor is also the line manager, the challenge is to ensure that professional supervision is not confused with line management supervision, and that the focus of supervision sessions remains on supporting the student's learning, though this may be easier said than done.

In the case study below, one student reflects on her experience of supervision and identifies ways in which line management supervision and professional supervision have been different.

Case study: Linda

In my experience, professional supervision was quite different from line manager supervision. My line manager was more concerned with whether the task was completed, whereas the professional supervisor was able to focus on 'how' the task was achieved. For me, the supervision sessions were the 'glue' that joined my working practice to the course theories. During the sessions we focused on the topics that were important to me. Professional supervision enabled me to discuss topics openly with someone who would be objective and non-judgemental and who also fully understood how to enable me to see the theory at work in my practice. I felt that I was talking to a peer and not to a manager and my views and opinions were understood and respected – even if I could not remember the exact name for the theory I was describing.

Whatever the position of the supervisor in relation to the student's practice setting, the relationship that they build with each other is crucial. In the next section of the chapter we will look at some of the issues that you need to consider and ways you might approach establishing a good supervisory relationship. We will be focusing particularly on supervision which takes place in the context of a professionally qualifying course, but the issues we will be examining will also be relevant to supervision in other contexts.

Developing the supervisory relationship

There is general agreement that the quality of the relationship between the supervisor and the student is the single most important factor in the effectiveness of the supervision (Kilminster and Jolly, 2000). Both parties need to focus on developing a good relationship from the start.

Developing good communication and trust within the supervisory relationship is particularly important (Tsui, 2005). The supervisor and the supervisee also need to be clear about the roles and responsibilities they each have within the relationship, and clear about the boundaries of the relationship. Establishing 'shared meaning', a shared understanding about the purpose of supervision and the factors that help to make supervision successful, are important aspects of developing effective supervision (Kaiser, 1997: 60). If you are beginning a new supervisory relationship, it is important to spend time discussing and agreeing how you will work together, just as you would if you were working with a new group of young people.

If supervision is going to be a process that supports your learning, you will need to be prepared to be questioned and challenged. Part of the role of a supervisor is to challenge practice that puts someone at risk or is inappropriate, oppressive or discriminatory. Where there is good communication between the supervisor and the supervisee, this will help to ensure that the messages conveyed as part of the challenge do not have a negative impact on the relationship, but rather help the supervisee to recognise bad practice, learn from the mistakes they have made and identify appropriate practice (Sapin, 2013).

As a supervisee, you also need to be prepared to receive feedback from your supervisor, including more negative feedback. Constructive criticism forms part of a healthy and successful professional supervision relationship, and the ability to receive and act on it will help you to learn and move forward.

Differences in power are a feature of many relationships; as someone who works with young people you will be aware of this. Issues of power will inevitably have an impact on the supervisory relationship and how this develops. Even if the supervisor is not your line manager, they are still in a position of authority, particularly through their role in assessing your practice and making recommendations to your university about whether you have met the practice requirements for successfully completing your course. Rather than trying to ignore this, Poole suggests that we 'need to acknowledge this power differential, be open about it, and work positively with it' (Poole, 2010: 69).

Making supervision work

Given the emphasis placed on the importance of supervision in professional education and practice, what can you do to make the most of supervision and supervision sessions?

An important starting point is to begin by identifying what you want from supervision and from a supervisor. Depending on your context, you may have a choice about who you approach and ask to be your professional supervisor. If you are in this position, you might decide to opt for a supervisor who has a specialism in an area of practice that you are particularly interested in. You might ask a colleague or former student if there are any recommendations or suggestions that they can make based on their contacts and networks. Issues of gender, language and culture might influence your choice of supervisor. However, the reality for many students is that the choice of a supervisor may be limited, perhaps because of a shortage of qualified workers in your organisation or a lack of willingness or time. At the very beginning of the relationship, whether it is one that you have consciously chosen or not, an important starting point will be to arrange an initial meeting with your supervisor where you can discuss each other's roles, responsibilities and expectations for supervision. It also might be useful to spend some of the session discussing each other's practice backgrounds and experiences, as well as what you want from supervision and whether there are any particular areas of practice that you would like to focus on.

It will be helpful to agree on some very basic practical arrangements. These include how often and where you will meet. It is useful to identify a quiet space which is as free from interruption as possible, and to identify a time of day that is mutually convenient. It is also important to discuss and agree on how you will conduct your working relationship, for example, who needs to create the agenda for supervision and by when does it need to be shared with the other party? After the meeting, who will write up the notes and what is the timescale for doing this? As a student, you will probably be expected to produce notes and recordings after supervision; they will form part of the evidence of practice that you will need to submit for assessment, and they will also help you to reflect back over the supervision session. What will you do to inform each other if a session needs to be cancelled or postponed because one of you is ill? The importance of these very practical arrangements should not be underestimated as they can severely impact on the quality of supervision sessions and the experience overall.

Conclusion

Supervision is an important tool that supports good professional practice, and that can help us to work with young people more effectively. It can help us to analyse and make sense of our experiences, and also provide us with support which enables us to do work that is often demanding and sometimes distressing. Effective supervision is based on the development of a good relationship between supervisor and supervisee, and on a mutual commitment to making the supervisory relationship work. At its best, supervision can help to provide us as practitioners with those 'lightbulb' moments, when we suddenly see a situation more clearly, and 'what I did' and 'why I did it' become connected and therefore more meaningful.

Whether you are being supervised as part of your journey towards professional qualification, or as someone who has been through this process and is now qualified, good supervision can help to put you in a better position to support the development of the young people you work with. As practitioners who are committed to developing our professional practice with young people, we all have a responsibility to ensure that youth workers are supported by good quality supervision.

References

Carroll, M. (2009) 'Supervision: Critical reflection for transformational learning, part 1'. The Clinical Supervisor 28 (2): 210–20.

Davys, A. and Beddoe, L. (2010) *Best Practice in Professional Supervision: A Guide for the Helping Professions*. London: Jessica Kingsley Publishers.

Gopee, N. (2011) *Mentoring and Supervision in Healthcare* (2nd edition). London: Sage.

Hawkins, P. and Shohet, R. (1989) *Supervision in the Helping Professions*. Buckingham: Open University Press.

Holloway, E. (1997) 'Structures for the analysis and teaching of supervision'. In Watkins, C. (ed.) *Handbook of Psychotherapy Supervision*. Chichester: Wiley.

Inskipp, F. and Proctor, B. (1993) *Making the Most of Supervision: A Professional Development Resource for Counsellors, Supervisors and Trainees*. Twickenham: Cascade.

Kadushin, A. (1992) *Supervision in Social Work* (3rd edition). New York: Colombia University Press.

Kaiser, T. (1997) *Supervisory Relationships: Exploring the Human Element*. Belmont, CA: Thomas Brooks/Cole Publishing Co.

Kilminster, S.M. and Jolly, B.C. (2000) 'Effective supervision in clinical practice settings: A literature review'. *Medical Education* 34 (10): 827–40.

Lomax, R., Jones, K., Leigh, S. and Gay, C. (2010) *Surviving your Social Work Placement*. Basingstoke: Palgrave Macmillan.

Poole, J. (2010) 'Perspective on supervision in the human services: Gazing through critical and feminist lenses'. *Michigan Family Review* 14(1): 60–70.

Rowe, A. and Haywood, J. (2007) *Providing Effective Supervision: A Workforce Development Tool, Including a Unit of Competence and Supporting Guidance*. Leeds: Skills for Care and the Children's Workforce Development Council.

Sapin, K. (2013) *Essential Skills of Youth Work Practice* (2nd edition). London: Sage Publications.

Smith, M.K. (1996, 2005) 'The functions of supervision', *The Encyclopedia of Informal Education*. Available at: www.infed.org/biblio/functions_of_supervision.htm (last update: 3 September 2009; accessed 20 August 2012).

Tash, J. (1967) *Supervision in Youth Work*. London: YMCA George Williams College.

The Open University (2011) *A Guide for Supervisors*. Milton Keynes: The Open University.

Tsui, M.S. (2005) *Social Work Supervision: Contexts and Concepts*. Sage Sourcebooks for the Human Services. London: Sage.

Turnbull, A. (2005) 'Using line management'. In Harrison, R. and Wise, C. (eds) *Working with Young People*. London: Sage Publications.

Woods, J. (2001) 'Using supervision for professional development', in Richardson, L.D. and Wolfe, M. (eds) *Principles and Practice of Informal Education*. London: RoutledgeFalmer.

Index

Page numbers followed by the letter "n" indicate figures.